T0305324

"I wish I had been able to access this book five years ago when I started moving my business from the 'old model' to pricing up front. For those accountants and lawyers out there seeking a 'how-to' on design and implementation of value pricing, this is the bible. This book should be required reading for any person who owns, runs, manages, or works in a professional knowledge business. What they do with it then comes down to courage. Be courageous and learn from Ron's experience. A brilliant read and seminal text."

—Matthew Tol, FCA, Principal, mta optima,
www.mtaoptima.com.au

"Every professional must read this book. Be brave and trust that Ron Baker knows what he's talking about. You'll find comfort in reading the amazing real-life examples of the innovators that took the leap. You'll want to slap yourself for not believing in change sooner!"

—Brandy Amidon, CPA, Brains On Fire,
Greenville, South Carolina

"Ron Baker is already regarded by most professionals who understand the impending implosion of a time billing business model as the pricing guru. In *Implementing Value Pricing*, Baker manages to further cement his reputation by comprehensively answering the 'elephant in the room' question of every professional firm looking to price on value—that is, how it is *actually* done. The book is a truly compelling read for any professional wishing to implement or improve a value pricing business model based on selling intellectual capital rather than time."

—Matthew Burgess, Partner, McCullough Robertson—
Lawyers, Brisbane, Australia

"Ron Baker does it again. Just when you think you have heard all there is about value pricing, Baker produces yet more challenges as well as solutions in this informative, well-researched, and at times humorous book on the practical implementation of pricing by value. How any leader of a professional firm could lead their business in the future without both reading this book and adopting many of Ron's practical concepts is beyond me."

—John Chisholm, former Managing Partner and CEO of law firms,
and now Principal John Chisholm Consulting,
www.chisconsult.com

Implementing
Value Pricing

Implementing Value Pricing

A Radical Business Model for Professional Firms

RONALD J. BAKER

WILEY

John Wiley & Sons, Inc.

Published by John Wiley & Sons, Inc., Hoboken, New Jersey.

Published simultaneously in Canada.

For general information on our other products and services or for technical support,
please contact our Customer Care Department within the United States at (800)
762-2974, outside the United States at (317) 572-3993 or fax (317) 572-4002.

Wiley also publishes its books in a variety of electronic formats. Some content that
appears in print may not be available in electronic books. For more information
about Wiley products, visit our web site at www.wiley.com.

Library of Congress Cataloging-in-Publication Data:

Baker, Ronald J.
    Implementing value pricing : a radical business model for professional firms /
Ronald J. Baker.
        p. cm. — (Wiley professional advisory services ; 8)
    Includes bibliographical references and index.
    ISBN 978-0-470-58461-3 (hardback); ISBN 978-0-470-92955-1 (ebk);
ISBN 978-0-470-92956-8 (ebk); ISBN 978-0-470-92957-5 (ebk)
    1. Pricing. 2. Value. 3. Fairness. 4. Professional corporations—Prices. I. Title.
    HF5416.5.B34   2010
    658.8'16—dc22

                                                                2010024729

Printed and bound by CPI Group (UK) Ltd, Croydon, CR0 4YY

C9780470584613_171224

To my mother and father, for genetically encoding me to challenge the conventional wisdom, and providing the most immeasurable of all blessings: their love and unwavering support in everything I do.

"At every crossway on the road that leads to the future each progressive spirit is opposed by a thousand men appointed to guard the past."

—Maurice Maeterlinck (1862–1949),
Belgian Nobel Laureate in literature, 1911

"It does not take a majority to prevail, but rather an irate, tireless minority keen on setting brushfires of freedom in the minds of men."

—Samuel Adams

Contents

Foreword

This book should come with a warning label: Reading this book may cause a Ron Baker Headache.

Now, before you put the book down, let me explain: I'm not talking about a headache in a bad, migraine-y kind of way. Think of it more like what you get when you have an ice cream on a hot day, or drink a milkshake too fast. When you read Ron Baker, and even more so when you talk with him about value pricing, you get a feeling that your head is going to explode because you suddenly have too many thoughts and ideas in it. In other words, it's a good kind of headache. A Ron Baker Headache.

I run a Boston law firm called Shepherd Law Group (shepherdlaw group.com), which helps companies make easier workplaces. When employers get into situations where they need a lawyer, they often feel like they're losing control. My job as a lawyer is to help them get some of that control back. But the problem is that most of the time, dealing with lawyers makes the employers feel like they're losing even more control. This is because lawyers never tell them how much it's all going to cost, so the employers don't know what they're getting into.

The main cause of this problem is, of course, hourly billing. So when I founded my firm a dozen years ago, I started looking into how I could kill the billable hour and get rid of timesheets. I read everything I could find on the topic, which was of little use. There was no one I could consult to learn how to fix prices in an employment-litigation law firm.

And then I found Ron.

The first Ron Baker book I came across was *The Firm of the Future*, which he coauthored with Paul Dunn. And I promptly got my first Ron Baker Headache. In a good way. My head filled up with thoughts and ideas and questions. I was no longer alone in my quest to make a better law firm. I found someone who shared the ideas I had stumbled upon, but who then took them much further than I ever could.

I tore through Ron's other books (more headaches!), and then a few years ago, I had the opportunity to meet Ron. From that first conversation over dinner, through our many chats over the past couple of years, I've always felt, "Here is someone who just plain thinks differently." I've said it many times: Ron Baker is the smartest person I've ever spoken with, in any industry or walk of life.

How fortunate we are then that Ron has chosen to use that powerful intellect to make the world of professional firms a better place, both for professionals and for customers. And as you will see in this book, his intellect is completely accessible. Ron is equally comfortable quoting F. A. Hayek and Homer Simpson.

Thanks in no small part to Ron's wisdom, my law firm successfully abandoned hourly billing and the tyranny of timesheets. Our profit has risen dramatically as a direct result. But so too has our customers' value. As you will learn, hourly billing creates great waste and inefficiency. With value pricing, both professionals and customers win. This isn't just a theory; firms like mine are actually doing it. And trust me: it is better than the old business model that relegates professionals to merely "selling time."

When Ron asked me to write this foreword, he warned me that as a reader of his other works, I might not learn anything new in this book. As if. For example, I was reviewing Chapter 16 and got to the part where Ron reveals how hourly billing got its start in the legal profession almost a hundred years ago—in 1919. Suddenly I had a new weapon to use in my fight against the billable hour: that it was an antiquated, Industrial Age concept.

Ron and I have talked about the need for a business—a law firm, a CPA firm, a consultancy—to have a central purpose or belief to guide it: a reason why it exists. Ron's wisdom and insight helped me come up with my firm's "why," which is "to fix the practice of law through innovation." And what I learned in this book gave me the argument that a business model developed in 1919 is the opposite of innovation. I've already started using this concept in talking with clients.

As you will find in the pages that follow, Ron is a true thought leader. These days, so many lawyers are paying vague lip service to the concept of "alternative billing," it's refreshing to find someone who has actually thought through all this and proposed a better business model. But unlike so many thought leaders, Ron doesn't mind if you don't agree with him. All he cares is that you bring an open mind and be prepared to question your own assumptions. As he wrote in his seminal book *Pricing on Purpose,* "My goal is to have you think with me, not like me. ... Do not accept anything at face value, not even from an expert."

Ron Baker is the expert when it comes to pricing professional services. But don't just accept his wisdom from the pages that follow. Think about it. Of course, you'll get that Ron Baker Headache, but in a good way.

Jay Shepherd
clientrevolution.com
May 22, 2010
Boston, MA

Preface

People of the same trade seldom meet together, even for merriments and diversion, but the conversation ends in a conspiracy against the public, or in some contrivance to raise prices.

—Adam Smith, *An Inquiry into the Nature and Causes of the Wealth of Nations*, 1776

One of my mentors is the late Peter Drucker, who always insisted on asking himself before writing any book, "Why this book, now?" It is a good question to ask oneself before setting out to write a book.

This book is a Declaration of Independence to my colleagues in all of the professions—to once and for all free ourselves from the tyranny of time. The "We sell time" business model I was taught as a young CPA is outdated, suboptimal, and driving the best and brightest out of the professions. We simply must find a better path to take us into the future.

Since 1995, I have been speaking to leaders in the professions around the world on the shift from "hourly billing" to value pricing, and if an observer from outside the profession were to attend, Adam Smith's charge above would certainly seem true. In a sense, this book is about how to raise your prices. But it is emphatically not a conspiracy against the public. Indeed, the main message of this book is that the customer is the sole and ultimate arbiter of the value that we, as professionals, provide. Further, the customer, too, must earn a profit from the relationship with our firm. If we do not provide something of value to the customer from which they will profit, we have no business being in business.

This book is the culmination of a personal odyssey for me. In June 1989, I attended a four-day seminar titled "Increasing CPA Firm Profitability." In the tranquil setting of Lake Tahoe, Nevada, I learned three major strategies on how to increase my CPA firm's profitability:

1. Raise my hourly billing rate by at least $10.
2. Grade my customers "A," "B," and "C," and fire all the "Cs."
3. Offer my customers "fixed fee agreements" on all services, with an appropriate "weasel clause" to cover any scope changes.

Inspired, I immediately shared all of these ideas, and more, with my new partner, Justin H. Barnett. We talked about becoming a "winning firm," the term the instructor used throughout the seminar, which meant, by today's vernacular, going from good to great. The course provided me with the tools I needed to put some of these ideas into practice immediately. In other words, it taught me *how* to do it.

What it did not teach me is *why* I should do it. It was all case studies and examples, but had absolutely no theory. So when I returned to my firm I had a hammer—the tool I needed to implement some of these new concepts—and I started furiously hitting things. I raised my hourly rate but did not simultaneously convince my customers that my value rose commensurately with that increase. I began grading my customers, and ridding the firm of the "Cs," but it was not until I began researching the ideas behind Total Quality Service that I learned that *my customers were not going to get better until I did.* Without a solid theoretical foundation of *why* I was doing these things, I failed miserably.

This is one of the most glaring weaknesses in most business books and management ideas: They are all practice with no theory. Most do little else than propound platitudes and compose common sense into endless checklists and seven-step programs. Yet, all learning begins with theory. There is nothing as sterile as a fact not illuminated by a theory; we may as well read the telephone book.

Theories are powerful because they seek to do at least one of three things: explain, predict, or prescribe. Yet when one reads a typical business book today, the author will usually begin by saying something to the effect that "this book is not based on some 'ivory tower,' theoretical model, but based on practical, real-world experience and examples."

Beware when you read such a qualifier, because as Dr. W. Edwards Deming used to say, "Without theory, experience has no meaning. No one has questions to ask. Hence without theory, there is no learning. Theory leads to prediction. Without prediction, experience and examples teach nothing" (Deming 1994: 103). In a business environment, whether we admit it or not, we are guided to a large degree by theoretical constructs that have evolved to simplify—and thus explain, predict, or control—our various behaviors. Theories build buildings and bridges, fly airplanes, and put men on the moon. There is nothing more practical than a good theory.

I have tried to avoid this defect by having the theories presented herein drive the ideas, not the other way around. Therefore, the book you are about to read contains more theory than you may be used to if you are a regular reader of business books, or attend business seminars. I make no apologies for this, because there is nothing more practical than a good theory. I wish I had one back in 1989.

About This Book

As Herman Melville wrote in *Moby Dick*, "To produce a mighty book, you must choose a mighty theme." There are three mighty themes that run throughout this book:

1. Changing the predominant business model of the professional firm from "We sell time" to the radical "We sell intellectual capital," transforming them from *professional service firms* to *professional knowledge firms*. This is described as "radical" because *radical* is Latin for "getting back to the root." The root in this case is customers buy *value*, not time, a truth the professions appear to have lost sight of since the adoption of the billable hour and timesheet regime.
2. Strategies to enable your firm to *create* more value by offering Total Quality Service, and developing a value proposition for which customers will gladly pay premium prices.
3. A specific eight-step model for implementing value pricing so your firm can *capture* a fair share of the value it creates from selling intellectual capital, not hours.

There are two types of readers this book addresses:

1. *Readers not at all familiar with any of my prior books.* This book offers a one-stop, comprehensive read to help you make the transition to becoming a firm of the future. As the three themes above are getting much publicity within the professions, new readers are being exposed to these ideas, some for the first time. My objective is not just to illustrate *how* to implement a business model change, create more value, and price to capture a fair share of it, but to persuade you on the importance of *why* to do it, because if you want to make incremental changes, work on practices and techniques. But if you want to make significant advancement, you must work on your theories and paradigms—the way you see the world.
2. *Readers who have read one or more of my prior books.* If you have previously read *Professional's Guide to Value Pricing* (editions 1 through 6), or *The Firm of the Future*, you will find much new "how to" implement material here. I would suggest jumping directly to

Part V, "Eight Steps to Implementing Value Pricing," along with the Appendixes, for the specific tools and strategies that will assist you in making pricing on purpose a core competency in your firm. I would also encourage you to read the Appendixes outside of your profession since much pricing skill can be learned and applied from other sectors.

In addition, here is new material you will find throughout the book:
A discussion of business model innovation, which is what the firm of the future is all about (Chapters 2 and 36).

New research on the history of the billable hour and timesheets, introduced in 1919—earlier than originally believed—in law firms, inspired by Frederick Winslow Taylor's Scientific Management religion (Chapter 16).

The foundations of creating value, Part II (Chapters 3–15) are somewhat duplicative if you have read *The Firm of the Future*, *Pricing on Purpose*, or *Professional's Guide to Value Pricing*; though the astute reader will notice much new material. Though this added to the length of the book, I felt it necessary to include these chapters for new readers, because the only way to *capture* more value through value pricing is to *create* value in the first place through excellent customer service, and other principles of exceptional value creation.

Part IV (Chapters 18–26) deals with what, specifically, replaces hourly billing and timesheets—including a case study from a firm that has made the transition—and a chapter is included to discuss each replacement in either Part IV or Part V.

Part V contains a new eight-step model to assist firms in implementing value pricing. One major addition is the inclusion of project management written by VeraSage Institute Senior Fellow, and project management expert, Ed Kless. A new chapter also contains two frameworks for scoping complex engagements, such as litigation, IT installations, and other engagements where the scope is very difficult to define upfront. Developing different options to offer the customer is also presented.

Throughout the book there are several case studies from firms that have implemented the specific ideas and the consequences of doing so.

As with all of my prior books, an extensive bibliography is included to make it easier for those who wish to find the original source discussed in the book, and further their knowledge.

About the Web Site

There are seven Appendixes available for download as a companion to the book, available at www.wiley.com/go/valuepricing (password: baker).

The Appendixes include a summary checklist containing strategies firm leaders need to discuss and implement; strategies with respect to Request for Proposals (RFPs); an Appendix for each of the professional sectors—advertising agencies, CPA, IT, and law firms—containing specific issues, case studies, and checklists for each.

I would encourage you to read the Appendixes outside of your profession, since much pricing skill can be learned and applied from other professional sectors.

An extensive Suggested Reading list, sorted by topic and alphabetized by author, is also included.

About the Words Used in This Book

Words have meaning, and as Werner Erhard wrote, "All transformation is linguistic. If we want to change our culture, we need to change our conversation."

Throughout this book, I use the word *customer, price, invoice,* and *team member* in lieu of, respectively, *client, fee, bill,* and *staff* (except when quoting from other sources). I do this because I believe these words convey better images and evoke more positive emotions of what they are attempting to describe. According to my dictionary, "among the ancient Romans a *client* was a citizen who placed himself under the protection of a patrician, who was called his patron; a master who had freed his slave, and retained some rights over him after his emancipation; a dependent; one under the protection or patronage of another." Are these the type of images we want to invoke? The welfare state has *clients,* while businesses have *customers.* A *fee* is negatively associated with a tax or some other charge, while *price* is a benign term most customers easily comprehend, eliciting no positive or negative emotions.

Value billing is not used because billing takes place in arrears, after the work has been done, whereas pricing takes place up front, before the work is begun.

It is not my objective to change your vocabulary, though I hope you will seriously consider your choice of words. I am simply far more comfortable using words that elicit superior images in other's minds. Action is released by emotion, and emotion is stirred largely based on the words we use.

The professions are a noble calling and the predominant method of pricing for the services they provide is not worthy of professionals. There is a better way.

My odyssey has been an incredibly circuitous route, proving that sometimes you have to go a long way out of the way to come a short way correctly. Author and educator William Arthur Ward wrote, "The great teacher tells. The good teacher explains. The superior teacher demonstrates. The great teacher inspires."

If I can shorten your path by sharing my learning—and that of many others who have traveled to a new destination—while inspiring you to life-long learning, this book will have accomplished its purpose.

Ronald J. Baker
Petaluma, California
October 12, 2010

Acknowledgments

Someone once wrote that acknowledgments are the equivalent of tipping, but with Monopoly money. I hope those mentioned herein forgive my frugality—but I give my deepest and profound thanks to the following individuals.

Too many economists to mention taught me price theory, in which this book is grounded. The most significant are David Friedman, Steven Landsburg, Deirdre McCloskey, and Mark Skousen. I thank them all for their wisdom.

George Gilder is the most profound thinker I have ever encountered, and his insights of how an economy creates wealth permeate this book. Every century needs an Adam Smith, and Gilder is ours for the twentieth and twenty-first.

The late Peter Drucker deserves special thanks for always focusing on doing the right things, why an organization exists, and knowledge workers, all the while teaching me that business is really a branch of the humanities because you have to deal with real people, not efficient machines.

My mentor Reed Holden continues to teach me pricing skills, and much else. Thank you, Reed, for always supporting my work.

Another mentor is Sheila Kessler, who has imparted much wisdom to me over the years in a calming, yet insightful, manner. Thank you for everything Sheila.

Tom Finneran of the 4A's has been an indefatigable supporter of our work, as well as having the patience to teach a neophyte about the advertising world. His gracious permission to publish the 4A's Compensation Dialogue Process will greatly assist any advertising agency—indeed, any professional firm—serious about pricing for value. Thanks Tom.

Sarah Armstrong of Coca-Cola was kind enough to give me an individual tutorial on the Coca-Cola Value-Based Compensation model, which is an outstanding step in the direction of focusing both agency and advertiser on the right things.

Richard DelCore of Procter & Gamble has also innovated an agency compensation model that deserves to be replicated. Rich's constant challenges and penetrating questions have helped us refine our ideas to better serve agencies and advertisers.

William Cobb, father of the beloved Value Curve, has been kind enough to grant me permission to use his curve for over a decade. He is one of the few consultants to the legal profession who truly "gets it." Thanks Bill.

Bob Cross, a giant in the field of pricing, has been more than generous with his support of my work. I greatly value his counsel, and most of all, his warm friendship.

VeraSage Institute has created quite an active—and vocal—community of mavericks and trailblazers. Their comments, support, and even disagreements over the years have helped me present these ideas—hopefully— more effectively.

I would especially like to thank all of those knowledge workers who were kind enough to provide case studies and unselfishly share their experiences in these pages. In order of appearance: Karen Smart, David Littlefield, Brandy Amidon and Robbin Phillips, Matthew Tol, Kurt Siemers, Brent Uken, John Shaver, Brett Kreykes, Mark Chinn, and Jay Shepherd.

Special friends of VeraSage I am proud to call colleagues and friends: Mark Bailey, Mark Chinn, Ron Crone, Paul Dunn, Tom Hood, Art Jacob, Mark Koziel, Mike McCulloch, Bill Mees, Ed Miller, Shirley Nakawatase, Ric Payne, Brenda Richter, Clar Rosso, John and Amy Shaver, and Brent Uken.

Very special thanks to Jay Shepherd not only for his case study and generous permission to quote his blog posts, but also for writing the foreword—and for his friendship.

To my editors at John Wiley & Sons, Inc., John DeRemigis, Tiffany Charbonier, Chris Gage, and Amy Handy for taking the ultimate risk and publishing this book, improving every page with adept editing, and for tolerating another late manuscript by understanding that the first thing every writer needs is another source of income.

John Chisholm has been courageously carrying on the crusade in Australia ever since he met our late friend Paul O'Byrne. Any progress in killing the billable hour Down Under is due to this fearless attorney. Better yet, *in vino veritas*—"after a bit of the grape, people tend to reveal themselves," and the revelations have been wonderful. Thanks for everything John.

Self-taught philosopher Eric Hoffer wrote, "There are no chaste minds. Minds copulate whenever they meet." Nowhere is this more true than with my friends and colleagues at VeraSage Institute, who are often accused with being part of a religion. But "veracity"—the first word that makes up VeraSage, the second being "sagacity"—differs from the word "truth."

Veracity is the habitual pursuit of, and adherence to, truth. The truth has led us to the ideas in this book, empirically proven in the marketplace—the opposite of faith.

I am proud and humbled everyday interacting with my VeraSage colleagues: Scott Abbott, Justin Barnett, Peter Byers, Michelle Golden, Daryl Golemb, Brendon Harrex, Paul Kennedy, Ed Kless, Chris Marston, Tim McKey, Dan Morris, Paul O'Byrne, Tim Williams, and Yan Zhu. All of these folks think "outside of the box"—Pandora's.

A wise rabbi said, "Pay attention to the ways in which your relationship continues," in reference to those loved ones who have departed. This is profound as it applies to the late Paul O'Byrne, whose influence is everywhere in our hearts—and minds.

Groucho Marx said, "Those are my principles, and if you don't like them ... well, I have others," a secret sentiment I am sure my brother, Ken Baker, shares. For someone who always complains he cannot possibly live through another one of my books, he came through again, cracking me up in the process.

About the Author

Ronald J. Baker started his career in 1984 with KPMG's Private Business Advisory Services in San Francisco. Today, he is the founder of VeraSage Institute, a think tank dedicated to educating professionals around the world.

As a frequent speaker, writer, and educator, his work takes him around the world. He has been an instructor with the California CPA Education Foundation since 1995 and has authored fifteen courses for them.

He is the author of five books: *Professional's Guide to Value Pricing*; *The Firm of the Future: A Guide for Accountants, Lawyers, and Other Professional Services*, co-authored with Paul Dunn; *Pricing on Purpose: Creating and Capturing Value*; *Measure What Matters to Customers: Using Key Predictive Indicators*; and *Mind Over Matter: Why Intellectual Capital is the Chief Source of Wealth*. He also wrote *Burying the Billable Hour, Trashing the Timesheet*, and *You Are Your Customer List*, published by the Association of Chartered Certified Accountants in the United Kingdom (available at www.verasage.com).

Ron has toured the world, spreading his value-pricing message to over 100,000 professionals. He has been appointed to the American Institute of Certified Public Accountant's Group of One Hundred, a think tank of leaders to address the future of the profession, named on *Accounting Today*'s 2001, 2002, 2003, 2004, 2005, 2006, and 2007 Top 100 Most Influential People in the profession, and received the 2003 Award for Instructor Excellence from the California CPA Education Foundation.

He graduated in 1984, from San Francisco State University, with a Bachelor of Science in accounting and a minor in economics. He is a graduate of Disney University and Cato University, and is a member of the Professional Pricing Society. He presently resides in Petaluma, California.

To contact Ron Baker:

VeraSage Institute
707.769.0965
Ron@verasage.com
Web/Blog: www.verasage.com
LinkedIn: Ron Baker
Facebook: Ron Baker
Twitter: @ronaldbaker

Implementing
Value Pricing

PART I

A Radical Business Model

There is nothing like returning to a place that remains unchanged to find the ways in which you yourself have altered.

—Nelson Mandela

CHAPTER 1

The Firm of the Past

I'm willing to be occasionally wrong. But what I hate most in life is to *stay wrong*.

—Paul A. Samuelson, Nobel laureate economist

A business model is nothing more than a theory. I am defining a business model as follows:

How your firm creates value for customers, and how you monetize that value.

Let us analyze the predominant theory of professional firms. In Greek language, *analyze* means "unloosen, separate into parts." Almost every book that discusses professional firms is based on this equation:

Revenue = People Power × Efficiency × Hourly Rate

Since this model dominates the thinking of firm leaders to this day, it is worth explaining the model in greater detail to understand both its strengths and—as will be increasingly detailed—its fundamental weaknesses.

Consider a professional firm—such as accounting, legal, consulting, advertising, IT, and so on—the archetypal pyramid firm model rested on the foundation of leveraging people power, in effect their "capacity." The theory is this: Since the two main drivers of profitability are leverage (number of team members per owner) and the hourly rate realization, if each partner could oversee a group of professionals, this would provide the firm with additional capacity to generate top-line revenue, and thus add to the profitability and size of the firm. If a firm wanted to add to its revenue base, it had two primary choices: It could work its people more hours, or it could hire more people. It is no secret which choice the average

3

firm tends to choose, much to the chagrin of its already overworked team members.

Now compare this practice with other industries—this process of adding capacity *after* revenue is backward. If you think of any other industry or company—from Intel and General Electric to FedEx and Microsoft—capacity is almost always added *before* revenue. Consider specifically FedEx: Before Fred Smith could deliver his first overnight package, he had to have trucks, drivers, airplanes, and facilities throughout the country, all at enormous fixed costs. Most organizations operate with capacity to spare, which is vital to maintain flexibility in changing market conditions.

Next, let us look at the second element in the old theory—efficiency. Efficiency is a word that can be said with perfect impunity, since no one in his right mind would dispute the goal of operating efficiently. The problem is *there is no such thing as generic efficiency.* It all depends on what your purpose is, and how much you are willing to pay. In professional firms, the pendulum has swung too far in the direction of efficiency over everything else. It seems innovation, dynamism, customer service, investments in human capital, and effectiveness have all been sacrificed on the altar of efficiency.

The next component in the old model is hourly rates—a form of cost-plus pricing. The real antecedent of cost-plus pricing is the Labor Theory of Value, posited by economists of the eighteenth century and Karl Marx in the middle nineteenth, and falsified by the 1871 Marginalist Revolution.

Last, consider revenue. It is one thing to get *more* business; it is quite another to get *better* business. The "bigger is better" mentality is an empty promise for most firms. Acquiring more customers is not necessarily better. Growth simply for the sake of growth is the ideology of the cancer cell, not a strategy for a viable, profitable firm. Eventually, the cancer kills its host.

If market share explained profitability, General Motors, United Airlines, Sears, and Philips should be the most profitable companies in their respective industries. Yet they have all turned in mediocre profitability records, and two have been through bankruptcy. Growth in profitability usually precedes market share, not vice versa. Wal-Mart, for example, was far more profitable than Sears long before it had a sizeable market share. It seems profitability and market share grow in tandem with a viable value proposition customers are willing to pay for.

Peter Drucker once wrote, "Most business issues are not the result of things being done poorly or even the wrong things being done. Businesses fail because the CEO's assumptions about the outside provide decision frameworks for the institution which no longer fit reality" (Edersheim 2007: 243). Nowhere is this truer than in the professions. The "We sell time" mentality is not simply a wrong pricing strategy, but far more systemic—a flawed business model.

It is a valuable accomplishment in and of itself to point out defects in a theory—or falsify it entirely. Another way to advance knowledge is to posit a better theory—a new business model for the firm of the future.

CHAPTER 2

The Firm of the Future

Revamping a business model is not easy; it requires visible, consistent commitment from the top. It takes time. First, the more established an industry's norms, the more difficult it is to innovate business models. Everyone has a big stake in preserving the status quo, but it is critical to resist the temptation to do so.

—A.G. Lafley and Ram Charan, *The Game-Changer*, 2008

Only a theory can replace a theory. If we reject our old notions of the way the world works, we need a new place to go. Certainly we can make incremental improvements to the old business model presented in Chapter 1. Indeed, business books are full of such ideas—Total Quality Management, Lean, Six-Sigma, reengineering, benchmarking, and so on. But if we endeavor to make significant improvements in performance and effectiveness in today's intellectual capital economy, we have to move beyond tactics and techniques. We have to work on our theories. Doctors used to believe in leeches and bloodletting, and no matter how efficiently they executed those therapies based on those theories, they simply were not medically effective. There is no right way to do the wrong thing.

In the previous chapter, I described the flaws in the traditional professional firm business model. I want to be very specific about the charge I am making. I am *not* arguing that the old business model is not profitable. That would defy the reality of many profitable firms. Instead, I am saying it is *suboptimal*. Engineers, for example, use this term to describe the mindless pursuit of one goal to the detriment of broader organizational interests. This is certainly the case with the pursuit of billable hours at the expense of effectiveness, customer service, innovation, creativity, and professional morale.

I want to posit a more *optimal* business model—meaning the best solution relative to a stated set of objectives, constraints, and assumptions.

7

The Business Model of the Firm of the Future

The *correspondence principle* is what scientists use when comparing two theories. The new theory should be able to replicate the successes of the old theory, explain where it fails, and offer new insights. It is time to replace the old firm model of "We sell time," described in the previous chapter, with a radical business model.

Why radical? Because it comes from the Latin for "getting back to the root." In this case, the root means customers buy value, not time, which leads us to a more optimal business model:

Profitability = Intellectual Capital × Effectiveness × Price

Let us explore each component of the above equation; then we will discuss why it is a better theory for explaining the success of firms operating in today's intellectual capital economy.

Revenue Is Vanity—Profit Is Sanity

We start with profitability, rather than revenue, because we are not interested in growth merely for the sake of growth. As many companies around the world have learned—some the hard way, such as the airlines, retailers, and automobile manufacturers—market share is not the open sesame to more profitability. We are interested in finding the right customer, at the right price, consistent with our purpose and values, even if that means frequently turning away customers.

Adopting this belief means you need to become much more selective about whom you do business with, even though that marginal business may be "profitable" by conventional accounting standards. Very often the most important costs—and benefits, for that matter—do not ever show up on a profit-and-loss statement. There is such a thing as good and bad profits. Accepting customers who are not a good fit for your firm—either because of their personality or their unwillingness to appreciate your value—has many deleterious effects, such as negatively affecting team member morale and committing fixed capacity to customers for whom you simply cannot create value. Growth without profit is perilous.

Businesses Have Prices, Not Hourly Rates

Everything we buy as consumers we know the price upfront. The billable hour violates this basic economic law, and it does so at the peril of the professions. No customer buys time—it measures efforts, not results. Customers demand to make a price/value assessment *before* they purchase, not after.

The word *value* has a specific meaning in economics: "The maximum amount that a consumer would be willing to pay for an item." Therefore, **value pricing** can be defined as *the maximum amount a given customer is willing to pay for a particular service, before the work begins.*

Why Intellectual Capital Is the Chief Source of Wealth

The Intellectual Capital Management Gathering Best Practices conference in 1995 defined intellectual capital as "knowledge that can be converted into profits," which is an adequate definition for our purposes since it equates knowledge with a verb (Lev 2001: 155). Intellectual capital should not be confused with knowledge management, which is merely a process, whereas intellectual capital (IC) is an entity.

Today, intellectual capital is sometimes thought of as nothing more than another "buzzword." However, IC has *always* been the chief driver of wealth, as economists have argued since the term *human capital* was first coined in 1961, and as far back as the late eighteenth century when Adam Smith discredited the idea of mercantilism. Wealth does not reside in tangible assets or money; it resides in the IC that exists in the human spirit, which is then used to create valuable goods and services. For our purposes we are going to separate a company's IC into three categories, as originally proposed by Karl-Erik Sveiby, a leading thinker in knowledge theory, in 1989:

- **Human capital (HC).** This comprises your team members and associates who work either for you or with you. As one industry leader said, this is the capital that leaves in the elevator at night. The important thing to remember about HC is that it cannot be owned, only contracted, since it is completely volitional. In fact, more and more, knowledge workers own the means of your firm's production, and knowledge workers will invest their personal HC in those firms that pay a decent return on investment, both economic and psychological. In the final analysis, your people are not assets (they deserve more respect than a copier machine and a computer); they are not resources to be harvested from the land like coal when you run out. Ultimately, they are *volunteers* and it is totally up to them whether they get back into the elevator the following morning.

- **Structural capital.** This is everything that remains in your firm once the HC has stepped into the elevator, such as databases, customer lists, systems, procedures, intranets, manuals, files, technology, business models, and all of the explicit knowledge tools you utilize to produce results for your customers.
- **Social capital.** This includes your customers, the main reason a business exists; but it also includes your suppliers, vendors, networks, referral sources, alumni, joint ventures and alliance partners, professional associations, reputation, and so on. Of the three types of IC, this is perhaps the least leveraged, and yet it is highly valued by customers.

The crucial point to understand here is that it is the *interplay* among the three types of IC above that generates wealth-creating opportunities for your firm. Human capital, for example, can grow in two ways: when the business utilizes more of what each person knows, and when people know more things that are useful to the firm and/or its customers. And since knowledge is a "nonrival" good—meaning we can both possess it at the same time without diminishing it—knowledge shared is knowledge that is effectively *doubled* throughout the organization. That is why former Hewlett-Packard CEO Lew Platt said, "If HP knew what HP knows, we would be three times as profitable."

Another useful way to think about IC is by ownership. Human capital is owned by the knowledge worker; structural capital is the only component of IC that is owned by the firm; and social capital is owned by no one, though it can be leveraged, monetizing benefits to the owners of the firm. When Robert Goizueta, then CEO of Coca-Cola, was asked what the lesson was from the New Coke debacle, he replied that he learned that Coca-Cola did not own its brand—the consumer did (Tedlow 2001: 105).

A fascinating study by the World Bank, *Where Is the Wealth of Nations?*, finds that 75 percent of the world's wealth resides in human capital. In the United States, 82 percent of our 2000 per capita wealth resided in intangible capital (16 percent is produced capital, and only 3 percent in natural capital). The poorest country, Ethiopia, derives 50 percent of its wealth from intangible capital, 41 percent from natural capital, and 9 percent from produced capital (World Bank 2006).

Knowledge firms are the ultimate "asset-less" organizations, since 75 percent of their value-creating capacity is owned by the volunteers who work there. This is a tectonic shift not only in the nature of wealth-creation but in how firms need to think about how they work. So before we leave this brief discussion of IC, it is necessary to explain something that may, at first impression, not seem obvious.

Negative Intellectual Capital

When IC is discussed, it is normally done in a very positive context, as most of the examples used are from successes in leveraging IC, such as Microsoft or Pixar. But it is important to understand there is such a thing as *negative* human capital, *negative* structural capital, and *negative* social capital. Certainly, this sounds counterintuitive, but it is nonetheless true. Not everything we know is beneficial. Think of the IC a thief possesses; it is knowledge in the sense he knows how to perform his craft, just as much as United Airlines knows how to fly planes and transport people around the world. But that does not make the knowledge valuable, and with respect to thieves, the social loss they impose is a societal negative.

Think of countries that dogmatically adhere to the principles of socialism or Marxism, even though both of these theories of social organization have been repudiated by empirical evidence. There has been enormous negative social capital built up over the past five decades in Castro's Cuba, just as there was in the former Soviet Union. Castro thought he maintained the most crucial capital from the capitalists, all the stores and buildings and so on to create a great Cuban city. He did—in Miami, since the crucial human capital left Cuba.

Examples of negative intellectual capital in a professional firm would include a rigid adherence to old methods that are hindering your people from achieving their potential, and subtracting from value creation. High on this list would be cost-plus pricing, Industrial Age efficiency metrics, focusing on activities and costs rather than on results and value, and other forms of negative IC that have embedded themselves into the culture. These negative ideas have permeated each type of knowledge discussed herein—human, structural, and certainly social—and have become part of our tacit and explicit knowledge systems. One of the duties of this book is to point out how these legacy systems are indeed *negative* forms of IC and need to be replaced in the firm of the future.

Why Effectiveness Trumps Efficiency

Efficiency means focus on costs. But the optimizing approach should focus on *effectiveness*. Effectiveness focuses on opportunities to produce revenue, to create markets, and to change the economic characteristics of existing products and markets. It asks not, How do we do this or that better? It asks, Which of the products really produce extraordinary economic results or are capable of producing them? ... It then asks, To what results should, therefore, the resources and efforts of the business be allocated so as to produce extraordinary results rather than the "ordinary" ones which is all efficiency can possibly produce?

—Peter Drucker, *People and Performance*, 2007

This is a critical component of the new business model, probably more controversial than value pricing versus hourly billing. It goes to the heart of how we measure, judge, assess, and compensate our knowledge workers, and what we measure internally to understand if we are creating value for customers. Attacking the concept of efficiency is similar to attacking motherhood and apple pie, but I am going to do it anyway. The fact is, a ruthless focus on efficiency is the wrong talisman in a professional knowledge firm, or indeed in any business.

Since all transformations are linguistic, let us start with definitions. In his book *Reinvent Your Enterprise*, Jack Bergstrand, founder of Brand Velocity, Inc., provides the following definitions:

Efficiency focuses on doing things right.
Effectiveness concentrates on doing the right things.
Productivity is about doing them both at the same time (Bergstrand n.d: 7).

I am using Bergstrand's work since he is attempting to build a knowledge organization—a consultancy firm known as Brand Velocity—based upon the teachings of Peter Drucker, especially Drucker's concept of the knowledge economy and knowledge workers. He has many contributions to make in applying the teachings of Drucker, but I take exception with his definition of productivity above.

There are many examples of firms being inefficient yet still being highly effective. However, there are few, if any, examples of a firm increasing effectiveness by increasing efficiency. I know this sounds incredibly counterintuitive and goes against the grain of how most of us were taught in business school, especially the axiom "What you can measure you can manage."

We read and hear it repeated everywhere: Efficiency needs to be improved in professional firms. But nowhere is the term "efficiency" defined. What, exactly, does it mean to say that efficiency needs to be increased?

What, Exactly, Is Productivity?

Productivity and efficiency are *always* a ratio, expressed as the amount of output per unit of input. Mathematically, it seems straightforward, as if there was one widely agreed upon definition of the components of the numerator and denominator. In an intellectual capital economy, however, it is a conundrum.

Take the denominator in the ratio. Which inputs should be included? If we are dealing with wine, we could count the costs of the grapes, the bottles, corks, and so on, none of which would help us define—let alone value—the final product. As they say, it is much easier to count the bottles than describe the wine.

If we were dealing with Rembrandt's productivity, we could sum up the cost of paint, canvas, brushes, and even the amount of labor hours spent plying his craft. Would there be any relationship to the final value of the output? Would counting the number of paintings produced over a given time period help? We can calculate how many surgeries the cardiologist performs in a given number of hours, but it does not tell us anything about the quality of life for the patient. Was Einstein efficient? How would you know? Who cares?

Firms have learned that costs are easier to compute than benefits, so they cut the costs in the denominator to improve the efficiency. This is the equivalent of Walt Disney cutting out three of the dwarfs in *Snow White and the Seven Dwarfs* in order to reduce the inputs, making the resulting ratio look better. Efficient, yes; effective, hardly. The fact of the matter is, we do not know how to measure the efficiency of a knowledge worker. And this is true for a very fundamental reason.

There's No Such Thing as Generic "Efficiency"

Efficiency cannot be meaningfully defined without regard to your purpose, desires, and preferences. It cannot simply be reduced to output per man-hour. It is inextricably linked to what people want—and at what cost people are willing to pay. Consider the example of a hammer in a poor country. It is likely to drive more nails per year, since it is most likely shared among more people and sits idle less of the time. But that does not make the poor country more efficient; it just proves that capital tends to be scarcer and more expensive in those countries.

During the Cold War, the old Soviet Union used to boast that the average Soviet boxcar moved more freight per year than the average American boxcar. Yet this didn't prove they were more efficient. On the contrary, it proved that Soviet railroads lacked the abundant capital of the American industry and that Soviet labor had less valuable alternatives to engage in than their American counterparts (I am indebted to Thomas Sowell and his masterful book *Basic Economics* for these two examples).

When economists use the term "efficiency" they are not doing so in the technical sense that, for example, the most efficient car is the one that gets the most miles per gallon. Gasoline is not the only scarce good, and it is not the only purpose of owning an automobile. It is sometimes cheaper to waste gasoline to have more of other things we value greater, such as safety, room, style, or acceleration. Indeed, if we were to measure the "efficiency" of most automobiles based on an output/input ratio we would discover most cars are completely inefficient, since they are idle a majority of the time. So what? When we want to go somewhere, they are very effective, and we gladly pay the price of the reduced efficiency.

Princeton economist William J. Baumol asks this thought-provoking question: How would you go about increasing the productivity of a string quartet playing Beethoven? Would you drop the second violin or ask the musicians to play the piece twice as fast?

So, why all the fuss about efficiency? Most likely because it can be easily measured. But that in no way means we can *manage* it, let alone *change* it, especially when you're talking about knowledge workers. One does not change one's weight by having a more accurate scale, or by weighing yourself more frequently.

None of this is meant to suggest that firms ignore productivity tools, such as document management, faster computers, software, printers, dual monitors, PDA devices, and the like. We are not Luddites. No one is suggesting we return to typewriters and carbon paper, though the logic of the billable hour would reward that very behavior.

I am making a very different argument: Efficiency in a professional firm, in and of itself, is *not* a competitive advantage. It is the equivalent of having restrooms. If your firm is not using the latest technological tools, that is incredibly inefficient; but if it is, so what? All of your competitors are too. The differences in firm revenue and profit cannot be explained by efficiency, only effectiveness in customer service, as well as the ability to create, communicate, and capture value. Efficiency is a table stake—the minimum you need to be in the game. Real competitive advantage is built on effectiveness, not efficiency.

Simply stating that a firm wants to be more efficient is meaningless. They need to define what they are trying to accomplish long before they can begin to consider the best way to achieve their objectives. What are firms trying to accomplish? What is the goal? Is it simply to crank out more work per labor hour? If that is the case, then under the hourly billing model their revenue actually *decreases*. That seems ludicrous. Is it to crank out more work per labor hour to increase firm capacity? For what purpose? To add more low-value customers? That, too, does not make much sense.

The ruthless quest for increased efficiency, especially through inward-looking tactics such as Lean and Six Sigma, contains within it a grave moral hazard. It is encouraging behavior from firm leaders that is driving out creativity, innovation, dynamism, and customer service, as well as talent, from the professions.

In too many professional firms, efficiency has become a talisman. But firm leaders should agonize over *effectiveness*. Better still, focus on *efficaciousness*; meaning having the power to produce a desired effect. The term "efficaciousness" is used to describe the miraculous power of many drugs since it suggests possession of a special quality or virtue that makes it possible to achieve a result—exactly what we are trying to accomplish in firms for customers. In an intellectual capital economy, and within firms, where wealth is created using the power of the mind—as opposed to the brawn of the body—these characteristics better explain the value created by knowledge workers.

Where Do Profits Come From?

A ship in harbor is safe—but that is not what ships are for.

—John A. Shedd (1859 to circa 1928)

In seminars around the world, we have presented to participants the following three factors of production in any economy, and the type of income derived therefrom:

1. Land = Rents
2. Labor = Salaries and Wages
3. Capital = Interest, Dividends, and Capital Gains

We then ask a deceptively simple question: Where do profits come from? The answers range from entrepreneurs and value to revenue minus expenses and customers. Nevertheless, the real answer is that profits come from *risk*. The word *entrepreneur* comes from the French word *entreprendre*, meaning "to undertake."

When a business engages in innovation, it is taking a risk. In Italian, the word *risk* derives from *risicare*, which means "to dare," which implies a choice, not a fate, as Peter L. Bernstein points out in his outstanding study of risk, *Against the Gods*. In other words, risk is an economic positive. There are five possible responses when confronted with risk: avoid it, reduce it, transfer it, accept it, or increase it. A business cannot eliminate risk, because that would eliminate profits. The goal is to take calculated risks and choose them prudently. The dilemma in many firms is that they are allocating a disproportionate share of their resources in perpetuating yesterday and today rather than creating tomorrow. For example, by setting a nice comfortable *floor* under their earnings (via the hourly billing mechanism), they have commensurately placed an artificial *ceiling* over their heads as well. This is self-imposed, and it comes from the attempt to avoid risk and uncertainty.

Ponder labor unions, the epitome of an institution attempting to avoid risk. Talk with union members and you quickly discover they credit the union for their standard of living. Certainly, they are paid an above-market wage (Milton Friedman has proved this point), receive good benefits, a healthy pension, and generous time off. But have you ever met a wealthy rank-and-file union member? The trade-off they make for their union compensation package is an artificial ceiling they can never rise above, at least not while employed in a union job, since seniority and other stultifying restrictions limit their potential.

Risk avoidance is the antithesis to a successful enterprise, condemning it to mediocrity, perhaps even extinction. Risks need to be weighed against one another, not zero risk, or "acceptable" or "unacceptable" risk. Our cars go faster because they have brakes, a trade-off we are willing to risk. The firm's goal should be to maximize wealth-creating opportunities rather than to minimize risk.

Businesses have very sophisticated means of measuring the costs and benefits of risks, *once they have been taken*. But the risk occurs only *before* the event, and cannot be accurately measured until *after* it has occurred. If movie studios knew which movies were going to fail beforehand, they would not make them. There is no theory—in economics or finance—that measures the cost of *not* taking a risk. Yet it is precisely these losses that cost the firm the most.

For a firm to be truly innovative, it must not only do new things, it must stop doing old things. It is not possible to create tomorrow unless one first disposes of yesterday. Maintaining yesterday is always expensive. The human body has an automatic mechanism to discharge waste, but it appears the corporate body does not—that requires leadership and vision. Drucker was also fond of saying, "Results are achieved by exploiting opportunities, not solving problems. Solving problems only returns the company to the status quo" (Kames 2008: 56).

The word "profit" comes from the Latin noun *profectus* for "progress" and the verb *proficere* for "to advance." We must always remember that profits, ultimately, are derived from risk taking, and no equation, no matter how complex and intricate, will ever be able to capture the essence of an entrepreneur, an effective executive, or a profit-making enterprise with a distinguished purpose that advances progress for society.

If Only I Knew Then What I Know Now

The thirteenth-century Spanish king Alfonso X said with no apparent modesty, "Had I been present at the creation, I would have given some useful hints for the better ordering of the universe." Likewise, when I entered the accounting profession in 1984 as a young, eager, determined "staff" person in the ranks of one of the then Big Eight accounting firms, and believed my destiny was to become partner, I wish I knew then what I know now.

I was taught from day one what approximately two generations of accountants—and probably three or more of attorneys—had been taught before me: "You sell your time." I had no reason to believe this conventional wisdom was not true. After all, I now had an hourly rate, which defined my status and rank in the pecking order of the firm. I completed a timesheet every two weeks, in increments of a quarter-hour, or my paycheck was dutifully withheld. It seemed quite logical and rational that all I had to provide our customers was my time.

Then when I launched my own firm, I was the epitome of what statisticians call path dependent—that is, the older I became, the greater the chance that what I would be in the future would be influenced by what I was in the past. It was not until I had been out on my own for a few years that I started to wrestle seriously against the conventional wisdom of my chosen profession.

As they say, the results of a life are incalculable and unpredictable, as we make our journey toward the future. The years teach so much of what the days never knew. If I had known then what I know now, like Alfonso X, I certainly would have offered a better business model for the professional firm, along with a deeper understanding of the value that knowledge workers provide to their customers.

The new business model offered herein is not about predicting the future; it is about helping to shape and create the future. No one can predict the future, and only a fool tries. But we can influence the future based upon the decisions and choices we make. The world is not controlled by some ever-swinging pendulum of history or some outside fate. We create the future by the actions we take today. The Berlin Wall did not fall because of inclement weather—it was *pushed*. Ultimately, all history is biography, which is why I fervently believe that firms themselves must make these changes, not their customers. You are in charge of your own destiny.

Summary and Conclusions

This chapter has laid the groundwork for the remaining chapters. We have covered a lot of material here, and have presented some radical (Latin for "getting back to the root") ideas. I have argued that the old business model is not worthy of enterprises more and more comprising knowledge workers, because it leverages the wrong things and does not explain the elements of success in an intellectual capital economy. The new business model does all of these things and is a worthy paradigm for the noble calling of the professions.

Even better, if the model posited here is someday replaced with a better one, I will have contributed to the advancement of the professions— and nothing would please me more.

Let us now turn our focus to the foundations of *creating* value for customers by asking ourselves what is conceivably the most fundamental question any firm has to answer.

PART II

Foundations of Creating Value

"Price is what you pay. Value is what you get."

—Warren Buffett

CHAPTER 3

Why Are We in Business?

To know what a business is we have to start with its purpose. There is only one valid definition of business purpose: *to create a customer*. Because its purpose is to create a customer, the business enterprise has two—and only these two—basic functions: marketing and innovation. Marketing and innovation produce results; all the rests are costs.

—Peter Drucker, *People and Performance*, 2007

When participants in our seminars are asked why they are in business, more than 75 percent answer, "To make a profit."

Yet is the answer really that simple?

Any business needs to earn a profit to survive; indeed, profit is the measurement of how much value an organization adds to the lives of others. It is also a premium earned for risk and uncertainty. That said, to think that a business exists solely to make a profit is to confuse cause and effect—we must distinguish between the *purpose* of a business with its *goal*. As Peter Drucker indefatigably pointed out, not only is the notion that businesses exist to make a profit false, it is irrelevant. Profit is a *result* of customer behavior. More accurately, profit is a *lagging indicator* of customer behavior. The real results of any organization take place in the hearts and minds of its customers.

The Economist's Definition of Profit

Too many people think only of their own profit. But business opportunity seldom knocks on the door of self-centered people. No customer ever goes to a store merely to please the storekeeper.

—Kazuo Inamori, founder of Kyocera Corp.

Economists use a different definition of profit from that of the typical financial statement. They consider both parties to a transaction, because both parties must receive more value than each is giving up; otherwise no transaction would be consummated in the first place (assuming no fraud or coercion). United States Representative Samuel Barrett Pettengill (1886–1974) gave an excellent definition of *profit* from an economist's perspective:

> The successful producer of an article sells it for more than it costs him to make, and that's his profit. But the customer buys it only because it's worth more to her than she pays for it, and that's her profit. No one can long make a profit producing anything unless the customer makes a profit using it.

A most articulate expression of the above definition came from Stanley Marcus (1905–2002), chairman emeritus of Neiman-Marcus, one of the ultimate authorities on customer service:

> You're really not in business to make a profit, but you're in business to render a service that is so good people are willing to pay a profit in recognition of what you're doing for them.

Figure 3.1 demonstrates that for every voluntary transaction that occurs, both the seller and the buyer earn a profit. The total value the seller creates over and above its costs is the economic value added to society. The price the seller charges is the portion of the total value created it captures, while the excess value over price accrues to the buyer. To the extent the seller can add more total value, represented by the arrow, the price can more easily be increased to capture a fair share of that marginal value. In reality, there is no way for a seller to capture all of the economic value created— the buyer must also earn a profit. This economic fact provides a plethora

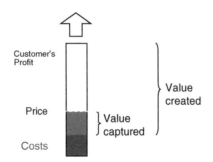

FIGURE 3.1 Value Creation and Capture

of opportunities for firms to increase profits by using a combination of value created and strategic pricing.

The Marketing Concept and Total Quality Service

Peter Drucker explained the same idea by what he termed the *marketing concept*, in the early 1960s. The purpose of any organization—from a governmental agency or nonprofit foundation, to a church or a corporation—exists to create results *outside* of itself. The result of a school is an educated student, as is a cured patient for a hospital, or a saved soul for a church. A business exists to create wealth for its customers.

The only thing that exists inside of a business are costs, activities, efforts, problems, mediocrity, friction, politics, crises, and a grapevine that would make Ernest and Julio Gallo proud. In fact, Peter Drucker wrote, "One of the biggest mistakes I have made during my career was coining the term *profit center*, around 1945. I am thoroughly ashamed of it now, because inside a business there are no profit centers, just cost centers" (Drucker, 2002: 49, 84). The only profit center is a customer's check that does not bounce. Customers are indifferent to the internal workings of your firm in terms of costs, desired profit levels, and efforts. Nobody wants to hear about the labor pains—they want to see the baby.

What makes the marketing concept so breathtakingly brilliant is that the focus is always on the outside of the organization. It does not look inside and ask, "What do we want and need?" but rather it looks outside to the customer and asks, "What do you desire and value?" While the marketing concept has existed for decades, it is regularly ignored because professional firms lose sight of the fact that the sole reason they exist is to serve customers outside of their four walls. In the final analysis, a firm does not exist to be efficient, control costs, perform cost accounting, or give people fancy titles and power over the lives of others. It exists to create results and value *outside* of itself. This profound lesson must not be forgotten.

The best professionals, in any of the professions, are those who care deeply about their customers as fellow humans. David Maister makes this very point in his splendid book *True Professionalism*, which should be *required* reading for all professionals: "The opposite of the word *professional* is not *unprofessional*, but rather *technician*. Professionalism is predominantly an attitude, not a set of competencies. A real professional is a technician who cares" (Maister 1997: 16).

Maister's definition is the embodiment of Total Quality Service, as defined by Karl Albrecht in his trailblazing book *The Only Thing That Matters*:

A state of affairs in which an organization delivers superior value to its stakeholders: its customers, its owners, and its employees (Albrecht 1992: 72).

Notice how this definition is a goal condition to be sought, not a particular method of operation. Methods are developed as a way to achieve the goal, not as ends in themselves. There is a sign in the textile plant of the Baldridge National Quality Award–winning Milliken & Company that reads: "Quality is not the absence of defects as defined by management, but the presence of value as defined by customers."

Summary and Conclusions

Perhaps another reason we lose sight of the truth that businesses exist to create wealth is that the language of business is drawn largely from war and sports analogies. In sports, a competition is usually zero-sum; meaning one competitor wins and the other loses. This is not at all relevant in a business setting. Just because your competitors flourish does not mean you lose. There is room for both FedEx and UPS, Airbus and Boeing, Pepsi and Coke, Ford and Toyota, and while their sparring might be mistaken as some war, as John Kay points out, "not in Pepsi's wildest fantasies does it imagine that the conflict will end in the second burning of Atlanta [the location of Coca-Cola's head office]" (Koch 2001: 73). When Coca-Cola changed their recipe to New Coke, company spokesman Carlton Curtis stated, "You're talking about having some guts—and doing something that few managements would have the guts to do." If you find it amusing that grown men talk about *guts* and *recipes* in the same sentence, then it should be obvious business has nothing to do with war.

Business is not about annihilating your competition; it is about adding more value to your customers. War destroys, commerce builds. Marketplaces are conversations, derived from the word for the Greek marketplace, the *agora*. It is where buyers and sellers meet to discuss their wares, share visions of the future, where supply and demand intersect with an invisible handshake. It is as far removed from war as capitalism is from communism, and perhaps these war analogies, too, need to be tossed onto the ash heap of history.

Any firm has to understand what customers truly value, since all economic value is in the eye of the beholder, the subject of our next chapter.

A Tale of Two Theories

In the final analysis, I find nothing as intellectually satisfying as the history of ideas. ... [W]ithout the history of economics, economic theories just drop from the sky; you have to take them on faith. The moment you wish to judge a theory, you have to ask how they came to be produced in the first place and that is a question that can only be answered by the history of ideas.

—Mark Blaug, *Not Only an Economist*, 1997

Adam Smith (1723–1790) was confounded. One of the greatest economic and social thinkers in the history of ideas struggled with the so-called diamond-water paradox, which Smith explained in Chapter 4 of Book I of *The Wealth of Nations*: "Nothing is more useful than water: but it will purchase scarce anything. ... A diamond, on the contrary, has scarce any value in use; but a very great quantity of other goods may frequently be had in exchange for it" (Skousen and Taylor 1997: 27). None of us would be able to live beyond a couple of weeks without water, yet its price is relatively cheap compared to the frivolous diamond, which certainly no one needs to stay alive. This conundrum led to some incredible discoveries, advancing our understanding of value.

Most people confronted with this paradox—including Smith—would resolve it by replying the supply of diamonds is sparse compared to water, and hence they command a higher price. This is an intuitive and very reasonable solution. Water *is* approximately 71 percent of the earth's surface, while diamonds are found in only a limited number of places in the world, and the supply is even further restricted by diamond cartels.

Yet the scarcity theory lacks explanatory power. If it was true, I, as the author of the book you are now holding, could sign your copy in pink crayon, attesting to the fact that only one copy exists of this book with my autograph in pink crayon. It is like a Picasso, one of a kind—in other words, scarce. How much is it worth? My autograph does not enhance the value of the book by even one cent. Just because something is scarce does not make it valuable. There must be a better theory that solves this puzzle, so let us explore the antecedents of the theory of value.

The Labor Theory of Value

Throughout history, man has always correlated labor with value, inputs with outputs. In medieval English, the word *acre* meant the amount of land a team of eight oxen could plow in a morning.

Even Smith identified two separate forms of value—"value in use" and a "value in exchange," which gave rise to the famous diamond-water paradox, since certain items for one's own use were highly valuable (e.g., water) but commanded little in exchange for other goods, like diamonds. In essence, Smith decided to ignore a commodity's value in use and just focus on value in exchange. Indeed, to this day, one sees various pricing books distinguishing value in use from value in exchange.

Yet Smith understood there were factors other than labor that went into the cost of producing commodities, such as the cost of capital, equipment, rent, and the risk the entrepreneur was assuming. All these factors also had to be compensated in the price of the final commodity, so Smith posited a "cost of production" theory of value, in effect "adding up" labor, profit, rent, and cost of capital to determine price. Of course, this still begs the question of how a company could ever lose money by following this theory, since even the most inept businessperson would be able to add up all of these factors to derive a price that generates a profit.

Here we have an eminent economist—although called a moral philosopher in his day—who struggled to develop a unifying and credible theory of value. It would take another influential economist to popularize a theory of value that appeared to advance his utopian objectives.

Karl Marx, False Prophet

The philosophers have only interpreted the world in various ways. The point however is to change it.

—Inscription on Karl Marx's tomb, Highgate Cemetery, London

Workers of the world … forgive me.

—Graffiti on a statute of Karl Marx, Moscow, 1991

"Go on, get out—last words are for fools who haven't said enough." So said Karl Marx to his housekeeper, who urged him to tell her his last words so she could write them down. Karl Marx is far from dead. His flock might have perished, but his church lives on. His labor theory of value still wields enormous influence over our present-day concept of value and price. Here is how Marx explained his theory in *Value, Price and Profit*, originally published in 1865:

> A commodity has *a value*, because it is a *crystallisation of social labour.* The *greatness* of its value, or its *relative* value, depends upon the greater or less amount of that social substance contained in it; that is to say, on the relative mass of labour necessary for its production. The *relative values of commodities* are, therefore, determined by the *respective quantities or amounts of labor, worked up, realized, fixed in them.* The *correlative* quantities of commodities which can be produced in the *same time of labor* are *equal* (Marx 1995: 31).

This, too, sounds quite reasonable, until you put this theory to the test of explaining how people spend their money in the marketplace.

Marx's theory cannot explain how land and natural resources have value, since there is no labor contained in them. Taken to its extreme, the labor theory of value would predict those countries with the most labor hours—such as China or India—would have the highest standards of living. But this is demonstrably false, and what we witness instead in countries with *less* labor inputs and more entrepreneurship—as well as secure private property and other institutions conducive to economic growth—are vastly higher standards of living, including shorter hours for workers.

If Marx's theory was correct, a rock found next to a diamond in a mine would be of equal value, since each took the same number of labor hours to locate and extract. Yet how many rocks do you see in the local mall's jewelry store? If you were to have pizza for lunch today, under Marx's theory, your tenth slice would be just as valuable as your first, since each took the same number of labor hours to produce. One glaring flaw in Marx's theory was that it did not take into account the law of diminishing marginal utility, which states that the value to the customer declines with additional consumption of the good in question.

Another Marxian flaw is the very nature of a transaction between a willing buyer and seller is not based on an equality of labor but rather the *inequality* in the subjective value of the good bought and sold. This takes us back to one of Adam Smith's central insights: that both the buyer and the seller must gain from an exchange, or it will not take place. Were this not so, a contractor could build any type of house *he* wanted, hire incompetent and lazy workers, tally up his costs, add a desired profit, and still receive his full price.

The Marginalist Revolution of 1871

Three economists, from three different countries, developed the theory of marginalism and created a revolution, which took approximately 20 years to become generally accepted theory: William Stanley Jevons (1835–1882), from Great Britain; Leon Walras (1834–1910), from France; and Carl Menger (1840–1921), from Austria. There were forerunners to the marginal theory, but it was not until these three came together that the theory was accepted as valid in the economics profession. "Swedish economist Knut Wicksell, who lived through the marginalist revolution, described it as a 'bolt from the blue'" (Skousen 2001: 169).

What made this new theory so revolutionary? As Menger explains in his book *Principles of Economics*, written in 1873 when he was 33 years old:

> Value is … nothing inherent in goods, no property of them. Value is a judgment economizing men make about the importance of the goods at their disposal for the maintenance of their lives and well-being. Hence value does not exist outside the consciousness of men. … [T]he value of goods … is entirely subjective in nature" (Ebenstein 2003: 23).

> The value of goods arises from their relationship to our needs, and is not inherent in the goods themselves. … Objectification of the value of goods, which is entirely *subjective* in nature, has nevertheless contributed very greatly to confusion about the basic principles of our science. … The importance that goods have for us and which we call value is merely imputed (Menger 1976: 120–121, 139).

Value is like beauty—it is in the eye of the beholder. This theory has enormous explanatory and predictive capabilities, because it explains, for instance, why people dive for pearls. Marx would say pearls have value because people dive for them (thus supplying labor). Menger would retort that people dive for pearls because other people value them.

Philip Wicksteed, a British clergyman, wrote a scientific critique of the Marxian labor theory of value in 1884, where he explained:

> A coat is not worth eight times as much as a hat to the community because it takes eight times as long to make it. … The community is willing to devote eight times as long to the making of a coat because it will be worth eight times as much to it (Howey 1989: 157).

Cause and effect is confused constantly on this principle. I remember taking a wine tour of Far Niente Winery in Napa Valley, where the guide was explaining how one particular vintage had to be bottled by hand, which was why it was more expensive—due to the extra labor this entailed. I could not help thinking of Wicksteed and the Marginalists, who would retort: No, you are willing to invest in the labor necessary to bottle the wine by hand because some customers find it valuable (and delicious!) enough to cover the extra labor costs. Yet there are endless examples of this confusion, especially in professional firms that indoctrinate their professionals to believe that value resides in billable hours.

None of this discussion is meant to imply businesses cannot *create* the demand for a product. No one "demanded"—or subjectively valued—a Sony Walkman or the Apple iPod before they were produced and offered in the market. Quite often, supply does indeed create demand, especially as it relates to innovations and new technologies. But there is no guarantee of consumer acceptance just because costs were incurred; the high rate of product failures is a testament to this fact. Nonetheless, in the long run, a product or service will *continue* to be produced only if people value it, and its price can cover its full costs of production.

Why Are Diamonds More Expensive Than Water?

Besides being abundant, water tends to be priced based upon the marginal satisfaction of the last gallon consumed. The German economist Hermann Heinrich Gossen (1810–1858) developed what is known as *Gossen's Law*: The market price is always determined by what the last unit of a product is worth to people.

While the first several gallons of water may be vital for your survival, the water used to shower, flush the toilet, and wash the dishes is less valuable. Less valuable still is the water used to wash your dog, your car, and hose down your driveway. The market price of water reflects the last uses of the good for the aggregate of all consumers of water. On the other hand, the marginal satisfaction of one more diamond tends to be very high (even for Elizabeth Taylor).

If water companies knew you were dehydrated in the desert, they would be able to charge a higher price for those first vital gallons consumed, and then gradually adjust the price downward to reflect the less valuable marginal gallons. Since they do not possess this information—the cost of doing so would be prohibitive—the aggregate market price for water tends to be based upon its *marginal* value.

As a consumer, if I'm dehydrated in the desert, near death, a bottle of Evian water is *priceless*, compared to the same quantity of water used to wash my dishes or dog. If my basement is flooded with water, now it has a *negative* value to me, since I will have to pay someone to remove it. Value is not only subjective, it is contextual.

One CFO of a top-tier law firm said to me, "You are right; we sell intellectual capital, but it is denominated in hours." Well, you might as well plunge a ruler in the oven to determine its temperature if you think hours spent is a good measure of value created. Thomas Sowell explains how the economics profession finally overcame this absurd notion:

> By the late nineteenth century, however, economists had given up on the notion that it is primarily labor which determines the value of goods. ... This new understanding marked a revolution in the development of economics. It is also a sobering reminder of how long it can take for even highly intelligent people to get rid of a misconception whose fallacy then seems obvious in retrospect. It is not costs which create value; it is value which causes purchasers to be willing to repay the costs incurred in the production of what they want (Sowell 2004: 177).

To argue that you can measure value in hours is to say the value of Jonas Salk's polio vaccine is based on how long it took him to develop it.

Wrong Theory, Suboptimal Results

As John Maynard Keynes said, "The difficulty lies, not in the new ideas, but in escaping from the old ones, which ramify, for those brought up as most of us have been, into every corner of our minds." To this, philosopher Bertrand Russell added, "The resistance to a new idea increases as the square of its importance."

Just as geologists fought for decades against plate tectonics theory to explain earthquakes, and germ theory remained on the fringes of medical science until the late nineteenth century, the subjective theory of value is not widely taught or practiced in professional firms. Yet when people see this theory explained, they intuitively understand it, because it comports to human behavior, including their own as consumers. And is not this part of what learning can be about—understanding something you have known all along, but in a new way?

Despite this lesson, we return to our offices and fall back to pricing our services using a cousin of Marx's labor theory of value—the billable hour. This method of pricing ignores the four Ps of marketing and the five Cs of value, which we turn to next.

CHAPTER 5

Four Ps and Five Cs

[S]elling concerns itself with the tricks and techniques of getting people to exchange their cash for your product. It is not concerned with the values that the exchange is all about. And it does not, as marketing invariably does, view the entire business process as consisting of a tightly integrated effort to discover, create, arouse, and satisfy customer needs.

—Theodore Levitt, *Marketing Myopia*, 1975

Shawn Fanning was a 19-year-old college dropout in 1999 when he created Napster. In the first three months of 2001, 2.5 billion files a month were being downloaded, validating the economist's theory of demand, which states the that lower the price, the larger quantity demanded, especially a zero price. Nevertheless, from the music industry's perspective, when you have millions of potential customers breaking the law, you do not have a crime wave; you have a *marketing* problem.

The point is not to argue the highly contentious legal issues of copyright and private property law, particularly as it relates to digitally downloaded music files. The more precise point is the lack of understanding of value by the music company executives. By keeping their focus on the *inside* of their companies, they completely ignored the *external* value potential of easily obtaining music files. It took Steve Jobs of Apple Computer to capitalize on this opportunity with iTunes—which at the time of this writing has a 70 percent market share on the legal downloadable music market—in an eerily analogous manner in which he capitalized on the personal computer opportunity invented at Xerox's Palo Alto Research Center.

Had the music company executives been focused on the *outside* of their companies—studying, analyzing, and innovating what their customers found valuable—they could have invested many millions into productive research and development rather than throwing away that sum down the judicial sinkhole. Yet the Napster saga is just one in a long history of revolutions taking place outside the confines of an existing industry, in what the Austrian economist Joseph Schumpeter labeled the "perennial gale of creative destruction." The reason entire industries can be brought down is because competitors offer more value to the customer than the status quo.

In their course "Pricing: Strategy and Tactics," at the University of Chicago Graduate School of Business, Thomas Nagle and Reed Holden taught the four Ps of marketing using the farming analogy. This is a powerful analogy because it treats the four Ps as an interdependent system whose components have to work together to achieve the maximum result. As VeraSage Institute Senior Fellow and advertising agency consultant Tim Williams points out:

The default purpose of marketing is not to increase revenue. It is to increase profits.

Take *product*—your offering to the customer. Not only does this encompass the tangible product but it also encompasses the intangibles of service, experience, and transformational aspects of what the customer receives. In the farming analogy, product is the seed, crop, and planting process.

Promotion is an integral part of marketing. Whereas selling focuses on the needs of the seller, promotion concentrates on the needs—and desires—of the customer. Procter & Gamble spends billions of dollars annually on advertising. Promotion expenditures are becoming more sophisticated in their informational content and how they communicate to various segments of customers with the aid of technology. In the farming system, promotion is the equivalent of fertilizing the soil and watering the crop.

Marketing and promotion have become much more important in the professions, especially in the aftermath of the *Bates* decision. Prior to that U.S. Supreme Court ruling, most firms spent virtually nothing on advertising, marketing, and promotion. Today, it is common for firms to spend somewhere between 2 and 10 percent of gross revenue on these items, and even to have in-house marketing departments—usually non-CPAs or nonlawyers—who assist in selling the firm's services. This was relatively rare even 25 years ago, and arose in response to the maturing market for professional services.

Place is not where the firm's offices are located, but rather which type of customer the firm is servicing—your market niche. No firm can be everything to everyone, and specialization has become more important in order to segment various customers so you can tailor a value proposition to suit their needs. Place in the farm analogy is the land where you plant and grow your crop.

Last, but by no means least, is *price*, perhaps the most complex of the four Ps. Because value is subjective—and solely determined by the customer—pricing is an *art*, never a science. In the past, pricing has been largely determined on a cost-plus basis, once again focusing on the *internal* costs and activities rather than the *external* value and results created. Such pricing policies are relying on a silent fifth P of marketing—*prayer*—by hoping internal costs plus desired profit has a direct correlation to value for the customer, an improbable reality.

In the farming analogy, your price is the harvest, when you reap what you sow. While there are many ways for money to flow out of a company, price is the only way you have to generate revenue by *capturing* the value from what you create. In the past twenty years, companies have begun to gain a deeper understanding of this discipline, recognizing it as a separate body of knowledge and skill set. The Pricing Institute was founded in 1987. Later, Eric Mitchell formed the Professional Pricing Society in Atlanta, and Fordham University has created the Pricing Center, all done in an effort to disseminate intellectual capital with respect to the pricing function.

Industries—from airline, hotel, rental car, and retail businesses, to manufacturing, sports teams, and software—have invested enormous resources and intellectual capital in developing revenue management models and dynamic pricing software. Professional firms are laggards in this revolution, having relegated their pricing to a rote administrative and organizational task of completing timesheets and printing invoices. Pricing needs to be returned to the exalted position it deserves in the marketing mix.

Compared to the other three Ps, price transmits the most important signal to the customer—what the firm believes it is actually worth. This message, in effect, is louder than any advertising and promotion, because it creates the ultimate acoustics in the marketplace. Pricing is a strategic function, which needs to be aligned with the other three Ps to create a viable value proposition for the customer. Yet most firm leaders will spend more time and resources on the other components of marketing, neglecting the importance of the pricing function.

This is a costly mistake. Two studies, one performed by McKinsey & Company and the other by A.T. Kearny, both consulting firms, demonstrated that a 1 percent improvement in the following areas resulted in net income increasing, as shown in Table 5.1.

TABLE 5.1 Pricing Function and the Net Income Effect

	McKinsey	A.T. Kearny
Reducing fixed costs	2.7%	1.5%
Increasing volume	3.7%	2.5%
Reducing variable costs	7.3%	4.6%
Increase price	11%	7.1%

Source: Marn et al. 2004: 82; Docters et al. 2004: 6–7.

In his book *The 1% Windfall*, pricing expert Rafi Mohammed calculates the percentage increase in operating profit for the following companies, assuming a 1 percent increase in price, with no change in demand:

Sears	155%
Tyson	81%
Whirlpool	34%
Amazon	23%
Wal-Mart	18%
Home Depot	16%

Source: (Moahmmed 2010: xiii).

The percentage for a 1 percent pricing improvement would be even more dramatic for a professional firm. Since most costs in a professional firm are fixed, you can see that the largest payoff comes from focusing on strategic pricing, not trying to increase efficiency by lowering fixed costs. Even rainmaking ("volume" in the studies) cannot have the impact on profits that pricing is capable of achieving. Rainmaking is all well and good, but if you bring in those new customers at the wrong price, you have done nothing but added layers of mediocrity to your firm.

The Five Cs of Value

The main function of your firm's marketing strategy is not simply to acquire revenue at any price but to gain your share of highly profitable work. It is not enough to price based upon a customer's willingness and ability to pay; you must increase that willingness by constantly communicating the value of your offerings. For pricing to become a core competency in your firm, it must understand the five Cs of value, as documented in *The Strategy and Tactics of Pricing*, by Thomas Nagle and Reed Holden (2002: 164):

- *Comprehend* value to customers
- *Create* value for customers
- *Communicate* the value you create
- *Convince* customers they must pay for value
- *Capture* value with strategic pricing based on value, not costs and efforts

These five components determine the wealth-producing capacity of any firm and will drive profits in the long run. Every job for every customer has value drivers, and the firm's job is to *comprehend* what those are. Why does the customer want you to provide the service? What is the motivation for hiring you? Most professionals do not pay enough attention to the actual motivations of the customer, thinking they already know why they are being engaged to perform a service. But there are almost always motivations other than simply "I have to get my tax return in by the due date" or "My banker is demanding a financial statement review." It is not enough to focus on the technical product; you must probe deeper to discover the customer's true expectations and desires.

Creating value for the customer is not merely providing high-quality technical work, but would also include the level of service the customer experiences. It could also include the transformation you are guiding the customer through, from where they are to where they want to be. Bundling your services into a Fixed Price Agreement, offering a service guarantee, providing payment terms, and utilizing Change Orders are all methods used to enhance the value of your offering. Since value is always subjective, you have to get close to the customer to understand exactly what she values.

Even if the firm does a stellar job in creating value for customers, there no doubt will be instances where the customer does not understand the value. This places the onus on the firm to *communicate* to the customer the full value of what it is delivering. Understand that most customers do not have an incentive to collect data on the value you are providing, since they purchase relatively infrequently. Your firm, on the other hand, sells frequently; therefore, you should make communicating your unique value a core competency among your professionals. Certainly the marketing function is the main way to communicate to your chosen customers.

Convincing customers to pay for the value is an integral part of any firm's responsibilities. Of course, this job is much easier with the right customers, which is why prequalification is so critical. There is no right way to value price the *wrong* customer. The fact of the matter is that you are going to have a price discussion at some point with your customer, either at the *beginning* of the engagement or at the *end*. It simply cannot be avoided, since price is a major factor in any customer's decision whether or not to purchase. You need to face this issue squarely, and be confident as to the value you are providing. Most of a firm's customers are adept negotiators, since this is precisely how they built their businesses. This is especially true if your firm has to deal with procurement; in effect, these are professional buyers. You need professional pricers to bring some equality to the process.

The final duty is to *capture* the value you provide by utilizing the appropriate pricing strategy. This is where the billable hour method fails miserably, since it treats all jobs and all customers equally, and it prices the services, not the customer. There is no effective mechanism that allows prices to rise commensurate with value of the service, only with the labor time involved in production. Value pricing offers a much wider range of strategic pricing options the firm can implement to capture value.

You Are What You Charge

Let us revisit the Xerox saga mentioned at the start of this chapter with an important question: Why did Xerox fail to capitalize on the innovations its Palo Alto Research Center developed? This included the computer technology that eventually led to the Apple computer and launched the personal computer revolution. But Xerox did not see the opportunity right in front of it. In *Dealers of Lightning*, Michael Hiltzik offers this hypothesis for the failure:

> In the copier business Xerox got paid by the page; each page got counted by a clicker. In the electronic office of the future, there was no clicker—there was no annuity. How would one get paid? The hegemony of the pennies-per-page business model was so absolute that it blinded Xerox to an Aladdin's cave of other possibilities (Hamel 2000: 112).

A business is what it charges for. More precisely, a business is the value it creates. Ultimately, it must offer a value proposition that a customer is willing to pay for. Xerox's business model prevented it from seeking new and emerging opportunities in the marketplace—the same myopia that blinded the music industry to Napster, and the same myopia that is keeping professional firms mired in the mentality that what they sell is time.

Since value is the ultimate arbiter of price, it is worth exploring how customers determine value, the subject we turn to next, as we explore what and how people buy.

CHAPTER 6

What People Buy

What customers think they are buying, what they consider value, is decisive—it determines what a business is, what it produces, and whether it will prosper. And what customers buy and consider value is never a product. It is always utility, that is, what a product or service does for them. And what is value for customers is ... anything but obvious.

—Peter Drucker, *People and Performance*, 2007

It is a deceptively simple question: What are we getting paid for? Still, many businesses arrogantly assume they know what their customers want and believe they have been giving them exactly that for years. This is a myopic vision, and potentially harmful, as there now exists a plethora of information on why people buy, how they buy, and the decision process they go through, all of which businesses ignore at their peril.

In his book *How to Win Customers and Keep Them for Life*, Michael LeBoeuf suggests that customers have the following motivations for these various purchases:

- Don't sell me clothes. Sell me a sharp appearance style, and attractiveness.
- Don't sell me insurance. Sell me peace of mind and a great future for my family and me.
- Don't sell me a house. Sell me comfort, contentment, a good investment, and pride of ownership (and a piece of the American Dream).
- Don't sell me books. Sell me pleasant hours and the profits of knowledge (LeBoeuf 2000: 22–23).

Advertising giant Leo Burnett used to say, "Don't tell me how good you make it; tell me how good it makes me when I use it."

Peter Drucker has advanced the notion the patient knows the *symptoms*, but the doctor knows the *meaning*. But both must be listened to for a value-added relationship to develop. Doctors must not complain that the patient did not attend medical school; similarly, it does no good for a firm to complain that its customers "just don't understand the value of what we do." It is their job to make them understand the value and they can only do that by understanding—at a very deep and meaningful level—the motivations of why customers select and stay with the firms they do.

Again, Michael LeBoeuf distilled his summation of customer statements and posited the following overall theory to explain what people really buy:

Despite all of the untold millions of products and services for sale in today's marketplace, customers will exchange their hard-earned money for only two things:

- Good feelings
- Solutions to problems (LeBoeuf 2000: 23)

This is a good theory, because it has a certain utilitarian streak to it—that is, the idea that individuals spend their time (and money) pursuing pleasure and avoiding pain. It is the old marketing axiom that says you really do not buy drill bits; you buy the *hole* it makes. Understanding that simple fact could help a company (such as Black & Decker) get into the laser beam business, since they, too, put holes in things.

Professionals are excellent at solving problems. Sometimes they are even too good, because they tend to jump right into the solution without first discovering what the customer really wants and expects, almost completely ignoring the creation of good feelings that are so essential to developing long-term relationships. Simply offering solutions to problems is not enough. The customer automatically expects problems to be solved, which is why they seek out a professional in the first place. More emphasis needs to be placed on the total customer experience.

Focusing on the total customer experience demonstrates not just *competency* but *distinction*. But the utilitarian view posited by LeBoeuf does not help a firm custom-tailor its service offering to its various customers; which is why I prefer Theodore Levitt's theory of what customers really buy. *Expectations.*

The Dynamics of Customer Expectations

There is a difference between getting what you pay for and what you hope for.

—Malcolm Forbes (1919–1990), American publisher

Theodore Levitt was a marketing professor at Harvard Business School and once the editor of *Harvard Business Review*. His expectations theory is useful because it forces the firm to focus on the utility the customer is trying to maximize.

By ascertaining customer expectations, the firm has the ability to manage—to a certain degree—those expectations. Southwest Airlines is a master at managing customer expectations. Customers understand very well that it is a *no-frills* airline: no food, no first class, and so on. However, since the airline has lowered customers' expectations in these areas, when they crack irreverent jokes, achieve a stellar on-time arrival record, and do not lose your luggage, all at a price comparable to driving yourself or taking the bus, most customers walk away with their expectations exceeded—and, more important, they come back to fly Southwest again. Compare these expectations to buying a first-class ticket on, say, United Airlines. The customer's expectations of every aspect of the flight are totally different.

It is hard enough to meet a customer's expectations, let alone exceed them, if a firm does not know exactly what they are. Becoming a customer and experiencing what they do is a good way to learn. The next best alternative is to constantly question the customer about their expectations.

Because expectations are *dynamic*, not *static*, it is also imperative to continuously ask customers what they expect. A firm should never rest on its laurels and assume it knows exactly what the customer is up to. Knowing your customer's expectations also enables you to ask Peter Drucker's deceptively simple question mentioned at the beginning of this chapter: What are we getting paid for? Often, if companies ask, "What job is the customer trying to get done?" they can innovate higher-value offerings. When General Electric asked this question for its jet engines, it innovated the "Power by the Hour" program for its aircraft engines, whereby it would be responsible for maintaining the engines and price for the serviceable usage the airline received.

Prior to every single engagement, a firm needs to know exactly what the customer's expectations are, providing the opportunity to manage those expectations and better control the outcome. For instance, if a millionaire anticipates paying no taxes, he has an unrealistic outlook. The options are to educate him, thereby lowering expectations, or to refuse the engagement altogether. No matter how technically proficient the firm's work is, if they do not satisfy the customer's expectations, they will fail to deliver value.

For instance, a CPA met for the first time with the CEO of two companies. Due to banking covenants, the CEO was required to prepare full-disclosure reviewed financial statements. During the meeting, the CPA asked, "What do you expect from us?" The CEO sat back and replied: "Obviously I need the financials, but what I really want from you is to develop a relationship with my banker. You see, during the year I tend to fall out of compliance with my loan covenants, [nothing sinister here; he has a cyclical business], and if my banker were comfortable with you it would make my life much easier." When the CPA heard that, he knew exactly what the customer expected. Upon returning to his office he immediately called the banker to set up a lunch. He also priced the services at three times his "standard hourly rate," based upon what he knew the engagement and the relationship with the banker was worth to the CEO. It would have been fairly easy to provide the solution to the CEO's problem—two reviewed financial statements. However, by focusing on his expectations, he found the hidden desire and was able to meet and exceed that specific expectation.

There is another major lesson with respect to customer expectations. Firms compete against *any* organization that has the ability to raise customer expectations. FedEx brought a new standard to the passenger airline business with respect to handling and tracking luggage, just as anyone who visits Disneyland or Walt Disney World has expectations raised when it comes to customer service. Once people experience premium service, they want more of it and are less and less tolerant of those organizations that do not deliver on the promise. This expectation dynamism, though, requires leaders to constantly look beyond their own four walls to learn from other industries.

Now that we have discussed *what* people buy, let us turn our attention to *how* people buy, because it certainly has ramifications for capturing the value your firm creates.

CHAPTER 7

How People Buy

Consumers judge the quality of a product by its price. The higher you price your product, the more desirable it becomes in the eye of the consumer. Most of the marketers I know are afraid of pricing their products above competition. The consumer is not a moron, she is your wife.

—David Ogilvy, *Ogilvy on Advertising*, 1985

The first concept is that people buy *emotionally* and justify *intellectually*. I live in California, and I understand the best time for earthquake insurance sales is right after one. This is curious, especially from an actuarial point of view. If people were willing to assume the risk prior to a quake, why would they not be willing to assume the risk after one strikes? The probability of another earthquake striking simply because one just did does not change, since fault lines do not have memories any better than dice at the craps tables in Las Vegas. The purchase is not made based upon the *intellectual* calculation of the statistical odds, but on the *emotional* desire for peace of mind. Customers are attempting to maximize their serenity. Neurologist Donald Calne says, "The essential difference between emotion and reason is that emotion leads to action while reason leads to conclusions" (Roberts 2005: 42).

People also do not like to admit being *sold*, but they brag about what they *buy*. Think of the last time you made a major purchase—a boat, car, or new gadget—and said to a friend, "Guess what I was sold today." People do not like to feel they are being sold because it makes them feel like they are out of control. The best salespeople in the world actually empower the customer to buy and help them envision their future with their product or service. Forget *selling*; focus on what the customer *buys*.

Relative, Not Absolute, Price Matters

It is helpful to suspend talking about absolute price in terms of dollars and cents. *Absolute price* is defined as "the number of dollars that can be exchanged for a specified quantity of a given good." Instead, economists deal with *relative price*, defined as "the quantity of some other good that can be exchanged for a specified quantity of a given good" (Landsburg 1996: 34). This is an important distinction because in the final analysis, we live in a barter economy.

The reason economists discuss *relative*, as opposed to *nominal*, prices can be illustrated by the example of married couples with young children deciding on a night on the town, versus the same decision made by couples without children. Suppose an expensive date, including dinner and a concert, is $150, whereas a cheap date is dinner and a movie, costing $75. Each couple faces the same two options. The childless couple would have to sacrifice the enjoyment of two movies and two dinners for one expensive date ($150/$75). The married couple, because they must hire a babysitter for, say, $50, no matter which date they decide on, will most likely choose the more expensive date. Why? Because the relative price is only 1.6 cheap dates ($150+$50/$75+$50), compared to two for the childless couple. Therefore, we would expect to see married couples on more expensive nights on the town. To illustrate, a letter to the editor of *BusinessWeek* said that Hollywood should price new movies at $30 for home viewing, because he compares it to $75 for a night out at the movies (babysitter, popcorn, tickets). Not a bad idea and an interesting opportunity for Hollywood, one that is certainly consistent with the concept of relative, not absolute, price.

In a purely rational sense, a price difference of $400 between two products is the same no matter what the total product price is. However, that same $400 is perceived to be a much larger difference for a $1,000 purchase that it is for a $20,000 purchase. In one study, 68 percent of the respondents said they were willing to drive to another store to save $5 on a calculator selling for $15; but if the same calculator cost $125, only 29 percent of the respondents were willing to do so (Nagle and Holden 1995: 300). The tendency of buyers to engage in this type of calculation is known as the *Weber-Fechner Law*, which states that *buyers perceive price differences in proportional terms, not absolute terms*. This refers to the percentage change in price, and not to the absolute level, and indicates that there is an upper and lower threshold of price in the mind of each customer. If the price falls outside of that band, customers ignore the offering. This is precisely why your firm can be a *price searcher*, rather than a passive *price taker*.

Another facet of the distinction between absolute and relative price is another deleterious effect of hourly billing. If a firm quotes $300 per hour as their standard rate, yet the people paying the bill are earning, say, $50 per hour, the comparison is the wrong anchor to put in the customers mind. Better to quote a fixed price, focusing the customer on the nominal price, rather than making them think in relative terms.

Price Psychology

All firms need to have an understanding of the role price psychology plays in influencing customers' buying decisions. Since people tend to buy emotionally and justify intellectually, the study of pricing psychology is a worthwhile endeavor, a field known as behavioral economics. There are two characteristics of price psychology:

1. Price leverage
2. Pricing emotions

Price leverage is not an advantage possessed by one party over the other. It is a question of who has the most (or least) price sensitivity at a given point of time during a transaction. A service *needed* is always worth more than a service *delivered*, and therefore most businesses provide a price to the customer *before* they buy, so they can make the all-important value versus price comparison. However, professional firms defy this psychology by pricing *after* the work has been done, thereby sacrificing leverage to the customer and hence pricing when they possess the least amount of leverage. This usually leads to write-downs, write-offs, and unhappy customers, not to mention that after an engagement is over is precisely the wrong time to discover the customer did not agree with your price since there is not much you can do at this point.

The second type of price psychology is *pricing emotions*, of which there are three that customers will experience at various times through a purchasing cycle:

1. Price resistance
2. Payment resistance
3. Price anxiety

As long as you are dealing with people, you will encounter *price resistance*—also known as *sticker shock*—usually at the beginning of the buying process, making it easy to identify. The best way to overcome it is by educating customers about the value being provided. By discussing value, rather than price, you lower a customer's price resistance. All customers have a natural incentive to *lower* your price but, at the same time, to *maximize* their value. It is far more strategic to have a discussion around what they are trying to maximize rather than what they are trying to minimize.

Price bundling is an effective way to overcome sticker shock as well, as it focuses the customer on the totality of the offering, rather than on specific components. Witness the success McDonald's has had with its Value Meals. Also product bundling increases a customer's switching costs, making it less likely they will defect to a competitor.

Prices should not be lowered for customers suffering from sticker shock, because this cheats your firm's best customers—those who value what you provide—and subsidizes your worst customers—those drawn to you by price considerations alone. These will be the first customers to defect once they find a provider with a lower price. Rather than lowering price, consider removing value from the offering, thereby forcing the customer to make a price/value trade-off. For instance, sometimes technology firms will lower prices, but only on older technology.

Payment resistance is simply the customer's unwillingness to cut the check. Who likes to pay their bills? Payment resistance is overcome by getting the customer to agree to the payment terms *before* the service is rendered. Lawyers can overcome this emotion by more consistently requiring retainers, as do firms that require customers to pay at an agreed-upon interval. The old axiom of business valuators applies: "I'll let you set the price if you let me set the terms." Always make payment terms an integral part of your pricing strategies. Be sure to make paying your firm as easy as possible for the customer by accepting credit cards, electronic fund transfers, and so on.

The last pricing emotion, *price anxiety*, is also known as *buyer's remorse*. Anytime a customer spends a relatively large amount of money— for a house, automobile, expensive jewelry, and the like—it is quite natural to experience this emotion. Luxury automobile advertisements, for instance, are targeted at existing owners, rather than potential owners, to provide reassurance that they made a good and prudent decision. Price anxiety is less likely to affect repeat customers. Offering excellent customer service, and a service guarantee, are also effective methods to ameliorate buyer's remorse.

Search, Experience, and Credence Attributes

From a marketing perspective, products and services can be separated into three useful classes: search products, experience products, and credence products. *Search products* or services have attributes customers can readily evaluate before they purchase. A hotel room price, an airline schedule, television reception, and the quality of a home entertainment system can all be evaluated before a purchase is made. Well-informed buyers are aware of the substitutes that exist for these types of products and thus are likely to be more price sensitive than other buyers, unless there exists some brand reputation or customer loyalty. This sensitivity, in turn, induces sellers to copy the most popular features and benefits of these types of products. Price sensitivity is high with respect to products with many substitutes, and since most buyers are aware of their alternatives, prices are held within a competitive band.

Experience products or services can be evaluated only after purchase, such as dinner in a new restaurant, a concert or theater performance, a new movie, or a hairstyle. The customer cannot pass judgment on value until after he or she has experienced the service. These types of products tend to be more differentiated than search products, and buyers tend to be less price sensitive, especially if it is their first purchase of said product. However, since they will form an opinion *after* the experience, if it is not favorable, no amount of differentiation will bring them back. Product brand and reputation play an important role in experience products, due to consistency of quality and loyalty. For instance, when customers travel, so does brand reputation, as with airlines, hotels, rental cars, and so forth.

Credence products or services have attributes buyers cannot confidently evaluate, even after one or more purchases. Thus, buyers tend to rely on the reputation of the brand name, testimonials from someone they know or respect, service quality, and price. Credence products and services include health care; legal, accounting, advertising, consulting, and IT services; baldness cures; pension, financial, and funeral services; and even pet food (since you have to infer if your pet likes it or not). Credence services are more likely than other types to be customized, making them difficult to compare to other offerings. Because there are fewer substitutes to a customized service and there is more risk in purchasing these types of services, price sensitivity tends to be relatively low—that is, the majority of customers purchasing credence services are relatively price insensitive compared to search or credence goods.

Understanding Customer Risk

Any purchase entails risk. Services are relatively riskier than products, especially credence services discussed above. If you buy a defective toaster, you take it back and get a new one. But if your veterinarian does more harm than good to your pet, there is not much you can do. This is one reason why there is greater loyalty to service providers than to product manufacturers. The seven types of customer risk are:

1. **Performance risk** is the chance the service provided will not perform or provide the benefit for which it was purchased.
2. **Financial risk** is the amount of monetary loss incurred by the customer if the service fails. Purchasing services involves a higher degree of financial risk than the purchasing of goods because fewer service firms have money-back guarantees.
3. **Time loss risk** refers to the amount of time lost by the customer due to the failure of the service.
4. **Opportunity risk** refers to the risk involved when customers must choose one service over another.
5. **Psychological risk** is the chance that the purchase of a service will not fit the individual's self-concept.
6. **Social risk** is closely related to psychological risk, and refers to the probability a service will not meet with approval from others who are significant to the customer making the purchase. Services with high visibility will tend to be high in social risk. Restaurants, hair stylists, and plastic surgeons are perceived to have a high level of social risk. Even for business-to-business marketing, social risk is a factor. Corporate buyers are concerned that a service they purchase will meet with approval of their superiors (thus IBM's famous slogan: "No one ever got fired for choosing IBM").
7. **Physical risk** is the chance a service will actually cause physical harm to the consumer (Kurtz and Clow 1998: 41–42).

It must be emphasized that the above risks are *perceived*, not necessarily *actual*, risks, and the perception is in the mind of the customer. The actual probability of service failure is immaterial. Usually, all things being equal, the service provider that offers the lowest perceived risk will be chosen, especially with credence services. FedEx's guarantee of "Absolutely. Positively. Overnight." was a strong factor that led to—and maintains—its dominant share of the overnight delivery market at a premium price. This guarantee was especially important when FedEx began, since no one knew whether it could actually deliver on its promise.

Be sure to perform a risk analysis using the above seven factors, and find ways to mitigate those risks, keeping in mind it is the *perceived* risk to the customer that is important. Most professional firms do an inadequate job of assessing and pricing risk from the customer's vantage point. It may make sense to employ the services of an actuary for this type of intellectual capital and to learn the actuary's famous axiom: There is no such thing as bad risks, just bad premiums.

The Four Ways to Spend Money

I like best the wine drunk at the cost of others.

—Ascribed to Diogenes the Cynic, c. 380 B.C.

According to Milton and Rose Friedman in *Free to Choose*, in any economy there are four ways people can spend money (Friedman and Friedman 1980: 116–17):

	On Whom Spent	
Whose Money	**You**	**Someone Else**
Yours	I	II
Someone else's	III	IV

Category I: When you spend your money on yourself, you will do everything in your power to maximize your utility. For example, if you are in the market for a car, you will download information from the Internet, talk to friends, visit dealerships, take test drives, read consumer reports, and so on. You will try to get the biggest bang for your buck.

Category II: Perhaps you're buying a gift for a spouse, friend, or colleague. You will still want to maximize your utility and theirs and to shop around and try to get the biggest bang for your buck. If you doubted your ability to maximize utility for the recipients, you might simply give them money and put them into Category I.

Category III: When you spend someone else's money on yourself, this is the greatest luxury of all. A corporate expense account is a perfect example. There is very little incentive to economize. You might fly first class, upgrade your rental car, not eat all of your dinner, even eat the cashews in the mini bar. This is why airlines, hotels, and rental car agencies discriminate in their pricing against business travelers, since they know these people are not paying their own bills. They are, by definition, less price sensitive. Businesses serving travelers would be missing an enormous opportunity if they did not charge these customers higher prices.

Category IV: When you spend someone else's money on strangers there is very little incentive to economize. Government programs are a perfect example, and are why government spending is out of control. Health-care spending has moved from Categories I and II to Categories III (private health insurance) and IV (government spending on health care, such as Medicaid and Medicare). If groceries were purchased in these categories, prices would most definitely skyrocket, and Fido would dine on top sirloin every night. There is no incentive for the spending party to make value/

price tradeoffs, nor is there an incentive for the party providing the money to insure they are meeting the expectations and utility of the receiving party. At least with a corporate expense account, my employer has the satisfaction of knowing I received a direct benefit from the more expensive rental car and upgraded hotel suite, but a government employee has little incentive to follow up with a recipient of a government sinecure.

These four categories hold many lessons about how businesses price their goods and services, and we will continue to refer to them throughout the rest of the book.

Understanding exactly *what* customers buy—expectations—will enable your firm to exceed those expectations and thus be able to charge premium prices for your services. Understanding *how* customers buy helps to focus on the decision-making process of the customer, enabling you to better manage the entire customer experience. Let us now put it all together by providing a value proposition to the customer.

CHAPTER 8

Your Firm's Value Proposition

> The secret of staying afloat in business is to create something people will pay for.
>
> —Thomas Edison (1847–1931)

Fortunately, more firms now realize it is not enough to focus on simply the value of the service being offered; they have to take into consideration the total experience from the customer's vantage point. They have to provide a value proposition that, when compared with the customer's viable alternatives, offers a better deal. The originator of the value proposition, Michael J. Lanning (a former Procter & Gamble executive and consultant with McKinsey & Company), defines it this way in his book *Delivering Profitable Value*:

> Essentially, a value proposition is the *entire set of resulting experiences*, including some price that an organization causes some customers to have. Customers may perceive this combination of experiences to be in net superior, equal, or inferior to alternatives. A value proposition, even if superior, can be a "Tradeoff," i.e. one or more experiences in it are inferior while others are superior (Lanning 1998: 55).

When most firms think about their value proposition, they usually include at least some of the following elements:

- Trusted advisors
- Long-term history
- Good reputation
- Technical expertise
- Knowledgeable and experienced personnel
- Utilize latest technology
- Wide range of customers served
- Committed to customer service

Note that none of the characteristics describe the *experience* the customer will have with the firm. No doubt, many of the above elements are essential, but they are not related to customer experiences. It is very difficult to catalogue all of the various experiences a customer will have with an organization. In fact, this is an exercise the firm would do well to carry out to enhance the value of the total experience for its customers. However, some generalizations can be made. The experiences a customer will have in interacting with a firm generally revolve around three areas:

- Quality
- Price
- Service

At the risk of changing Lanning's contribution, I would add one additional factor to the above three:

- Intellectual capital

I'm adding intellectual capital because your firm's value proposition is not limited to your services, your current customers, or even the sources of your firm's revenue. Intellectual capital encompasses your firm's social capital, which is an important component of how you add value to society. The associations you belong to, alumni, vendors, joint ventures, alliances, are all vital components of how your firm adds value to others. Take Google. Some 97 percent of its total revenue is from advertising, but most of its services are not designed to add value to advertisers, but rather to users of Google—think of Google Earth, Google Books, and so forth. (For more detail on your firm's intellectual capital, see my book *Mind Over Matter.*)

A firm must look at the interaction of all four of these variables and decide which combination of each it will deliver to its customers. Focusing on any one is not enough, since they are all interdependent and not mutually exclusive. That old canard of joking to the customer "Select any two" does not apply in today's world, where quality is a table stake and service standards have been raised by other excellent companies. The Japanese even have a term for this phenomenon: *atarimae hinshitsu*, which means *quality taken for granted.*

No firm can compete on quality alone. Who is going to stay with an incompetent professional? Besides, customers cannot easily judge the technical expertise of the professionals they use any more than you can be confident in the technical competence of your doctor. What customers do know is how they are treated—the bedside manner of the doctor—and based on the empirical evidence, this treatment determines whether the customer remains loyal. The number one complaint in firms is not bad quality but rather lousy service.

Neither is price enough to attract customers; if it were, books.com would have been a raging success, since it sold books cheaper than Amazon. Think of Southwest Airlines: By its own definition, it is the low-fare leader in the airline industry, but would that be enough to retain customers if they did not provide on-time flights and excellent service? As my friend Reed Holden points out, we do not even buy the cheapest toilet paper. Customers are not *price*-sensitive; they are *value*-conscious.

Firms have also started to think about their value propositions in terms of a SWOT analysis—strengths, weaknesses, opportunities, and threats. A SWOT analysis is indeed a useful concept for firms to work through, but it does not address customer experiences explicitly. The same can be said for benchmarking best practices. Unless you can relate these tools to what the customer actually experiences in dealing with your firm, they are half-measures at best. Overall, then, service excellence is an enormous fulcrum to develop your value proposition and create superior experiences for your customers.

Moments of Truth

Karl Albrecht, the modern founder of the Total Quality Service (TQS) movement in the United States, defines the Moment of Truth (MOT) as follows:

> Any episode in which the customer comes into contact with the organization and gets an impression of its service (Albrecht 1992: 116).

Utilizing the MOT method is one of the most effective ways to distinguish your firm's value proposition. The term has its roots in *the hour of truth* in bullfighting, to signal the third and final hour, the killing of the bull. In a business context, MOT certainly has a more prosaic meaning, but in terms of delivering excellent experiences to customers, and hence lengthening a firm's life, it is potentially just as fatal as to the bull.

Taken individually, each MOT is a minor event. Over time, however, each interaction is like a pebble placed on a scale, with one side being service excellence and the other being service mediocrity. Eventually, that scale will begin to tip in one direction or the other. Generally, there are three possible outcomes to each MOT:

- Neutral experience (rarest)
- Positive experience (moments of magic)
- Negative experience (moments of misery)

Few customers come into contact with an organization and walk away with a neutral perception. When developing your firm's value proposition, it helps to map out each potential MOT with the customer and be as inclusive as possible. Even mundane things like how accessible your parking is affects a customer's overall experience of dealing with your firm.

Karl Albrecht and Ron Zemke articulate this core principle of service excellence: "When the moments of truth go unmanaged, the quality of service regresses to mediocrity" (Albrecht and Zemke 2002: 55). No MOT should ever be taken for granted, for no matter how small it may be, in the long run, each one determines the destiny of your firm.

What Is Beyond Total Quality Service?

It may be premature to discuss what is beyond customer service excellence, considering Karl Albrecht has pronounced the revolution dead. One of the problems with excellence in customer service is that it is easier to discuss than to deliver. Although we supposedly live in a *service* economy, the level of customer service, by some indicators, has actually dropped in recent years.

Be that as it may, it is important to discuss a trend an astute observer can witness taking place in the marketplace today, as it is a level beyond Total Quality Service. Granted, you have to look at specific companies to find this trend, but it is worth exploring to obtain a broadened horizon of the professional knowledge firm's value proposition. Let us start by posing these two questions:

- What is next for organizations that already provide unsurpassed customer service?
- What do companies such as Disney, Ritz-Carlton, FedEx, and Nordstrom, among others, see as they peer into the future and strive to offer a value proposition to their customers that prevents them from falling into the so-called "commodity trap," while still allowing them to maintain their leadership role as price makers, not takers?

One compelling hypothesis comes from Joseph B. Pine II and James H. Gilmore, in their book *The Experience Economy*, wherein they put forth a futuristic value curve for businesses, with the following echelon of customer value:

- If you charge for *stuff,* then you are in the *commodity* business.
- If you charge for *tangible things,* then you are in the *goods* business.

- If you charge for *the activities you execute*, then you are in the *service* business.
- If you charge for *the time customers spend with you*, then you are in the *experience* business.
- If you charge for the *demonstrated outcome the customer achieves*, then and only then are you in the *transformation* business (Pine and Gilmore 1999: 194).

What is interesting about this proposed hierarchy is not only where professional firms are on it, but where their greatest potential is on the curve. Most firms would think of themselves as service providers, offering intangibles to their customers, and no doubt this is true. Very few accounting and law firms view themselves as being in the experience business, let alone the transformation business. Visiting a professional firm is not often thought of as an enjoyable experience and is certainly not equated with visiting Las Vegas or a Disney theme park.

It is interesting to speculate how firms could be in the experience business. This does not mean to charge for the time—as in billable hours—the customer spends with you, but rather charge for the experience you create for the customer. As crazy as it may seem, how about this idea:

Charge an admission price to enter your firm.

This is not as uncommon as you might think. Wineries in the Napa Valley charge for tasting. What would you have to do differently to provide a value proposition worth paying for? Think of the difference between entering a Disney theme park and one of its retail stores in a mall. Although the mall store provides good service, it is nowhere near the standard of an amusement park experience. One of the reasons for this, perhaps, is that Disney does not charge you to enter the store. What would it have to do differently to induce customers to pay an admission? Would it result in a better and more lasting experience? My conjecture is that it would.

You can apply this thinking to a *minimum* price for all new customers. What is going to be included in your firm's standard offering to entice a customer to pay a minimum to do business with you? It is an interesting thought experiment and one worth thinking about seriously. However, the main point to make is the firm of the future—and the future of the professions—is poised at the top of the value curve, since they are already offering their customers *transformations*, even though they may not think of themselves as doing so. To prove this, let us see how Pine and Gilmore define *transformation*:

While commodities are fungible, goods tangible, services intangible, and experiences memorable, transformations are *effectual*. All other economic offerings have no lasting consequence beyond their consumption. Even the memories of an experience fade over time. But buyers of transformations seek to be guided toward some specific aim or purpose, and transformations must elicit that intended effect. That's why we call such buyers *aspirants*—they aspire to be some one of some *thing* different. With transformations, *the customer is the product!* The individual buyer of the transformation essentially says, "Change me." (Pine and Gilmore 1999: 171–172, 177, 192).

Think of the difference between a fitness center, one that charges for membership, versus personal trainers. The latter earn more because they take personal responsibility for the *outcome* of their customer's fitness regimen. And because they take responsibility for the demonstrated outcome the customer achieves, they are more selective about whom they accept as customers, as well as more diligent in performing an up-front analysis of each customer's expectations and willingness to change. This is a critical analysis, because if the customer is not willing to follow the trainer's advice, his or her attempt at transforming the customer is bound to fail. The point is, today's sophisticated customers are demanding more from their professionals than merely providing services and a good experience; they want transformations and they hold the professional accountable for guiding the transition.

Professionals such as accountants, financial planners, attorneys, and advertising agencies already effectuate many transformations for their customers. For example, they can help their customers become millionaires, retire at a specific age, finance a child's education, grow and enhance the value of a business and brand, and carry out a customer's last wishes through estate and gift planning. These are inherently personal transformations, guiding the individual into their preferred vision of the future— guiding them from where they are to where they want to be. There is no similarity between this offering and a commodity or even a bundle of intangible services. You are touching your customer's soul, forging a unique relationship with them virtually impervious to outside competition and commanding prices commensurate with the value of the results you are creating.

By emphasizing Total Quality Service and transformations, your firm will offer a superior value proposition to its customers, allowing it to charge a premium price, one commensurate with the value you are creating. In order to capture this value from each customer, a firm must capture the consumer surplus, the topic of the next chapter.

CHAPTER 9

The Consumer Surplus and Price Discrimination

> When a reflective man buys a crowbar to open a treasure chest, he may well remark to himself that if necessary he would have been willing to pay tenfold the price. ... Marshall gave the odd name of "consumer's surplus" to these fugitive sentiments.
>
> —George Stigler, Nobel Prize–winning economist (1911–1991)

Imagine you are booking a flight for the entire family. Most likely you will select the cheapest fare possible, even if you must sacrifice flying out of your nearest airport, departing or returning on the exact date and times you want, or a multiple-stop versus a nonstop route. What is interesting about this situation from a pricing perspective is how the notion of demographics, or even psychographics, does not offer much help in predicting your price sensitivity. During the 1960s, marketing managers paid a lot of attention to segregating their customers based on demographics—income, neighborhood, race, gender, and so on. Then in the 1970s, an article was published asking a provocative question: "Would you treat Tricia Nixon Cox the same as Grace Slick?" (The former is the daughter of the late president Richard Nixon, and the latter was the lead singer of Jefferson Starship). Demographically, these two women at the time were indistinguishable—both were 25 to 34 years old, family size of three, urban residents, and college educated. Psychographics opened up a whole new way of thinking about customer behavior, and many companies started to pay attention to it.

And yet, in the decision to purchase a flight for business or leisure, this way of segmenting customers does not offer much help in capturing the true value of the flight. What really determines the value of the flight is what you are doing at your destination. Taking an enjoyable family vacation provides value, but flying on a necessary business trip is usually more valuable. It also cannot be planned very far in advance, and usually needs to be at exact times, particular airports, and during the week (no Saturday layover). Demographically and psychographically it is exactly the same customer making both purchases, but the value proposition is totally different in each case. The airlines know this, and they have developed very sophisticated yield management systems enabling them to segregate customers and offer different value propositions depending on the customer's relative price.

For another reason a business traveler is willing to pay more for a flight (thinking back to Chapter 7, "How People Buy"), recall Category III, spending someone else's money on yourself. Most of the people sitting in business class are not paying their own airfares, but rather flying on a corporate expense account, as opposed to you paying for your family to fly to a favorite vacation destination (Category I). The incentive to shop for the cheapest flight, sacrifice a nonstop route, depart from a distant airport, or give up earning frequent flyer miles is simply not as keen. The airlines, hotels, rental car companies, resorts, and restaurants certainly take this into account in their pricing strategies.

Price Elasticity

Cambridge economics professor Alfred Marshall (1842–1924) drew the supply and demand curves you studied in your introductory economics course. With the supply curve reflecting a cost of production concept of value, and the demand curve the utilities of buyers, Marshall merged the classical and marginalist schools together in one diagram—the Marshallian Scissors, as seen in Figure 9.1.

To be included on a demand curve, customers must meet two specific requirements: (1) They have to be *willing* to buy the product and (2) they have to be *able* to buy the product. For instance, a customer may not be on the demand curve for a Rolls-Royce because, although he is *willing* to buy the car, he is not *able* to buy it.

Keep in mind that Marshall's demand curve does not represent how much you *value* a good, but rather how much of a good you want, at various prices. The former is determined by marginal utility and the subjective value you place on the good; while the latter is depicted by the demand curve showing various quantities demanded over a range of prices. A price is paid because someone values the good in question, and the price cannot exceed that value no matter what the cost of producing it is. Hence the supply curve—tallying up costs—does not *cause* prices to be paid. You can spend a lot of money producing something customers reject.

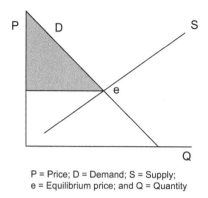

P = Price; D = Demand; S = Supply;
e = Equilibrium price; and Q = Quantity

FIGURE 9.1 The Marshallian Scissors
Source: *Pricing on Purpose*, Ronald J. Baker, p. 80 (John Wiley & Sons, 2006).
Reprinted with permission of John Wiley & Sons, Inc.

And since there are rarely "single price" markets, businesses have the capability of segmenting customers and charging different prices to different groups based upon subjective value.

Marshall also developed the concept of *elasticity*, another name for responsiveness (for more on price elasticity, see my book *Pricing on Purpose*, or any college economics textbook).

Even if a firm possesses a precise elasticity calculation it knows is accurate, it would only be a small part of the puzzle of pricing. Since elasticity normally lumps "consumers" together, it does not help us in segmenting customers into different value propositions, thereby offering individuals different options to maximize another concept Alfred Marshall developed—the consumer and producer surplus.

Consumer Surplus

Notice the shaded area above the equilibrium price on the demand curve. Marshall pointed out that some customers are *willing* and *able* to pay more than the market price, represented by the shaded area, what he called *consumer surplus*. Specifically, consumer surplus is defined as *the amount by which customers value a product over and above what they pay for it.* This is the buyer's profit, as we discussed in Chapter 3.

On the other hand, there is also a *producer surplus*, the difference between the price for which a producer would be willing to provide a service and the actual price at which the good or service is sold. The consumer's and producer's surplus provides a measure of the gain to both parties, with the sum of both being the social gain, or welfare gain, due to the existence of the market. While the consumer surplus is the gain the buyer receives from trade, the producer surplus is sometimes referred to as *economic rent*—the amount received by sellers of an item over and above what they would have accepted. Michael Jordan received an enormous amount of economic rent above what would be needed to induce him to play basketball. There is also a *consumer detriment*, representing the customers who are willing to pay more than cost but less than the market price. While consumer surplus makes customers happy, it is economic rent that makes firms—and individuals—rich.

In fact, because of this fact, some economists believe Marshall should have called his scissors "sales curves" and "bid curves" rather than supply and demand curves, since what they are really depicting is the highest price an individual would be willing to pay, or the lowest a seller would accept, for a given amount of product.

If a firm can identify those customers willing and able to pay more, it can capture a portion of this consumer surplus. It is there for any firm with a downward sloping demand curve, which is present even for the most elastic demand curves. Consider an airline with 100 passengers willing to pay $400 for a particular flight, and another 100 willing to pay only $200. If the airline charges $400, it will generate $40,000 in revenue (100 × $400). If it charges $200, it will generate the same $40,000 (200 × $200). But if it can charge what each passenger is willing to pay, it can generate $60,000, a 50 percent increase (100 × $200 + 100 × $400).

Identifying these particular customers is only part of the puzzle, however, since then you have to charge different prices to different customers, and this presents some challenges, although not insurmountable.

Price Discrimination

Charging different prices to *different* customers is the definition of *price discrimination*, a term coined in 1920 by Arthur Cecil Pigou in *The Economics of Welfare*. Price discrimination occurs when a good or service is sold at different prices that do not reflect differences in production costs. Firms engage in this practice to extract a portion of the consumer surplus from various customers.

Because the word *discrimination* has become a pejorative in today's vernacular, marketers have developed euphemisms for price discrimination, such as *market segmentation, yield management,* or *revenue management*. Since this book rests on the broad shoulders of the history of economic ideas, I do not have the temerity to alter the language of an entire academic discipline. It is the approach to the topic, in any case, with which we are here interested. It is worth reiterating that price discrimination does not imply discriminating against people based on race, gender, religion, ethnicity, and so forth, but only on their willingness and ability to pay, which is based on the subjective value they are receiving.

Requirements to Price Discriminate

In a perfect market (from the seller's perspective anyway), customers would each pay their *reservation price* for each service, defined as the maximum amount they are willing and able to pay for a service. This would be the ultimate expression of pure price discrimination. Unfortunately for sellers, the marketplace is not perfect and other methods must be devised to ascertain how much different buyers value their offerings. Successful pricing strategies are designed to induce customers to better reveal their reservation price, thereby capturing a larger percentage of the consumer surplus. To achieve price discrimination, four requirements must be met:

1. **The firm must have market power.** Not monopoly power, but a downward-sloping demand curve, so a firm can raise prices *without* losing all of its customers—as would happen with a completely horizontal demand curve—imperfect, as opposed to perfect, competition.
2. **Buyers with different demand elasticities must be separable into submarkets.** Differences arise from income disparities, preferences, locations, and so on.
3. **The transaction cost is less than the potential profit.** Costs associated with separating buyers with differential demands must be lower than the differential gain in profit expected from the multiple-price as compared with the one-price strategy.
4. **The seller must separate buyers to avoid arbitrage.** Otherwise, products sold more cheaply in one location can be purchased there and transported to a higher-price location (Skousen and Taylor 1997: 57–58).

These four requirements present barriers to engaging in price discrimination, but they are surmountable, and many companies have developed very imaginative and creative ways to overcome these challenges. Let us explore each of the four requirements. First, companies must have market power, meaning a downward-sloping demand curve. Even the most elastic services meet this requirement, which means the firm has some ability to control the price they charge rather than merely being a *price taker.*

Second, to judge the marginal value, separating buyers with different demand elasticities requires a firm understand its customers' motivations, how they benefit from its service, how it will be used, and other similar considerations. If you sell in business-to-business markets, understanding your customer's business model, how they make money, and how you can help them be more successful is essential in separating them into various value segments. This is obviously easier with long-term customers, with whom a deep relationship has been established.

The third requirement is that the potential profit must be greater than the costs of separating buyers for price discrimination purposes. A case in point where this requirement became a barrier to charging different customers different prices was Disneyland's A–E ticket system (E stood for *exciting*), used to price its attractions. From a pricing perspective, the A–E ticket system was a pure price discrimination strategy, whereby the park charged the highest prices to those guests who simply had to ride the most exciting rides, and some rode multiple times. However, over time the problems with the A–E system began to outweigh the benefits. Disney had to print the tickets, its guests had to wait in long lines to purchase them (thus diminishing the fun and experience of the park visit), and the cast members at each ride had to handle and police the tickets, sometimes turning away guests carrying the wrong ticket. The total costs of engaging in this type of customer segregation began to exceed the marginal profits derived from it, and in 1982 Disneyland changed to the Disneyland Passport, a fixed-price, unlimited use of attractions, all-day pass.

The fourth, and final, requirement, avoiding arbitrage, is much easier for service providers to meet than product sellers. If a bakery were to sell pies in two nearby towns, and price them $20 in one town and $10 in the other, eventually customers would buy in the lower-price location. Some customers might even buy pies in the lower-price location and transport them back to the higher price location and sell them, thus keeping some of the consumer surplus for themselves, a process known as arbitrage.

But one cannot arbitrage services. You cannot send your butler, who may be charged on a sliding scale based on his income, to get your kidney transplant. A customer cannot sell his or her tax return or legal services to someone else. Services consumed on location, such as haircuts or medical and dental care, are not susceptible to arbitrage, making it easier for professional firms to engage in price discrimination.

We have studied the four requirements necessary to price discriminate. Let us now examine the three degrees of price discrimination:

1. **First-degree price discrimination.** Charging each customer the most that he or she would be willing to pay for each item purchased, thereby transferring all of the consumer surplus to the seller.
2. **Second-degree price discrimination.** Charging the same customer different prices for identical items.

3. **Third-degree price discrimination.** Charging different prices in different markets (Landsburg 1996: 363–65).

Due to the high transaction costs of determining what each and every buyer is willing to pay, auctions and negotiable price markets are the closest approximation to first-degree price discrimination. Whether it is the late Princess Diana's dresses or articles from the Kennedy estate, buyers line up and identify the maximum amount they are willing to pay, and thus the item is sold to the individual who *values* it the most.

Second-degree price discrimination exists when businesses charge the same customer different prices for identical items, such as Procter & Gamble giving Wal-Mart a discount on Pampers for large-quantity orders.

An example of third-degree price discrimination—charging different prices in different markets—is coupons. If Procter & Gamble can make a profit selling a box of Tide detergent with a 50-cents-off coupon, what are they making when a customer buys a box without a coupon? Not everyone redeems coupons, and that is the point, for if everybody did, they would be superfluous. The manufacturer would simply discount the price of the product by the coupon amount and be done with it, saving the costs of printing, distributing, and redeeming the coupons.

Once you understand pricing, you can notice for yourself just how ubiquitous and clever price discrimination strategies are among all businesses, as the following examples illustrate.

Hardcover vs. Paperback Books

John Grisham, Steven King, J. K. Rowling, and other best-selling-authors' novels are priced at nearly $30 in hardback and around $10 in paperback. Would you be shocked to discover the production cost to the publisher is approximately the same for both books? What the publisher is doing is having those fans of *Harry Potter* who simply cannot wait for the paperback version, due out in twelve months, self-identify themselves and buy the hardcover, thus extracting an additional $20 in consumer surplus. The fact that serious book lovers prefer hardcover books to paperbacks (they last longer and look more impressive in one's library) is simply icing on the cake and merely adds to the perceived value of the hardcover. The real goal is *charging different prices to different customers* based upon their individual demand elasticities, not upon cost.

Senior Discounts

The one demographic group in the United States least in need of discounts is seniors. As a group, they are the wealthiest people in society. They have worked all their lives, have had longer to save, and thus have more to show for their accumulated years. So why do businesses offer these wealthy individuals discounts? Seniors have one thing on their hands a lot of other customers lack: time. They tend to seek out and patronize establishments that offer them discounts, even if they must arrive at certain times or clip coupons, referred to as *hurdle pricing*. If a restaurant can make a profit serving a senior citizen a prime rib dinner at $7.95, what are they earning from a customer who pays $12.95?

Children's Prices

At the fair, Disneyland, and movies, and on planes, trains, and buses, kids take up the same amount of capacity, yet they are charged a lower price than adults. This is done to prevent discouraging parents from bringing their families, and because children have a more elastic demand curve than their parents. But from a cost standpoint, is it any cheaper for the airline to fly a child than an adult?

Cosmetics

Cosmair manufacturers both L'Oréal and Lancôme cosmetics, among others, which contain virtually identical ingredients; the former selling in drug stores while the latter sells at much higher prices in department stores.

Value—Not Cost—Drives Price

Cost and value are sometimes inversely related. Laser printers are valued by the printing speed per page; the less expensive printers have higher-priced components to slow them down. FedEx's two-day and three-day service is priced lower than overnight service, but arrives at the depot the same day and must be held, raising the cost of handling (albeit minimally). It costs airlines more to fly minors, due to increased security and monitoring costs, yet they pay less.

These examples could go on and on, and I would encourage you to become observant of how businesses innovate pricing strategies to extract a larger consumer surplus. It is the holy grail of pricing.

In terms of degree, professionals, more than any other business, have the capability of implementing first-degree price discrimination, since they do not inhabit a single-price market, such as water or food. They also meet with each and every customer, enabling them, at very little marginal cost, to determine each one's particular demand elasticity. It merely takes asking the right questions and educating the customer about the value of what you do. Professionals occupy a market that most sellers would die for, with the ability to establish a price for each customer, at a nonprohibitive cost. The professions need to start taking advantage of this enormous opportunity to move toward first-degree price discrimination.

Now that we have explored the consumer surplus and price discrimination, let us turn our attention to a few other macro pricing strategies.

CHAPTER **10**

Macro Pricing Strategies

However beautiful the strategy, you should occasionally look at the results.

—Winston Churchill

At the macro level, there are only three pricing strategies: skim, penetration, and neutral. There is no doubt price can be an effective way to compete for some companies. Think of Wal-Mart, Southwest Airlines, Costco, Dell Computers, or Timex watches—all use a penetration pricing strategy. All of these companies have used price as an effective competitive differentiation and have relentlessly driven out needless costs from their operations, passing the savings on to its customers.

On the opposite side of the spectrum there are Apple, BMW, Bose, Disney, FedEx, Godiva, Gucci, Lexus, and Nordstrom, all of which command premium prices—a skim pricing strategy—because they offer premium quality, Total Quality Service, and exceptional experiences.

In the middle are companies such as Buick, Kodak, Seiko and Casio watches, JC Penney, Sony televisions, and Toyota, where price plays a more neutral role.

Not only does this apply to new services your firm may be offering, but also to newly established firms. Far too many professional firms assume they need to offer a lower price than the competition to establish itself. This results in attracting low-value customers, which the firms usually regret in the long run. Far more consideration should be given to which of the three generic pricing strategies will guide the firm's pricing. Let us examine them to gain an understanding of which strategy is appropriate given the realities of the marketplace.

Skim Pricing

In any market, there is a certain segment of buyers who are relatively price insensitive because they value the offering so highly. Think of early adopters in the technology industry who rush to purchase the latest and greatest gadgets, newest high-speed computers, printers, and audio equipment, such as the 500 videophiles who purchased the first VCRs—made by Ampex—from Neiman-Marcus between 1963 and 1968 for $30,000.

Skim pricing is a conscious decision to sell to this segment at premium prices more commensurate with value, thereby earning more profit than could be made selling at a lower price to an albeit wider market. The firm is not so much interested in market share as it is in extracting the perceived value from this smaller segment of the market. When Apple launched its iPod in October 2001 they priced it at $399, more than double the price of competing MP3 players. This launch coincided with the nadir of the dot. bomb economy, Intel admitting it could not successfully enter the consumer electronics market, lawsuits being filed over downloadable music, and the country still reeling from the 9/11 attacks. Internet discussion boards wittily suggested iPod meant "idiots price our devices," and "I prefer old-fashioned discs."

Hardly. By mid-2005, Apple had shipped its 16 millionth iPod, providing a profit to Apple for each iPod almost equal to the profit from the flagship iMac computer, while costing a fraction of the iMac to manufacture (proving, once again, value drives price, not costs). The iPod's complementary music store, iTunes, has achieved a 70 percent market share for legal, downloadable music.

Penetration Pricing

Penetration pricing is when the firm decides to set the price below the service's value to the customer, thereby ensuring a larger customer base. It is the trade-off of higher revenue versus higher margins and can be a very effective strategy especially for new entrants into particular markets.

Penetration prices are not necessarily cheap, but they are low relative to perceived value. For instance, Lexus used a penetration pricing strategy to bring Mercedes, Audi, BMW, and Porsche to its knees when it launched its LS (luxury sedan) 400 in early 1989 at $35,000, 40 percent less than BMW, Mercedes, and the same as Cadillac. The Lexus was relatively inexpensive compared to its value, and it was also less expensive relative to its competitors, and thus was perceived to offer a higher value.

Penetration pricing can be used at any stage in the service life cycle and is usually deployed after a steady customer base is established to drive revenue. To reiterate, though, it is a price set relative to the service's value, not a competitors' price. Do not let your competitors determine your price, as they have no interest in your firm's long-term viability.

Neutral Pricing

The neutral pricing strategy is generally a default strategy. In effect, this strategy minimizes the role of pricing in the marketing mix, not utilizing price to gain or restrict market share. A firm may select this strategy when it knows its service, promotion, or distribution offers other more powerful advantages to the customer. The neutral price does not mean a price in between that of competitors, but in relationship to the firm's value. Apple laptop computers and Sony televisions, for example, are consistently priced above competitor levels, but because they offer such excellent value, the market still perceives the price as neutral.

Many new boutique law firms and advertising agencies have been launched in recent years specifically to take advantage of the discontent over hourly billing. These firms are offering a broad array of pricing strategies, from fixed prices to risk-sharing plans based on creating results. The problem is many of them are positioning themselves as "cheaper alternatives" to their larger competitors, since they have smaller overheads—in effect, justifying price based on costs, not value. Some have selected a penetration pricing strategy to gain acceptance among customers.

This is a strategic mistake. If these firms are truly offering new and innovative pricing policies, then at the least they should be utilizing a *neutral* pricing strategy. An enormous component of their value proposition lies in the fact that they are aligning the incentives of the firm with that of its customers, which is an enormously valuable offering in and of itself. It is folly to provide a cheaper price simply because your firm has less fixed overhead. What matters is the value you can create, and if you have remarkable intellectual capital—especially human capital—then offering it for a lower price is to sacrifice an enormous amount of profits. A case could also be made that these firms should be using a skim strategy to send the message to those customers frustrated with the billable hour and willing to pay a premium for certainty in pricing.

Two More Curves for Value

Just as all customers are not the same and all hours are not the same, all services are not of equal value. Another way of analyzing this is by

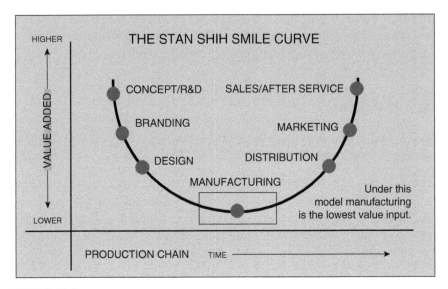

FIGURE 10.1 The Stan Shih Smile Curve

pondering two curves, the Smile Curve and the Value Curve. The Stan Shih Smile Curve is shown in Figure 10.1.

The idea is that the lowest-value item in the production chain is the manufacturing of the product. Even though the Apple iPod and iPhone are manufactured overseas, we should not care. The real value of these products is in the R&D, branding, design, and end use. It is estimated that of the $400 price of an iPhone a mere $5 goes to manufacturing in China, about $45 goes to Japan for parts, the other $350 to Apple. This is why every iPod and iPhone say, "Designed by Apple in California. Assembled in China."

Another conclusion to take away from the Smile Curve is controversial but no doubt true in our intellectual capital economy:

Ideas have always and everywhere been more valuable than the physical act of carrying them out.

Of course, the Smile Curve can be adapted to the various professional sectors—legal, accounting, IT, and advertising agencies. VeraSage Senior Fellow Ed Kless has adapted the Smile Curve to IT firms, as shown in Figure 10.2.

For advertising agencies, the Smile Curve would contain the elements as shown in Figure 10.3:

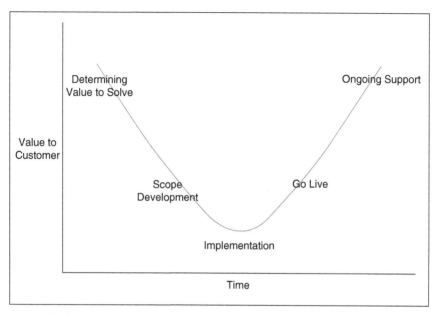

FIGURE 10.2 Smile Curve for IT Firms

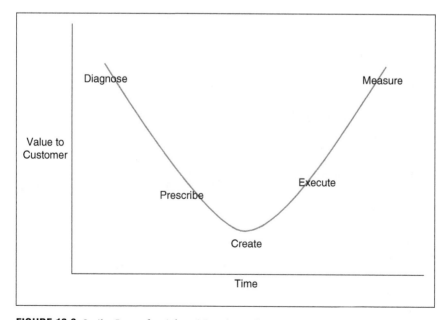

FIGURE 10.3 Smile Curve for Advertising Agencies

- Diagnose
- Prescribe
- Create
- Execute
- Measure

If you want to create wealth and remain relevant there may be no more important question to answer than this:

How much of your firm's human capital is devoted to creating and testing new ideas versus merely executing old ones?

Another useful framework for thinking about value from a macro perspective is the beloved Value Curve, originally published for law firms, as shown in Figure 10.4.

The Value Curve was originally published in the seminal work by the American Bar Association Section of Economics of Law Practice, *Beyond the Billable Hour*, edited by Richard C. Reed. Let us examine each component on Cobb's curve:

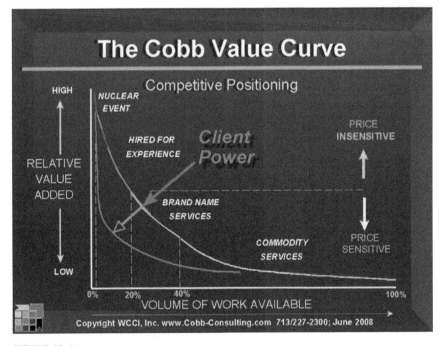

FIGURE 10.4 The Cobb Value Curve
Source: Copyright WCCI, Inc. www.Cobb-Consulting.com.

1. **Nuclear event.** These services are typically distinctive to a particular customer and add high value because either they avert a major catastrophe or they have a significant impact upon the customer's future. Examples are succession planning, major tax litigation, a merger or acquisition, and high-profile divorce. Cobb estimated that less than 4 percent of work in any given market is unique.

2. **Experiential services.** This is work of high-risk or high-impact nature, and the customer typically selects the professional perceived as best able to handle the matter effectively. Such services include real estate services, litigation support, and divorce. Cobb originally estimated approximately 16 percent of work in any given market fits this category.

3. **Brand name services.** This work, while perhaps routine, is important to the customer and tends to go to firms that have well-established reputations in a particular area. The Big Four accounting firms, for example, get a share of their work based simply upon their reputation in the marketplace, and they are major players in SEC and initial public offering work. National, regional, and local firms that may have a reputation for a particular niche, such as health care, construction, or automobile dealerships, tend to earn brand-name recognition over time. Cobb originally estimated about 20 percent of work is of this nature.

4. **Commodity services.** This includes write-up, tax return compliance (income, payroll, sales, etc.), compilations, and basically any other work that the customer expects their firm to be able to provide. Cobb estimated that this is the largest slice of work in any market, at approximately 60 percent.

Implications of the Curve

Regardless of whether the originally estimated percentages of work in each category are correct, there is no doubt that the Value Curve is a useful way of thinking about where your customer is on the curve. This can shed light on their relative price sensitivity. Ample opportunities exist to engage in value pricing no matter where a customer is on the curve. A firm that does nothing other than provide "commodity" services is still able to engage in the value pricing strategies discussed in this book.

A customer's position on the curve can change. Many professionals, when they examine the curve for the first time, tend to sell themselves short, seeing the majority of what they do as "commodity," or low-end, type services. The empirical evidence does not support these self-assessments. Practically all but the most low-end compliance-driven firms perform some experiential services, such as IRS audits or divorce work, and at one time or another, some customers will demand a unique service, tailored to their particular situation. A major mistake professionals make is treating all customers equally by pricing their services with one hourly rate method, no matter where they are on the curve.

Another implication of the value curve is what economists call umbrella pricing. For example, when Walt Disney World in Orlando, Florida, under the new leadership of Michael Eisner, engaged in a series of price increases at the theme parks, the surrounding competition—Busch Gardens, Sea World, Universal Studios—followed with their own increases. Likewise, within a firm, when value-added services are offered, this serves to place an umbrella over the prices of the more traditional low-end services. If you focus on the totality of the value that your firm provides the customer, and the services are bundled into a Fixed Price Agreement (FPA), commanding prices toward the top of the curve becomes easier.

We have examined the macroeconomics of pricing—the three generic pricing strategies, consumer surplus, price discrimination, and the Smile and Cobb Value Curves—that are all integral pieces to implementing a value pricing mindset in your firm. But as useful as these macro models are, they deal with customers as averages, not as individuals with subjective perceptions of value. It is now time to explore how firms need to change their pricing paradigms from pricing their services to *pricing their customers*, the subject we turn to next.

CHAPTER 11

Price the Customer, Not the Service

If I have 2,000 customers on a given route and 400 different prices, I'm obviously short 1,600 prices.

—Robert Crandall, former CEO, American Airlines

The most common pricing mistake among professional firms, alongside underpricing, is pricing the service, *not* the customer. Studying elasticity, consumer surplus, demographics, and psychographics, as discussed in the previous chapters, are not the full story of a customer's perception of value. To establish an optimal price, you must understand the value drivers of your customers, and what causes them to be more or less price sensitive. This is not as precise as computing price elasticity, but it is far more valuable when dealing with something as subjective as value. Value pricing is different than the concept of elasticity, since it is not concerned with how changes in price will affect revenue. It is more concerned with setting a price commensurate with the value you are creating for a flesh-and-blood customer—not some amorphous notion such as a "market"—to drive profit.

Ten Factors of Price Sensitivity

To assist those who are in charge of pricing in ascertaining and judging price sensitivity, the following ten factors should be examined to see which apply to your particular customer circumstances. There are many factors that influence a customer's price sensitivity, and pricers need to understand these factors long before setting a price for any individual customer. Nagle and Holden identify ten factors affecting price sensitivity (Nagle and Holden 1995: 95–99).

1. Perceived substitutes effect

This effect states that buyers are more price sensitive the higher the product's price relative to its perceived substitutes. New customers to a market may be unaware of substitutes, and thus pay higher prices than more experienced buyers. Restaurants in resort areas face less pressure to compete based upon price (which locals may describe as "tourist traps"). Branding can also overcome, to a certain extent, the substitute effect. Woolite, for example, has maintained a relatively expensive price because it positions itself as an alternative to dry cleaning, not a substitute to regular laundry detergent. Customers have a reference price when there are many substitutes, and as long as the offering is within that range—sometimes referred to as a zone of indifference—it will be considered acceptable, the point being that your marketing can influence which products customers will compare yours with, possibly pushing up the price they are willing to pay.

2. Unique value effect

Buyers are less price sensitive the more they value the unique attributes of the offering from competing products. This is precisely why marketers expend so much energy and creativity trying to differentiate their offering from that of their competitors. Heinz ketchup, for example, developed a secret formula for making its product thicker and was able to increase its market share from 27 to 48 percent while maintaining a 15 percent wholesale price premium.

3. Switching cost effect

Buyers will be less price sensitive the higher the costs (monetary and nonmonetary) of switching vendors. Airlines that have a fleet of Boeing airplanes may be reluctant to switch to Airbus because of the enormous investment they have in operating a certain plane. Personal relationships are most susceptible to this type of perceived cost, due to the emotional investment the customer has made in the relationship.

4. Difficult comparison effect

Customers are less price sensitive with a known or reputable supplier when they have difficulty in comparing alternatives. Cellular phone companies employ this strategy by offering different features among their myriad calling plans, making it deliberately very difficult to compare one company's offering to another.

5. Price quality effect

Buyers are less sensitive to a product's price to the extent a higher price signals better quality. These products can include image products, exclusive products, and products without any other cues as to their relative quality. It is said that only 15 percent of Rolls Royce customers ask about price before purchasing (Docters et. al 2004: 220).

6. Expenditure effect
Buyers are more price sensitive when the expenditure is larger, either in dollar terms or as a percentage of household income. A one-office accounting firm may not pay much attention to the price of paper clips, but an international firm that buys in large quantities will. Business purchasers look at the total amount of the purchase, while households will compare the expenditure to total income.

7. End-benefit effect
The larger the end-benefit, the less price sensitive the buyer. This effect is especially important when selling to other businesses. What is the end-benefit they are seeking? Is it cost minimization, maximum output, quality improvement? The fulfillment of the end-benefit is often gauged by its share of the total cost. For instance, steel suppliers selling to auto manufacturers know the price of the steel comprises a large component of the cost of the car; on the other hand, when steel is sold to a luggage manufacturer, the steel cost is relatively minimal compared to the other material used.

The end-benefit effect is also psychological. Think of going out for a romantic anniversary dinner and paying with a two-for-one coupon. Most people view price shopping as tacky when the purchase involves something emotional. Wedding florists, caterers, and bands certainly understand this principle.

8. Shared-cost effect
Chapter 7 looked at the fact that when you spend someone else's money on yourself, you are not prone to be price conscious. This is one reason airlines, hotels, and rental car companies can all price discriminate against business travelers, because most of them are not paying their own way. This also explains some of the success of the frequent flyer and other reward programs. Many business travelers value these rewards and will not accept alternative offerings, especially since they are reimbursed anyway.

9. Fairness effect
Notions of fairness can certainly affect customers, even when they are not economically (or mathematically) rational. If a gas station sells gas for $2.90 per gallon and gives a $0.10 discount if the buyer pays with cash, and another gas station offers the same gallon at $2.80 but charges a $0.10 surcharge if the customer pays with a credit card, which station will sell more gas to credit card users? The economic cost is exactly the same, but most people will psychologically

prefer to deal with the first station and not the second because there appears to be something inherently unfair about being assessed a surcharge.

10. Inventory effect

The ability of buyers to carry an inventory also affects their price sensitivity. Amateur cooks with large pantries will stock up on a good deal, but a single person living in a small apartment will not. The perishability of the item in question is another factor to consider.

Analyzing price sensitivity is certainly an important task for any firm that wants to capture the value it receives from its offerings. Taking into account these ten factors of price sensitivity is a good start to formulating your firm's pricing strategy.

All of the price segmentation and sensitivity strategies discussed in this chapter explicitly recognize that not all customers are created equal. Charging different prices to different customers based upon the subjective value they place on your offerings is one of the most effective ways to increase a firm's profits, without adding proportionately to overhead. Developing the strategies necessary to take advantage of price discrimination takes innovation, creativity, and experimentation—the same characteristics needed to avoid the so-called "commodity trap," which we turn to next.

CHAPTER **12**

There Is No Such Thing as a Commodity

There is no such thing as a commodity. All goods and services are differentiable.

—Theodore Levitt

During the days of Prohibition, 25 of Chicago's top bootleggers were rounded up in a surprise raid. During their arraignment, the judge asked the usual questions, including the occupation of each suspect. The first 24 were all engaged in the same activity. Each claimed they were a lawyer. "And who are you?" the judge asked the last prisoner. "Your honor, I'm a bootlegger," he said. Surprised, the judge laughed and asked, "How's business?" "It would be a lot better," he answered, "if there weren't so many lawyers around."

G. K. Chesterton once wrote, "Competition is a furious plagiarism." Yet the fact of the matter is there is *no such thing as a commodity. Anything* can be differentiated, which is precisely the marketer's job. Believing your firm—and the services it offers—is a commodity is a self-fulfilling prophecy. If *you* think you are a commodity, so will your customers. How could they believe otherwise? This notion of selling a commodity is one of the most pernicious beliefs, which leads to price wars, incessant copying of competitor's offerings, and lack of innovation, creativity, and dynamism, not to mention suboptimal pricing strategies. Consider this story from the *Tom Peters Seminar.*

Transformation. Breaking the mold. Anything—ANYTHING—can be made special. Author Harvey Mackay tells about a cab ride from

Manhattan out to La Guardia Airport: First, this driver gave me a paper that said, "Hi, my name is Walter. I'm your driver. I'm going to get you there safely, on time, in a courteous fashion." A mission statement from a cab driver! Then he holds up a *New York Times* and a *USA Today* and asks would I like them? So I took them. We haven't even moved yet. He then offers a nice little fruit basket with snack foods. Next he asks, "Would you prefer hard rock or classical music?" He has four channels. [This cab driver makes an above-average amount per year in tips.] (Peters 1994: 235–36).

If a taxi cab driver can establish a rapport with a complete stranger in a 15-minute ride to the airport, what is possible with a customer relationship over the course of a lifetime? Note how the cab driver differentiated himself with low-cost items (newspaper, snacks, and so on). It is not the cost that counts, but the value *perceived* by the customer; and in this instance the little touches make all the difference. If a taxi cab driver can be this imaginative and creative, what is the excuse of today's professional firm leaders?

The potential for competitive differentiation is limited only by your firm's imagination. Many leaders lament that since their professions are mature, commoditization is inevitable, despite all the empirical evidence surrounding them that this is simply not so. Consider candles, an industry literally in decline for the past 300 years. Yet Blyth, Inc., custom-tailors its candles for the specific location, companion, and occasion, growing from $3 million in sales in 1982 to over $1 billion in 2009. Candles!

Even the declining lettuce business has been differentiated by prewashing it, cutting it up, and packaging it—along with some salad dressing on the side—for the customer to save time. As a result, from the late 1980s to 1999, a $1.4 billion industry was created. Lettuce!

A. G. Lafley, former CEO of Procter & Gamble, wants design, not simply price or technology, to become a key differentiator for the company. In a *Fast Company* interview he was asked, "How do you respond to the notion, popularized by Wal-Mart and others, that price rules the world?" He answered:

> I think it's value that rules the world. There's an awful lot of evidence across an awful lot of categories that consumers will pay more for better design, better performance, better quality, better value, and better experiences. Our biggest discussion item with a lot of retailers is getting them to understand that price is part of it, but in many cases not the deciding factor. Design is part of brand equity (*Fast Company*, June 2005, 57).

Jim Stengel, former global marketing officer of Procter & Gamble, is even more vigorous about the commodity cop-out:

I hate it when someone says they're in a commodity category. We don't accept that there are any commodity categories. We are growing Charmin and Bounty very well and if there is any category that people could say is a commodity, it's paper towels and tissues. We have developed tremendous equities, tremendous loyalties from our consumers. So, no, I think that is a cop-out. That is bad marketing and an excuse. We are not in any commodity categories. ("Selling P&G," *Fortune*, September 2007).

Would you ever pay more for a share of stock—whose price is publicly listed and traded on the New York Stock Exchange—to one broker over another? After all, how can a share of stock be differentiated? It may be one the few examples of a pure commodity. Before you answer, visit www. oneshare.com, where you can only purchase *one* share of stock at a time, valued primarily as gifts for babies and teenagers. Included in the most popular-selling shares, which you can have framed for an additional price, are Disney, Harley Davidson, Krispy Kreme, DreamWorks Animation, Tiffany & Co., Ford, Microsoft, Playboy, Coca-Cola, and Starbucks. You pay the market price for the stock (minimum $15), a $39 one-share fee, and a frame ranging from $34 to $600 depending on your style choice, the latter being for an American-made pewter frame plated in 18-carat gold (www. oneshare.com, accessed January 14, 2010). A share of stock!

Basic economics teaches that it is very difficult to sell something someone else is giving away for free. Yet notice bottled water. Water covers nearly three-fourths of the earth's surface. Could there be a larger commodity than water? You wouldn't think so until you realize that it is an $11 billion market in the United States alone. Perhaps this is why Evian is naïve spelled backward.

There is a corollary to "There is no such thing as a commodity": There is no such thing as a market either. Markets do not set prices—sentient humans do. There is no invisible computer that dictates prices in a dynamic economy, for if there were, certainly companies would not employ expensive professional pricers. Do not fall into the trap of believing that your prices are dictated by the invisible hand of the market. Prices are established by very visible hands.

If only professional firm leaders had more imagination, then maybe they would not suffer from the commodity trap thinking that drives down their prices. Instead, most firms seem content with gazing at each other's navels and copying them rather than innovating.

The Perils of Benchmarking

One cause of the commodity trap is ruthless imitation on the part of firms, cloaked in the names of benchmarking and best practices. Rather than investing in research and development and experimenting with innovation, a lot of companies are spending precious executive resources trying to figure out where they are relative to the competition by studying financial indicators and other forms of competitive intelligence.

While no doubt useful for some applications, benchmarking is not a way to build a strategic advantage. It is as if entire professions are gazing at each other's navels and bathing in the same bathwater, rather than looking for ways to change the rules of the game. Pouring over lagging indicators such as financial ratios—realization rates per hour, per partner net income, net profit percentages, and so on—rarely spurs innovation and dynamism within a profession. Comparative financial information has a place, but it must be tempered with a theory of what is being observed if we are to gain an understanding of the underlying causes.

The major problem with benchmarking studies and best practice reports is that one is studying the *results* of an interdependent system, not the process itself. They tend to confuse cause and effect.

Financial averages can be devastatingly misleading without understanding the underlying causes of the results one is observing; I can prove statistically that everyone in the world has, on average, one testicle. Furthermore, there is a *selection bias* in the data being analyzed; rarely is it a truly random sample or a statistically significant sample size.

Avoid benchmarking your competitors—why benchmark mediocrity? Truly effective benchmarking usually takes place outside of one's profession, such as when Henry Ford was inspired to create the assembly line from a visit to a slaughterhouse where he observed the overhead trolley system. What was standard in one industry became a revolution in another— old ideas in new places.

Purging the Commodity Word

Robert Stephens, founder of the Geek Squad, said, "Advertising is a tax for having an unremarkable product." This is true whether you sell to business or consumers. As Sean Finn, Senior Vice President of Public Affairs and Chief Logistics Officer of Canadian National Railway Company in Montreal, said about its law firm, "Any time a law firm realizes that we don't view their services as a commodity, we get a better product. It's not just a question of money ... we look at the value provided." Why do so many firms ignore this message?

There is absolutely no excuse—none—for professional firms to think of themselves as commodities. Any firm can compete on price; it is truly a fool's game. On the other hand, competing based on Total Quality Service, positive customer experiences, and transformations requires more thought, creativity, and investment. The commodity trap is a self-fulfilling prophecy, breeding cynicism and stifling creativity, dynamism, and innovation.

More sophisticated customer selection can assist you in tailoring various value propositions to different customer groups, while reserving capacity for your best customers, a topic we turn to next.

CHAPTER 13

Baker's Law: Bad Customers Drive Out Good Customers

We hold these truths to be self-evident, that all men are created equal.

—Thomas Jefferson, The Declaration of Independence,
July 4, 1776

Whenever anyone quoted those immortal words from the Declaration of Independence—"all men are created equal"—Federalist Fisher Ames, an ardent opponent of Thomas Jefferson and a superb congressional orator, would retort, "And differ greatly in the sequel." While Fisher's admonishment might not be the best way to administer a country's laws—before which all should be treated equally—it is profound when it comes to understanding that no two customers are equal. A German Proverb teaches, "He who seeks equality should go to a cemetery."

All firms have a theoretical *maximum* capacity and a theoretical *optimal* capacity. From a strategy perspective, it is essential to see how that capacity is being allocated to each customer segment. Ensuring a proper amount of capacity is allocated to various customer segments, while offering a differentiating value proposition within each segment, is an essential element of implementing price discrimination strategies. It also prevents bad customers—those who are not willing to pay for the value you deliver—from crowding out good customers.

Customer Grading Criteria

It has become common for firms to grade customers and focus attention on the "A" and "B" customers and even hold out incentives to the "C" customers to upgrade to higher status. In this section, two distinct methods of applying this customer grading strategy in a more sophisticated and rigorous manner will be discussed. Along with your human capital selection, your customer capital criteria are the most important aspect of crafting your firm's success.

The traditional customer grading criteria are most likely familiar to you. They usually include:

Amount of annual revenue
Prompt payment history
Potential for growth
Potential for future referrals
Actual referrals
Profitability of customer
Risk of having customer in portfolio
Timing of work (fiscal or calendar year)
Reasonable expectations
Willing to take advice
Profitable and not undercapitalized

Certainly these are important criteria and should be made part of any firm's prequalifying process. Ric Payne, Chairman and CEO of Principa, advocates the following 12-point criteria for selecting customers:

In business for at least three years.
Pleasant, outgoing personality.
Willing to listen to advice.
Positive disposition.
Technically competent.
Business is profitable.
Business is not chronically undercapitalized.
Business is not dominated by a small number of customers or suppliers.
Clearly established demand for the product or service.
Business has a scope for product or service differentiation through innovative marketing.
Business has scope for improved productivity through innovative management planning and control.
Business has a strategic plan.

These are all good criteria to judge potential new customers because there is no point in working for and with people whom you do not like or are indifferent about. Paul Dunn, co-author of *The Firm of the Future*, wrote this about customer selection and deselection, as described in Case Study 13.1.

Case Study 13.1: Grading and Firing Customers

If there was just one phrase from this book that readers should pin up on their walls, it would be "Bad customers drive out good ones." In every gathering of professionals I'm asked to address, I always ask, "How many of us have customers we wish we didn't have?" I've never yet seen a gathering where fewer than 99 out of every 100 raised their hands in the air, most of them held up in what you might call an enthusiastic way, along with a dramatic eye roll, as if to say, "Yes, I have them and what a drag it is."

You know the customers they're thinking of—the ones who don't pay the bills, the ones who sap your energy rather than build it, the ones you simply don't like being with—the list goes on and on.

Or consider this: Imagine you could put the work you do into these three categories:

I really love doing this type of work.
I can tolerate it.
If I'm brutally honest, I hate it.

How much of your typical week would be in the bottom two?

It may come as no surprise for you to read that, for many professionals, the number in those bottom two categories is frequently around 80 percent. Or, to put it another way, they're only loving what they do 20 percent of the time. Yet they smile through it because they're getting paid. As David Maister points out in his book *True Professionalism*, there is another "profession" that says, "Pay me the money and I'll fake it" (Maister 1997). Some call it the oldest profession in the world.

So why does the profession prostitute itself so frequently? Maybe it's because many (most?) in the profession have been, as one practitioner in the United Kingdom put it to me, "indiscriminate" about the customers they work with. To put that more bluntly, if it looks like the customers have a checkbook, they take them on. Some don't.

Take Tom Weddell of the Newburgh- and Poughkeepsie-based practice Vanacore, DeBenedictus, DiGovanni & Weddell (try answering the phone there!). Weddell, forty-two years old [at the time] and the youngest of the partners, had been appointed managing partner just six weeks before he attended a four-day program I presented in Chicago. Weddell *really* got the message. On the way home from the program, he said to his partners, "Clearly, there's so much for us to do

Continued

to implement this material. I want to know right now if you're with me."

It was a completely general question with no implied reference to "reorganizing" the firm's customer list. "Well, yes, of course Tom," they replied. "Are you certain?" Weddell asked. "Yes, we're really with you, Tom."

So the next day, Tom went into his office early. He got a full list of the firm's customers and copied it 27 times (the number of team members he had at that time). He gave it to each member with the instruction, "Circle everyone's name on this list whom you don't like dealing with and give it back to me by 11:00 A.M., please." That was his only criterion. The other partners had no idea he'd done this at the time (Weddell presumably was taking them at their word that they were "with him").

That afternoon, Weddell took every customer whose name was circled and fired them (nicely). He even recommended another accountant they might like to try, who would welcome them with open arms. By 4:00 P.M., the job was done. Weddell had gotten rid of the customers—along with $64,000 worth of revenue.

When Weddell told the team what he'd done, they cheered! At 4:15, the other partners, who by now realized what had happened, called a meeting. In essence, the message was, "We're not sure we're with you, Tom!" But three months later, the partners were absolutely sure.

Weddell showed me his financials and pointed to the additional $300,000 worth of revenue the practice had generated in the period. And he made this wonderfully simple point: "We couldn't have gotten that unless we'd created $64,000 worth of space."

Do you have any customers taking up space? Many firms are trying to be all things to all people. Yet they're advising their clients to be "selective" when those clients choose customer segments. The answer really does come back to that earlier comment about professionals choosing their clients "indiscriminately." Want to prove it? Take out your latest firm brochure (if you're still one of the people who believe in brochures) and mark anywhere on it where it specifically says something like, "You've got to be special to be one of our clients." I doubt you'll find it. Even your brochure or your Web site probably implies that all customers have to do is breathe and you'll take them on.

After years of "preaching" this message, I've never known any firm to regret that they took action in the way that Tom Weddell did. You won't either. Bad customers drive out good ones.

When a firm accepts a new customer, it is not merely *closing* a sale; it is beginning a lifelong relationship. We select our spouses, friends, and other important relationships very carefully; why would we not perform a proper amount of due diligence before selecting a customer? If the customer is worth having, then that customer is worth investing some time and resources in determining if he or she is a good fit for your firm.

It is no longer wise to accept new customers simply because they have a checkbook and are alive. The most successful firms in the world all have very rigorous prequalifying standards, and they do not accept all comers (in fact, they report that they turn away more business than they accept). This is not out of arrogance, but from the recognition that the firm cannot be all things to all people. It is not possible to value price the wrong customer. Reed Holden has a wonderful saying: **The price isn't wrong—the customer is!** The essence of strategy is choosing what *not* to do. Saying no to a new customer is not necessarily easy, but it is vital if you want to accept only those customers who are pleasant to work with, have interesting work, and enhance your firm's intellectual capital. Complexity kills a business, and by accepting any customer—especially those who do not fit your purpose, strategy, and value proposition—you are adding a layer of bureaucracy that will starve your best customers and put them at risk of going elsewhere.

To manage this inevitable effect, let us now explore the Adaptive Capacity Model for professional firms.

The Adaptive Capacity Model

Think of your firm as a Boeing 777 airplane, similar to Figure 13.1. When United Airlines places a Boeing 777 in service, it adds a certain capacity to its fleet. However, it goes one step further, by dividing up that marginal capacity into five segments (the percentages shown are suggested capacity allocations for a professional firm):

1. First class (5 to 8 percent)
2. Business class (15 to 24 percent)
3. Full fare coach (30 to 50 percent)
4. Coach (15 to 35 percent)
5. Discount/Priceline.com (10 to 20 percent)

Your firm has a theoretical *maximum* capacity and a theoretical *optimal* capacity, and it is essential to see how that capacity is being allocated to each customer segment. Your maximum capacity is the total number of

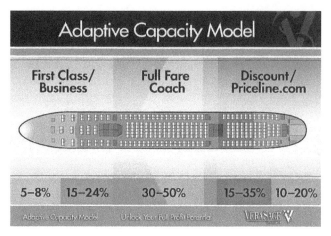

FIGURE 13.1 Adaptive Capacity Model
Source: The Firm of the Future: A Guide for Accountants, Lawyers, and Other Professional Services, pp. 22–24 (John Wiley & Sons, 2003). Reprinted with permission of John Wiley & Sons, Inc.

customers your firm can adequately service (not how many hours you have), while the optimal capacity is the point where customers can be served adequately and crowding out does not affect customer behavior. Usually, for most professional firms, optimal capacity is between 60 and 80 percent of maximum capacity.

Too many firms will, in fact, add capacity—or reallocate capacity from higher-valued customers—to serve low-valued customers. Furthermore, firms will turn away high-value, last-minute work for its best customers because it is operating near maximum capacity and usually at the low end of the value curve for price-sensitive customers. This is common during peak seasons, where high-value projects will arise from customers but the firm is at maximum capacity and cannot handle the marginal work. The lost profit opportunities because of this are incalculable.

Firms worry about running below optimal capacity and cut their prices to attract work, especially in the off-season. This strategy is acceptable but you must understand the trade-off you are making. Usually, that capacity could be better utilized selling more valued services to your first-class and business-class customers. This way, the firm does not degrade its pricing integrity to attract price-sensitive customers. According to most pricing consultants, one of the leading causes of pricing mistakes is the result of misallocating capacity to low-value customers due to the fear of not running at optimal (or maximum) capacity.

Remember, the objective of pricing is not to fill the plane; it is to maximize the profit over a given time period. If that can be done at 60 percent capacity, so much the better, as the excess capacity can be invested elsewhere.

Firing Customers

What happens when your plane becomes filled with too many "C," "D," and "F" customers? Many consultants to firms estimate that the average firm contains between 10 and 40 percent of "F" customers. It is never easy, but it is necessary, to remove these customers from your firm. Start with those customers whose personalities clash with the culture of your firm, or whose character is in question. Once that is completed, then you can focus on removing other low-valued customers (such as the "C" and "D" customers). These customers are usually the ones who complain most vociferously about your price; and the debilitating effect is that we tend to listen to them the most and this effects how we price our "A" and "B" customers. One caveat: Be sure you have done everything within your power to turn a low-value customer into a high-value customer. The fact of the matter is that *your customers are not going to get better until you do.*

All that said, how should you fire a customer? There are many strategies, some more effective than others. Many firms in the early days of implementing this strategy would simply raise their prices by a factor of two or four, and to their surprise, a super-majority of the customers remained with the firm (an indicator of just how much money professional firms leave on the table through suboptimal hourly billing). Nevertheless, it is strongly advised that you not utilize this strategy. The goal is to remove the customers, not simply increase their price. Getting two or four times more from an "F" customer does not make him a "C," "B," or "A" customer (this is the ethic of the world's oldest profession, not of true professionals).

A phone call or a meeting is the best—and most dignified—strategy. You may line up other professionals as potential referral sources (one of your "D" or "F" customers could be his "A" or "B" customer); some firms have even sold off these customers to other firms. Here is an example from a CPA firm of a possible conversation you might have:

> "Mary, we need to talk about how well we're working together. We need to be sure that the range of services we offer matches your needs. Here in the firm we want to work with people where we can add

significant value to their business, rather than just crunching some numbers and filling in some tax returns for them.

"This means we are reducing the number of customers we work with and increasing the range of services we provide for them. We're working with them on growing their businesses by offering consultative services. Naturally, this means that our price levels are increasing, too. Many of our customers are comfortable with that extra investment because of the value we are providing them in return.

"Mary, unless I'm very mistaken we simply can't provide you with that value. It seems to me that your needs would be better served by an accountant who just wants to stick to the numbers. How do you feel about that?"

The Forced Churn

In the mid-1990s, Lake Tahoe began a major renovation, where many older motels, stores, and other buildings were bulldozed down by the lake, just on the California side of the state line. A local newspaper article claimed that for every new room added, somewhere between two and three would be lost. Obviously, the developers were shifting up the value curve by constructing higher-end hotels, time-shares, condominiums, and so forth. Why shouldn't (some) firms remove somewhere between one and four customers for every new one added? This led to the concept of what we have since labeled the *forced churn*.

As a way to upgrade your firm's customer base from "C," "D," and "F" customers, each time a new customer is obtained, you would fire somewhere between one to four old customers. Of course, the exact ratio would depend on how many "C," "D," and "F" customers your firm has and what factor the leaders are comfortable with. Not only would this free up capacity to serve new customers, it would shift the firm up the value curve, allowing your plane to add more full-fare coach, business-class, and first-class seats. By implementing this strategy gradually, many firms feel more comfortable upgrading their customer base, and their sense of security is not jeopardized by firing a large number of customers all at once.

For a firm that did fire a large number of customers over a period of two years, see Case Study 13.2, authored by my British VeraSage colleague, the late Paul O'Byrne, in 2003.

Case Study 13.2: O'Byrne and Kennedy LLP—Firing Customers

In 1998 we were much like any other small firm of accountants. A ten-person firm in Hertfordshire, eight accountants dealing with the usual mix of work. Accounts and audit of small owner-managed businesses with their tax computations and returns and lots and lots of personal tax returns. We had nearly 500 customers with an average fee of about £1,000.

That average hid a wide spread. As with most customer portfolios there were some stars: customers whose work involved regular contact, sometimes weekly contact and attendance to help with management accounting or particular projects. There was also a large number of very small customers. When the Inland Revenue Self Assessment came in, we believed the market had set the price of a personal tax return at between £100 and £150 and we offered that fixed price accordingly. So for many of our clients, hundreds of them, the fee was £125.

We had come back from the Accountants Boot Camp with their injunctions to stratify customers ringing in our ears. So loud was it ringing, we took a good six months before doing it! We did it first off by gut feel; the two partners went down our respective customer lists and gave the customer a rating from "A" (the best) through "D." We discovered we had just 20 "A" customers, and over 100 "D" customers! Somehow though, it didn't seem right: We are professionals, and should we even be doing this? And how could we justify our rating unless it was more objective than gut feel? Not that anyone asked to justify it, but we were brought up in an evidence-based profession. So we did what any accountant would do; we devised a spreadsheet (of course!) and initially identified five categories that we thought mattered and ended up with a table like this:

Customer	Gut score	Calc score	Volume	Speed of payment	Profit	Potential	Like 'em	Partner input
A001	A	B	4	1	4	5	5	3
A002	B	D	3	3	2	2	4	1
C003	A	C	5	2	2	4	4	1
C005	C	B	3	5	4	3	3	4

Continued

Readers may ask how we decided to attribute scores, and where to set the thresholds between "A," "B," and so on. And how could we score profitability accurately? Well, we didn't know either, so we resolved to just get on and do it as best we could, using proxies where we could, and see what the results told us.

There were many surprises in the results, and we explored where the scoring system gave a different score from the gut-feel rating. This led to some adjustments to boundaries and re-ratings. But mostly it led to some valuable insights. The column for "Partner input" was an after-thought, as with most bottles, the bottleneck is at the top, and we recognised that how demanding a customer is of partner time was a feature of how good the customer was for the firm. The scoring system showed us that we had just one "A" customer and nearly 200 "Ds." Not an impressive spread of 500 customers!

So we decided to do something about it and we were determined to sack the lowest of the low "Ds." Our determination was immediately tested when we were confronted with the fact that many of the lowest were customers for whom the partners had acted for many years, and often had strong personal relationships with the customers and their families—indeed, often were family!

What did we do? Obviously as intelligent, committed professionals we wimped out and invented reasons why we should really keep many of the "Ds" and diverted our attention to sacking the ones we didn't like!

Even this wasn't easy. There seems to be a belief in an unwritten law that whereas customers can sack their accountant as they choose (fair enough) accountants can't ever, ever sack their customers. There is no such law, but nonetheless we found difficulty with actually doing it. There was nothing inherently wrong with these customers; many of them were perfectly good, reasonably well-behaved customers that other firms would be pleased to have. But our new determination to concentrate our efforts on higher-value customers meant we had to free up our precious fixed capacity. So we did two things. First, we identi-fied other firms in the area we would be prepared to recommend, so if the customers wanted a recommendation they had some clue whom to transfer to. Second, we worked up a system to break the news and carry through the transition in a professional and reasonable way. We wanted to do it slowly—after all, we wanted to be able to eat!

We drafted a letter to send to customers in effect saying—as one might well have done to a former girl/boy friend—"It's not you, it's me." We explained that we had chosen to concentrate our efforts in different areas and were not best placed to serve them any longer (whilst giving an opportunity for them to say they wanted more from us). However, we continued, there are many firms that were set up to carry out their type of work and they were free to choose from any of them, and we would be happy to recommend another firm if they would like.

Once we got started, the first 10 percent of customers went quite quickly. Team morale jumped, the pressure on our filing and storage facilities eased, and the chore of invoicing and collections seemed a little less onerous. Partners' morale soared. We had considered a radical idea—sacking customers—made a choice, faced the difficulties, and implemented it. Not a common feeling in our professional lives! We made the decision initially as much for quality of life as for profits. But profits didn't suffer even while we were putting a lot of effort into smoothing the transition of customers out of the firm. And we had time to seek out and welcome in new customers—of the type we wanted.

So we resolved to do more. And more. As we worked up our stratification list, we realised some of the customers we were choosing to dispose of were actually quite good customers, ones that in the past we would have happily paid to acquire. So we approached other firms (many of whom thought we were crazy getting rid of customers), saying, "We've got some good ones, if they want to transfer to you and we make it as easy as could be, what would that be worth to you?" It was worth the going rate for a block of revenue! So we revised our message to the next tranche of customers, telling them that we could recommend other firms, but one in particular we had come to know and we had a close working relationship with. If they transferred to this firm, we would be available to them for any issues they might care to take up with us, have access to our workings, and so on, and in consideration of this, the new firm would make some compensation to us.

We got paid for not doing work for customers we didn't want! This cash bonus sped up the reengineering process in our firm and allowed us to market more to the type of customers we wanted.

From that initial stratification of our customer list in 1998, we have taken this further than we ever envisaged and certainly further than you may be thinking now. Two years after starting this process, we met Ron Baker and he explained, with great passion and logic, the theories of why this was all right and what would happen. Many of the assertions Ron Baker makes in this book we have found to be true. I exhort you to test this for yourself.

You owe it to yourself to take a hard look at your customer list and ask yourself if you would be better off without some of them.

Continued

Have you added capacity that is soaked up servicing low-paying (slow-paying?) customers who will never grow into customers of the type you truly want? Have you left room in first class, for when those urgent, price-insensitive, once-in-a-while jobs come along? Have you ever tried to sack a customer? It's not as hard as you fear.

If you are an intelligent, educated, professional person with integrity and conscientiousness capable of delivering great value, is that reflected in your customer list?

Tom Peters is fond of making this point: "It's axiomatic: You're as good—or as bad—as the character of your Customer List. In a very real sense, you are your Customer List." My colleague Tim Williams likes to say that a firm is defined by the customers it *doesn't have*. The most successful firms in the world today turn away more customers than they accept because they have a rigorous prequalifying process and they understand that, ultimately, bad customers drive out good customers.

Let us now discuss carrying over this deliberate and strategic customer selection (and deselection) criteria to another vital characteristic of creating and capturing value—your level of self-esteem.

CHAPTER 14

Value Pricing and Self-Esteem

A man had better overvalue than undervalue himself. Mankind in general will take his own word for his own merit. ... [K]now your own value, whatever it may be, and act upon that principle; but take great care to let nobody discover that you do know your own value. Whatever real merit you have, other people will discover; and people always magnify their own discoveries, as they lessen those of others.

—Lord Chesterfield

When Larry Page and Sergey Brin were students at Stanford they developed technology that was designed to search Stanford University's Web pages, which immediately became popular among the students and faculty. This was 1996, and everyone thought that Yahoo! was the dominant search engine and there could never be another one. Larry and Sergey did not think their technological innovation was the basis for the company they wanted to start, so they put it on the market—at a price of approximately $1 million.

Fortunately for the rest of us, there were no takers. Had they found a buyer, Google probably never would have been born. It is an excellent example of how overpricing can have salutary effects.

Unfortunately, most professionals underprice their intellectual capital. They justify this with a variety of excuses:

- We do not have enough quality customers.
- Customers view what we do as a commodity.
- Customers do not understand the value we provide.
- Our people do not understand their worth.
- When customers engage in hardball negotiation tactics, we capitulate.

- Our profession has too much capacity, which drives prices down.
- We operate in what economists call "perfect competition," where no one firm is a price maker; rather, we are all price takers.

As we have discussed, most of these are nothing but excuses to explain away a lack of purpose, strategy, marketing effectiveness, and poor customer selection. But I believe there is a deeper reason, which I truly did not understand until I began teaching value pricing to my colleagues. Many participants in my courses have commented that they would "feel guilty" about charging a substantial multiple of their hourly rate. This attitude is especially prevalent after they hear about the TIP Clause discussed in Chapter 20. They say this as if they are taking advantage of the customer. This attitude is shocking. Not only is it a misunderstanding of how wealth is created—both sides to a transaction profit—it is a telling sign of low self-esteem.

The epiphany for me was that this was not a strategic, or even a pricing, competency issue, but rather a low self-esteem issue. Some of these professionals truly did not believe that they were worth more than costs plus some arbitrary profit margin. Yogi Berra has often said that 90 percent of the game is half mental, and the same applies to pricing, since it is a skill played between your ears.

Then I read an article by the late Timothy J. Beauchemin, titled "No More Begging for Work: Self Esteem Is the Key to a Better Practice," which appeared in the August 1996 issue of the *CPA Profitability Monthly Newsletter*. What he wrote resonated deeply with me, as well as the colleagues I began to discuss this issue with:

> I see too much of what I call "begging" in our industry—begging for work (especially by under pricing) and then begging to get paid. I have never really understood why this is, particularly when you consider the training, hard work, and risk that accountants go through. The only explanation I can see is that accountants tend to have rather low self images, unfairly and unreasonably low, but low just the same (Beauchemin 1996: 4).

Low self-esteem (or self-respect) does go right to the heart of why professionals question the value of the service they provide. Do you truly believe the benchmark of your value is the hours you spend? What about the years of experience that stand behind that $1 million marketing idea that took 15-minutes to create? Is the value really one-quarter your hourly rate? Professionals are so imprisoned by the hourly billing method that it has affected their own concept of self-worth and has lowered their self-esteem. Do other businesses "feel guilty" about pricing based upon value?

Does Cosmair feel guilty about charging seven times the cost of L'Oréal cosmetics as it does for Lancôme, even though they are made from essentially the same ingredients?

The lesson is vital, and it is this: **Before you can charge a premium price, you first have to believe, internally, that you are worth it. If you do not think you are worth multiples of your hourly rate, your customers never will believe it either.**

Have you ever dealt with a professional, such as a doctor or a consultant, who came highly recommended? When you learned of the price, did you try to negotiate it downward? Most highly recommended professionals will not budge on their pricing because they know they deserve it and are worth it. They are secure and confident in their worth, and they price above the market as a result. Obviously, not everyone can do this. But the ones who do all possess a common characteristic: *high self-esteem.* Psychologist Nathaniel Branden has done extensive work on self-esteem. His treatise on the subject is *The Six Pillars of Self-Esteem*, wherein he defines it as:

1. Confidence in our ability to think, confidence in our ability to cope with the basic challenges of life; and
2. Confidence in our right to be successful and happy, the feeling of being worthy, deserving, entitled to assert our needs and wants, achieve our values, and enjoy the fruits of our efforts (Branden 1994: 4).

In his book *Self-Esteem at Work*, Branden discusses the critical role self-esteem has in the success of enterprise:

> A simple example is the fact that analyses of business failure tell us that a common cause is executives' fear of making decisions. What is fear of making decisions but lack of confidence in one's mind and judgment? In other words, a problem of self-esteem (Branden 1998: xii).

Branden further points out: "[Self-esteem] is directly affected by how we act. Causation flows in both directions. There is a continuous feedback loop between our actions in the world and our self-esteem. The level of our self-esteem influences how we act, and how we act influences the level of our self-esteem" (Branden 1994). And please do not believe your level of self-esteem is set, once and for all, in childhood. It is not. You can increase it, and you can decrease it as well; Branden's book covers this subject well and is recommended reading for anyone interested in this subject (see Suggested Reading and Bibliography on the accompanying Web site.)

In his article, Beauchemin told of the changes he and his partner implemented to get over their "inferiority complex." They enhanced their office, bought a Mercedes, increased their prices to near the top of the market, and told prospects, "If you want the best, you have to pay for it" (Beauchemin 1996: 4). Probably the biggest change they made was to grade their existing customers "A," "B," "C," "D," and "F," firing all of the "F" customers, including one that was a large portion of their revenue—they were referred to the competition. They also referred customers who did not pay, who were rude to the team members, and who were not managing their business in an ethical manner.

By surrounding yourself with only "A" customers and excellent team members, you will begin to feel better about yourself and your firm. Branden says "Self-esteem is the reputation we acquire with ourselves" (Branden 1994: 69). That is profound. Professionals are deeply concerned, and rightfully so, with their reputations: They care what their customers think of them, of their firm, of their integrity. But what about their reputation with themselves? Most professionals were never taught even to ask the question. According to Branden:

> If low self-esteem correlates with resistance to change and clinging to the known and familiar then never in the history of the world has low self-esteem been as economically disadvantageous as it is today. If high self-esteem correlates with comfort in managing change and in letting go of yesterday's attachments, then high self-esteem confers a competitive edge (Branden 1994).

Yet how can people feel good about themselves, their work, and their service to the customer and the greater community if they believe they are commodities whose value is measured by a discredited labor theory of value? I have had countless professionals tell me, in no uncertain terms, they could *never* increase their prices, and yet we know countless others who have and the customers not only do not leave, they appreciate the extra level of service, and all the other salutary effects of pricing based on value, not costs.

There Is No Standard Price for Intellectual Capital

In today's world, intellectual capital is the chief source of all wealth. Shelly Lazarus, former chairman and CEO, Ogilvy & Mather Worldwide, explained what advertising agencies are really selling:

> Advertising is an idea business: That's all we are. And ideas don't come from the air, they come from human beings.

Napoleon Hill wrote in *Think and Grow Rich*:

There is no standard price on ideas. The creator of ideas makes his own price, and, if he is smart, gets it.

According to the *New York Times*, Merv Griffin (and his estate) has made between $70 million and $80 million in royalties from the *Jeopardy!* theme song, which he wrote in less than one minute.

People with high self-esteem are not threatened by the success of others. On the contrary, they are truly happy for another's success and will go out of their way to learn from them. The person who is not afraid of competition does not have any. Customers want their professionals to be successful because *they* want to be successful. Do not feel guilty or ashamed of your success, and do not let low self-esteem interfere with being paid what you are worth.

CHAPTER 15

Ethics, Fairness, and Value Pricing

Market Competition leads a self-interested person to wake up in the morning, look outside at the earth and produce from its raw materials, not what he wants, but what others want. Not in the quantities he prefers, but in the quantities his neighbors prefer. Not at the price he dreams of charging, but at a price reflecting how much his neighbors value what he has done.

—Friedrich A. von Hayek

Capitalism offers nothing but frustrations and rebuffs to those who wish—because of claimed superiority of intelligence, birth, credentials, or ideals—to get without giving, to take without risking, to profit without sacrifice, to be exalted without humbling themselves to understand others and meet their needs.

—George Gilder

Throughout history the morality of profits and a just price has been debated endlessly, as it should be. The late Father Richard John Neuhaus, in his book *Doing Well and Doing Good*, explains the ancient debate of a "just" price:

The idea that there is a right amount or a "just" amount always runs up against the question, Compared to what? The conventional answer is that one pays what the market demands, or what the market will bear. From Athens to Elizabethan England to the Great Terror of the French Revolution, societies have experimented with "sumptuary laws"

101

setting limits on people's income and expenditures. The experiments have never worked out very well, the obvious reason being that it is almost impossible to agree on standards. Few egalitarians, even among the well-to-do, propose a top income limit that is less than what they themselves receive (Neuhaus 1992: 193).

During the Dark Ages, merchants could be put to death for exceeding the communal concept of a "just" price (*justum pretium*, the right price). In A.D. 301, the Roman emperor Diocletian issued an edict fixing prices for nearly 800 items and punishing violators with death. Severe shortages transpired, as any economist would be able to predict when you place an artificial ceiling on market prices.

In ancient China, India, Rome, and almost everywhere throughout the Middle Ages, all interest charges were called "usury" and were prohibited entirely, making economic progress through lending and risk-taking all but impossible. Today, so-called "price gougers" are subject to societal condemnation, regulatory harassment, and editorial vitriol. Oil companies are frequently a prime target of public outrage, especially when prices at the pump vary from one city to another. Pharmaceutical companies are held in special contempt when they charge $5 to $100 (or more) per pill, even if the dosage reduces more costly medical intervention by other means, such as surgery. In May 2000, the late Senator Paul Wellstone claimed, "We have an industry that makes exorbitant profits off sickness, misery, and illness of people, and that is obscene." So what? Orthopedists profit from people breaking their leg skiing, just as professors' profit from students' ignorance. Farmers profit from our hunger, but in reality they keep us from hunger. Drug companies profit by making us healthy.

The problem with a "just" price is who gets to decide what is just? The free market already provides an answer to this question—*whatever someone is willing to pay.* There is no objective standard for "fair," which is why we have *free* speech rights, not *fair* speech rights. Although it sounds heretical, it is not. An old legal maxim teaches: *Emptor emit quam minimo potest, venditor vendit quam maximo potest* ("The buyer buys for as little as possible; the seller sells for as much as possible"). Ultimately, the customer is sovereign, spending his or her money only when it provides value.

To believe the free market is imperfect with regard to the fairness of prices is to grossly underestimate your own sovereignty as a customer while putting your faith in some anonymous third party—usually a governmental regulatory agency or the courts—to determine what is "fair." Yet prices contain a wealth of information that no central agency can possibly possess, which is why wage and price controls have failed *everywhere* they have been tried. (See Case Study 15.1, "A Fair Price Utopia Gone Wrong.") If it is immoral for a company to charge premium prices to customers, does it

Case Study 15.1: A Fair Price Utopia Gone Wrong

Once upon a time there was a fair price utopia. In it, prices were set according to a theory of fair pricing. The price was based on the average product cost of all firms plus a standard percentage markup. Even if the costs of production for an identical good varied, the price was kept uniform for the customer. Although prices responded dynamically to changing average costs of production, this dynamism was tempered to maintain price stability. There were no unpleasant surprises. Buyers were supposed to enjoy complete transparency and control: By law, they could review the producer's accounting and participate in determining the price. And the prices of basic staples like bread were subsidized to help the needy.

Beginning to sound familiar? That is because this utopia was the pricing system of the former United Soviet Socialist Republic. It was a pricing system designed to be fair. So what went wrong?

In might have been fair in theory, but not in actuality. Prices did not reflect the value as perceived by the consumer. The determination of value was done by overblown governmental departments based on complex calculations of cost and profit plus distribution costs, as well as consumption value and utility. Consumers had no idea how prices were actually determined. Supply did not respond to demand. Consumer goods were always in short supply no matter how strong the demand.

The system was imposed from above so that consumers had no voice. They consequently felt no compunction about flouting it. The black market flourished. Although in theory all consumers paid the same price, in actuality they did not.

The pricing system was inequitable, unequal, uncontrollable, and opaque. The prices were wrong—and that's not fair.

From *The Price Is Wrong: Understanding What Makes a Price Seem Fair and the True Cost of Unfair Pricing,* by Sarah Maxwell (John Wiley & Sons, 2008, page 164).

---

follow that it is also immoral for customers to pay low prices? If prices are deemed "unreasonable," why do people pay them? Only unreasonable people pay unreasonable prices.

Why is an oil or pharmaceutical company condemned for earning windfall profits when market conditions change, while an individual homeowner who realizes a tidy profit off of a hot real estate market is applauded? Popular movie stars, directors, and entertainment companies can earn above-normal profits without so much as a whisper of public protest. Premium ice creams and chocolates are very expensive and yield profit margins that would have made the "robber barons" of yesterday blush. Very few of us would continue working at 50 percent of our present salaries. Are we not charging what the market will bear? Why are individuals and corporations held to different standards?

To believe prices are determined by greed is to believe sellers can establish prices at whatever level they desire, in effect never having to suffer losses or bankruptcy. Homes along the oceanfront command high prices, but this does not prove fresh air causes greed. Prices convey information, while allocating resources and distributing income. If sellers are greedy then the counterargument can be made that buyers are also greedy and selfish, since they value seller's products more than they do their money. Yet only the seller gets blamed. Probably because greed and selfishness do not, at all, explain this behavior.

Perhaps it is not so much *price* that bothers people as it is *profits*. Profits have a bad reputation because most people simply do not acknowledge where they come from. Profits come from *risk*. The entrepreneuse gives long before she receives. She pays wages, vendors, landlords, and the other costs of running a business in advance of having anything left over (profits). Very few individuals work for 100 percent stock options, yet business owners, in effect, do exactly this, since profits are only left over after everyone else has been paid. If it were true that profits caused high prices, then we should witness lower prices in those countries with no profits, such as socialist or communist countries. Yet all of the empirical evidence is to the contrary. Even though profits comprise only 10 percent of national income, they are crucial in allocating the other 90 percent. Whenever someone laments a particular industry (or company) is making obscene profits, there is an effective retort: If you believe that, you would be crazy not to sell everything you own and buy its stock.

Peter Drucker pointed out, "If archangels instead of businessmen sat in director's chairs, they would still have to be concerned with profitability, despite their total lack of personal interests in making profits." Profits are an indicator that a useful social purpose is being filled and needs are being met. In a free market, no profit could exist without people voluntarily entering into a transaction where each receives more than they give up, what Harvard philosophy professor Robert Nozick cleverly termed "capitalist acts between consenting adults." This is why George Gilder compares profits to altruism, since in enterprise gift giving *precedes* voluntary exchange—*alter* in Latin means "other." For you to exchange you have to *create* something to exchange. The essence of giving is not the absence of an expectation of earning a return, but the absence of a *predetermined* return. Profits are not guaranteed, and are determined by consumers, not greed. Gilder explains this eloquently:

> A profit is the difference between what inputs cost the company and what they are worth to somebody else. It's the index of the altruism of the process.
>
> The moral code of capitalism is the essential altruism of enterprise. The most successful gifts are the most profitable—that is, gifts that are worth much more to the recipient than to the donor. The most successful givers, therefore, are the most altruistic—the most responsive to the desires of others.
>
> The circle of giving (the profits of the economy) will grow as long as the gifts are consistently valued more by the receivers than by the givers. A gift is defined not by the absence of *any* return, but by the absence of a *predetermined* return. Unlike socialist investments, investments under capitalism are analogous to gifts, in that the returns are not preordained and depend for success entirely on understanding the needs of others. Profit thus emerges as an index of the altruism of a product (Gregorsky 1998: 113, 302–303).

This view of capitalism being a moral system is certainly not one that is propagated in the mainstream popular culture, where a populist refrain is "People before profits," and the "bad guy" is portrayed as a businessman twice as much as any other occupation, as if profits and social responsibility are mutually exclusive. They are not. This view is pernicious and completely out of touch with human behavior. In fact, given the realities of free-market exchanges—where both parties are better off after the exchange—profits are actually an indicator of social value created. Those who believe that earning a profit is morally neutral rather than a morally *superior* way for a corporation to discharge its responsibility should be asked if they believe deliberately running losses is ethical—particularly if it is with someone else's money?

Honesty and ethical standards do not always pay off. One definition of ethics is to do the right thing even when it will cost you more than you want to pay. For moral reasons alone, these costs are worth paying. Reputation is a priceless asset, and loss of reputation is the single biggest risk a firm faces. As Oscar Wilde reminded us, no one is rich enough to buy back their past. The Greek senator Plenides said, "To lead a moral life one must do more than is required and less than is allowed." No doubt businesses act in a social context, as do all individuals, and should be held accountable for doing the right thing for the right reasons. None of this is inconsistent with the pursuit of profit and meeting human needs and wants.

Ethical conduct, integrity, trust, and honesty are not just moral principles, they are also major economic factors, and one all professionals should be judged against and held accountable for.

The Morality of Price Discrimination

This book has documented countless cases of price discrimination while also providing several strategies to implement it, all the while understanding that this method of pricing is similar to playing with fire, since it can be perceived as being grossly unfair. A. C. Pigou, the first economist to use the term *price discrimination*, understood the perceptual problems intrinsic with this form of pricing, noting businesses had to be careful in setting pricing policy: "Since a hostile public opinion might lead to legislative intervention, [the company's] choice must not be such as to outrage the popular sense of justice" (Pigou and Aslanbeigui, 1920).

Certainly we witnessed this public outcry when in 2000 the online retailer Amazon.com was found to be offering different prices on DVDs to different customers. Customers thought it unfair that customers from wealthier locations were being charged a higher price.

Rather than analyzing the *consequences* of actions, as utilitarian philosophers argued, the philosophical theory known as deontology holds that one should do what is right—*deontology* is Greek meaning "duty." Deontologists believe in universal principles (thou shall not steal, murder, etc.) and consequences should not be the only criteria used to judge moral behavior. The leading deontologist is the German philosopher Immanuel Kant (1724–1804). Kant's theory places *motives* for actions as higher importance than the *consequences* of those actions. In other words, one should do what is right, for the right reasons. If one is honest only because one believes that honesty pays, it is not as moral as those who are honest because it is the right thing to do. Here is what Kant had to say with respect to a merchant's pricing policies in *Grounding for the Metaphysics of Morals*:

> ... [T]hat a dealer should not overcharge an inexperienced purchaser certainly accords with duty; and where there is much commerce the prudent merchant does not overcharge but keeps a fixed price for everyone in general, so that a child may buy from him just as well as everyone else may. Thus customers are honestly served, but this is not nearly enough for making us believe that the merchant has acted this way from duty and from principles of honesty; his own advantage required him to do it. He cannot, however, be assumed to have in

addition an immediate inclination toward his buyers, causing him, as it were, out of love to give no one as far as price is concerned any advantage over another (Bowie 1999: 121–22).

Kant most likely would not approve of price discrimination. Of course, that may be a premature judgment, since it was not as ubiquitous a practice in his day as it is presently, and economists' understanding of welfare economics has improved to the point where it has been confirmed to have beneficial effects, especially for lower-income and poor customers. For instance, if pharmaceutical firms did not engage in price discrimination, poor countries would not get as many live-saving drugs that are produced in rich countries.

The analogy of progressive taxation may help to clarify this issue. James Coffield, in *A Popular History of Taxation*, asked, "What would you say of a baker or a grocer or any merchant who would demand for the same commodity a price varying with the wealth of the purchaser?" Coffield was actually leveling a charge against the progressive income tax, a valid charge, in my opinion. The question then is this: Is it a valid criticism of the free market? There is a profound difference between taxes paid to government and prices paid in the free market for goods and services. Paying taxes is guided by the Ability-to-Pay Principle, which basically means tax burdens should be assigned not on the basis of who benefits from government programs, but rather on the basis of who has the ability to pay—therefore, taxes should rise with income. Free market transactions, on the other hand, are guided by the Benefit Principle, which says prices are seen as a quid pro quo for the services provided to the purchaser. With taxes, there is no correlation between benefits received and the amount paid. Taxes are forced exactions; they are not voluntary; they are not debts because there is no principle of fair value received. Even the U.S. Treasury Department defines a tax as "a compulsory payment for which no specific benefit is received in return." Prices in the free market, in contrast, are established by people's willingness to pay (subjective value).

It is hard to see how even Immanuel Kant could argue with the welfare effects of price discrimination, complaining against the practice of charging children and seniors a lower price, or offering discount coupons to fixed-income, or merely frugal, customers. Nobel Prize–winning economist Milton Friedman was fond of saying that there is no such thing as a free lunch, yet the consumer surplus is, in effect, a free lunch, especially beneficial to the poor and lower-income members of society.

Even though economists can justify the practice of price discrimination with social welfare empirical evidence, businesses still must take into account the perceptions of fairness in establishing its pricing policies. Although customers are assumed to be rational economic agents, there is no doubt that emotions and perceptions of fair play influence their behavior. A strategic pricing policy takes these perceptions into account. Fortunately, there is now some guidance to assist in taking into account another dimension of human behavior beyond maximum utility calculations and the theory of rationality.

Prospect Theory

Israeli psychologists Daniel Kahneman and Amos Tversky created in 1979 what has become known as behavioral economics—they labeled it *prospect theory*. It sets out to describe how people evaluate losses and gains. Prospect theory maintains that people give more weight to losses than to gains. In fact, *loss aversion* posits that we feel the pain from a loss twice as keenly as we feel the pleasure from a similar-sized gain.

It appears that many actions people take are done with the full knowledge they are *irrational*. People will reject transactions whose terms they perceive to be unfair, even though the exchange would make them better off in an absolute sense, and rationality would predict they should accept the deal. Consider these scenarios:

> A hardware store sells snow shovels for $15. The morning after a large snowstorm, the store raises the price to $20 (quoted in Poundstone 2010: 105).

If you are like the overwhelming majority (82 percent), you feel this is unfair. Or think back to 1983 when the Cabbage Patch doll was in short supply during the Christmas season:

> A store has been sold out of the popular Cabbage Patch dolls for a month. A week before Christmas a single doll is discovered in a storeroom. The managers know that many customers would like to buy the doll. They announce over the store's public address system that the doll will be sold by auction to the customer who offers to pay the most (Poundstone 2010: 105–106).

Seventy-four percent of the public thought this unfair. Notice how self-serving these concepts of "unfair" are. No one ever complains when they get a great deal on an item.

How a price is framed can make all the difference in dealing with perceptions of fairness. It is more acceptable to list peak season prices and then discount from those than to add premiums to a lower listed price. Gas stations learned it is better to offer a discount when customers pay in cash rather than charge a premium for using a credit card. Even though these transactions have the exact same economic consequences, since they are perceived as being fair, they are more accepted.

There is no doubt pricers need to understand how prices affect their customers' perceptions of fairness, and whether there are superior ways to frame prices, payment terms, or other conditions of the transaction that will not violate people's subjective and emotional determinations of fairness.

Ethics and pricing cannot be separated, nor should they be. The concept of a "just price" will most likely not be solved anytime soon. Companies should be prepared to defend and justify their pricing policies, and the most efficacious way to do this is based on value, not costs. If you knew a cancer drug was 50 percent more efficacious, would you refuse to pay more than 50 percent of its nearest substitute?

Let us now subject the billable hour to the same ethical and fairness standards as all other pricing strategies.

Is Hourly Billing Ethical?

Ethics—originating from the Greek word *ethos*, meaning "habit"—is a branch of philosophy that explores and analyzes moral problems, concerned with questions such as: What kind of moral principles and values should guide our actions? What do we mean by right and wrong? Morality is not a personal choice but a social construct. Hitler probably thought he was ethical.

You would not need to study morality or ethics if you were stranded on an island, since there would be no one to be "just" or "unjust" to. The Josephson Institute of Ethics defines ethics this way:

> Ethics is about how we meet the challenge of doing the right thing when that will cost more than we want to pay. There are two aspects to ethics: The first involves the ability to discern right from wrong, good from evil, and propriety from impropriety. The second involves the commitment to do what is right, good and proper. Ethics entails action; it is not just a topic to mull or debate.

Immanuel Kant proposed broad principles to provide a framework for making moral decisions, described as categorical imperatives:

1. Act only on that maxim by which you can at the same time will that it should become a universal law (e.g., no stealing).

2. Act so that you treat humanity whether, in your own person or in that of another, always as an end and never as a means only. (People are to be respected because they have dignity. Moral agency is what gives humans dignity.)

3. Kingdom of Ends formulation: You should act as if you were a member of an ideal kingdom of ends in which you were both subject and sovereign at the same time.

If you apply this test to hourly billing, you find it fails miserably on all the questions, especially the first and third. Would you want hourly billing to become universal? Would you want all businesses to utilize it? If the Golden Rule is true—treat others as you yourself would want to be treated—how can one defend the morality of hourly billing? Would you accept that method of pricing from a hotel, an airline, or a grocery store?

Aristotle wrote, "It's not easy to be a good citizen in a bad society." Hourly billing creates a bad culture, focused almost exclusively on the convenience of the seller, not the customer. It is not how you purchase anything else in your life. You would not tolerate it for one minute if any other business tried to price this way. Hence, it is unethical. I think Kant would agree.

Part II has dealt with the foundations for *creating* value. In Parts IV and V, we will deal with *capturing* value by pricing on purpose. The first step is eliminating the billable hour and timesheets, replacing them with more strategic tools for professional knowledge firms. But before we get there, it is helpful to take a historical detour and explain the genesis and consequences of hourly billing and timesheets, the subject of Part III.

The Genesis and Consequences of Hourly Billing and Timesheets

Custom is the whole of equity for the sole reason that it is accepted. That is the mystical basis of its authority. Whoever tries to trace this authority back to its origin, destroys it.

—Blaise Pascal, *Pensées*, 1670

CHAPTER 16

A Brief History of Hourly Billing and Timesheets

Ages are no more infallible than individuals—every age having held many opinions which subsequent ages have deemed not only false but absurd.

—John Stuart Mill

Benjamin Franklin is often cited by businesspeople for his much-repeated saying "Time is money." This little adage has certainly infected the way professionals view the value of the services they deliver; unfortunately, it is taken out of context. The sentence was written in 1748—over 100 years prior to Marx's labor theory of value—and it was in a letter Franklin sent to a young businessperson just starting out, and who had sought Franklin's advice. Here is what Franklin wrote in its entirety on the subject of time in a letter entitled "Advice to a Young Tradesman":

To my friend, A.B.:

As you have desired it of me, I write the following hints, which have been of service to me, and may, if observed, be so to you. Remember that *time* is money. He that can earn ten shillings a day by his labor, and goes abroad, or sits idle, one half of that day, though he spends but sixpence during his diversion or idleness, ought not to reckon *that* the only expense; he has really spent, or rather thrown away, five shillings besides (Krass 1999: 283).

Note that Franklin was not speaking of value, nor price; he was articulating the concept of *opportunity cost*—that is, a forgone opportunity, the road not traveled, coined by the Austrian economist Friedrich von Wieser (1851–1926). In reality, every cost has an opportunity cost, an alternative you could have chosen. It is an important economic principle, but a seller's opportunity cost has little to do with the value provided to the customer. In fact, Franklin's statement has been misinterpreted as validating the labor theory of value, yet it does no such thing. Opportunity cost, like the supply curve, may influence the *quantity* of a good offered, not its *value*. Time is certainly precious, because it is a nonrenewable, precious resource. But even resources are useless until a purpose is found for them that people will value. Oil was worthless to the farmer—indeed it was a nuisance—until the invention of the combustion engine.

A direct derivative of the labor theory of value can be found among the thinking of cost accountants after World War I. One of the century's most influential accounting theorists was William Paton, who in a 1922 treatise described what he thought was the cost accountant's chief activity:

> The essential basis for the work of the cost accountant—without it, there could be no costing—is the postulate that the value of any commodity, service, or condition, utilized in production, *passes over* into the object or product for which the original item was expended and *attaches to* the result, giving it its value (Johnson and Kaplan 1991: 135–136).

But in a speech Paton gave at a conference in 1970, he repudiated this notion that costs attached to a product as it moves through the factory:

> The basic difficulty with the idea that cost dollars, as incurred, attach like barnacles to the physical flow of materials and stream of operating activity is that it is at odds with the actual process of valuation in a free competitive market. The customer does not buy a handful of classified and traced cost dollars; he buys a product, at prevailing market price. And the market price may be either above or below any calculated cost figure (Johnson and Kaplan 1991: 139).

Even prior to Paton's erroneous 1922 treatise on cost accounting, the industrial barons—such as Andrew Carnegie, Pierre du Pont, Alfred Sloan, and other engineers of the Scientific Management movement—were the leaders in pioneering cost accounting for their operations. Prior to World War I, the DuPont Powder Company was using nearly all of the management accounting principles for operating a company known today: cost accounting for labor, material, and overhead; cash, income, and capital budgets; and flexible budgets, sales forecasts, standard costs, variance analysis, transfer prices, and operating division performance measures. The most significant contribution made to management accounting theory was the invention of the return on investment (ROI) measure.

The importance of the DuPont ROI cannot be overemphasized, since it was the dominant theory taught to at least three generations of accountants and MBAs. Once the MBAs began to migrate into the professional firms, they brought with them the idea that firms could perform cost accounting and measure efficiency with timesheets, similar to the manufacturing industries. The theory was that by tracking time, the firms could perform cost accounting—not pricing—to determine if any one job, or customer, was profitable.

The Father of the Billable Hour and Timesheet— in the Legal Profession

The first person to introduce the idea of the billable hour and recording time was Reginald Heber Smith, a lawyer and author of *Law Office Organization,* published in 1943. This book was actually a series of four articles published in the *ABA Journal* from May to August 1940 (written by Smith during his Christmas vacation in 1939). They were so popular they were reprinted in pamphlet form in 1943, with continued printings up to 1983 by the Economics of Law Practice Section (ELPS) of the American Bar Association. The pamphlet I am quoting from here is the 11th edition (1983, 51 pages), with a foreword by James E. Brill, chairperson of the ELPS, 1982–1983.

Reginald Heber Smith graduated from Harvard Law in 1914, after which he became chief counsel of the Boston Legal Aid Society. This is where he implemented his Frederick Taylor–inspired ideas of Scientific Management principles into a law firm—specifically, completing a timesheet to track efficiency and perform cost and profitability accounting. In 1919, Smith joined the Boston law firm of Hale and Dorr as managing partner, where he practiced until his death in 1966.

Since my book is dedicated to dismantling what Reginald Smith implemented, I came to his book with an incredible bias, expecting to lay waste to Smith's ideas and policies. Yet I attempted to keep an open mind, as always, and hear him out. This was a fortunate attitude because the book is better than I expected, containing much wisdom. Even though I have major disagreements with Smith, I have learned to appreciate his counsel, and can forgive his sins as a result of the intellectual ideas in the zeitgeist at the time he practiced. As you will see, he even implemented many of the ideas that are contained in this book.

Here's how Smith described what lawyers sell:

> The service lawyers render is their professional knowledge and skill, but the commodity they sell is *time,* and each lawyer has only a limited

amount of that. Efficiency and economy are a race against time. The great aim of all organizations is to get a given legal job properly done with the expenditure of the fewest possible hours (Smith 1983: 3).

A race against time? Is that why you went to law school to become a lawyer—to constantly race against time? In spite of Smith's insistence to keep timesheets in tenth-of-hour increments, and his belief that the commodity lawyers sold was time, his views on pricing are more nuanced, since he also knew there was more to pricing than the labor involved.

Even though he is credited with creating the billable hour in law firms, he primarily used the timesheet as a cost accounting tool, not a pricing method. Smith then goes on to argue that, in reality, it is the customer who has the final say regarding the price. His firm allowed customers to fix their bills, in alignment with value received. His firm actually informed the customer of this policy up front, usually after the customer asked, "What will it cost?" He qualified this by stating that most customers were honest, but if the firm believed a customer was being unfair, they would respectfully decline to accept further work.

Now, of course, Smith goes on to justify not being able to answer the cost question by analogizing an architect building a house. He cannot give you a price until he sees all the specifications, and no attorney can know the specifications in advance, especially in litigation. Of course, there are solutions to this—phasing, change orders, offering different levels of protection to the customer as with insurance, as we will discuss in Part IV.

Nevertheless, you have to hand it to Smith and his firm for informing the customer of this policy up front. Talk about transparency. It may very well be the first explicit, up-front service guarantee offered by a professional firm.

Smith was inspired by Frederick Taylor's time-and-motion studies and his Scientific Management revolution that began in the 1880s. This is what led Smith to impose time recording in hours and tenths. He wrote, "Efficiency and economy are a race against time" (Smith 1983: 3). Recent scholarship has called into question Taylor's so-called "scientific studies" of efficiency—see, for instance, Matthew Stewart's book *The Management Myth*. Positing a universal science of efficiency as Taylor did was nonsense, for the reason we discussed in Chapter 2: There is no such thing as generic efficiency. Taylorism was a tautology: "An efficient shop is more productive than an inefficient shop." So what? Efficiency and effectiveness are worlds apart, and we will return to Taylor's work in Chapters 22–24.

All said, as Smith's book makes clear, the timesheet was introduced mainly to perform cost accounting, not for pricing. It was a way to *manage* and *cost* the inventory, but after lawyers became acclimated to completing a daily timesheet, it *became* the inventory lawyers sold. It was the ultimate quantification of Abraham Lincoln's erroneous utterance "Time is an attorney's stock in trade."

Summary and Conclusions

Reginald Heber Smith imparted much wisdom in his book, but he also embraced the Gospel of Efficiency at the expense of effectiveness by subscribing to Frederick Taylor's discredited Scientific Management ideas. Yet despite the fact that the billable hour and timesheet are antiquated, if Smith had not introduced these tools to the legal profession, someone else, somewhere else, most certainly would have.

But I also think Smith would be the first to embrace new ideas, as he did with Taylorism and Scientific Management. I think he would have supported value pricing and an alternative to timesheets, since he believed systems in law firms were nothing but a means to an end. And what was that end? Here is what he wrote in the 2nd Epilogue, Author's Note, in December 1963:

> What I reproach myself for is that, in my enthusiasm to set out the principles of a system for a law office, I failed to make it plain that any system is only a means to an end. The end, the goal, is to enable a group of people to work together happily and without friction, secure in their belief that the system is just and their good work for clients will be immediately reflected in the records (Smith 1983: 51).

The ideas and ideals advocated in this book have the same purpose in mind—that is, to maintain and advance the dignity and honor of professionals everywhere, while acknowledging that we are knowledge workers, and hence any system needs to be our servant, not our master. It is up to future generations of professionals to carry on Smith's innovative and visionary spirit. Are we up to the challenge?

In the final analysis, time is not money (or value) and customers do not buy hours. Pricing by the hour is causing professional firms to focus on the wrong things, with deleterious consequences—the subject of our next chapter.

CHAPTER 17

The Deleterious Effects of Hourly Billing

Custom doth make dotards of us all.

—Thomas Carlyle, *Sartor Resartus,* III, 1836

Nothing is more damaging to a new truth than an old error.

—Goethe, *Proverbs in Prose,* 1819

We have explored the fallacy of Karl Marx's labor theory of value and how it fails to explain value, and how it has been adopted by professional firms. The reader is justified in asking the following question: If people are supposedly rational—the assumption of rationality, which is the bedrock of economists—why is it that intelligent members of various professions have continued to apply the wrong theory to the value of their services?

The fact that hourly billing is so deeply entrenched and has been widely used for decades proves that is has some advantages. This is another case of cognitive dissonance. The only way to eradicate this paradox is to explain why hourly billing is a rational policy. The case against the billable hour is not that it is not a profitable pricing policy. Rather, the case being made is that hourly billing is *suboptimal* (if profitability is your goal), and its disadvantages outweigh its advantages. Therefore, before listing the disadvantages, we will now discuss what is right about hourly billing.

The Advantages of Hourly Billing

Hourly Billing Is Easy and Efficient

Hourly billing can be handled simply with appropriate time and billing software, turning the pricing function into an administrative task handled by less costly personnel, freeing up the professional team to take care of what is more important—customer relations.

Hourly Billing Is Perceived as Fair

Since hourly billing is largely justified based on a firm's costs and a "reasonable" profit margin, it is perceived as "fair" by customers. Prices set above this fair markup would attract competitors, as well as put any one firm at a disadvantage against competitors who do not similarly mark up to this level. Prices set below this level could set off a devastating and unsustainable price war. In addition, with all the talk of "transparency," our customers know our costs and would be aware of prices beyond a reasonable profit. Supernormal and windfall profits are perceived as unfair by many executives, unless, of course, they earn them.

Hourly Billing Provides Market Stability

Firms and customers understand hourly billing, making comparisons among firms easier. Since hourly rates remain relatively stable, this provides a desirable stability and predictability among buyers and sellers, as opposed to widely varying prices that may arise under a value pricing scenario.

Sometimes the Customer Demands Hourly Billing

It is rare but there are instances when customers will insist on being charged by the hour. One encounters this attitude most frequently in the legal profession, and to a lesser extent, in the accounting profession. Probably because the people hiring the firm were themselves alumni, raised on the virtues of hourly billing. But it is folly to turn this type of power over to your customers. You, not your customers, control your pricing strategy. They judge your value but cannot dictate how you price. This is not a large barrier to overcoming hourly billing. The problem is not with the customers; it is with the professionals.

Hourly Billing Is Required in Case of Litigation

Certain court cases require time recording due to legal precedent, fee shifting, and legal ethical rules. Bankruptcy requires attorneys to keep time in six-minute increments. If your firm does a majority of this type of work, then you may very well be stuck with the billable hour. However, this does not preclude your firm from pricing other services on a value basis. Slowly but surely, the rules of the game are starting to change, and even courts are beginning to recognize this reality. Eventually value pricing will be a common enough practice in the legal profession, and the threat of litigation as justification for tracking every minute will wane. We will discuss this issue further in Appendix F.

Hourly Billing Leads to Higher Volume

Higher prices would dampen demand for professional services, and some projects simply cannot be quoted up front without a high price being specified. This may lead to some customers not utilizing professional services, and thus not gaining the benefits of working with professionals.

Hourly Billing Is a Cost-Accounting, Productivity, and Project Management Tool

Combined with timesheets, this is the single largest perceived advantage of hourly billing. Leaders wonder, "If you did not keep time reports, how would you know if you are making money on a particular job? How would you measure the 'efficiency' of your people? How would you perform project management without analyzing time?" These are all valid questions that go right to the heart of why Reginald Heber Smith began tracking time in 1919—to measure *efficiency* and *profitability*. There are, of course, alternatives to performing all of these functions.

Hourly Billing Transfers Risk to the Customer

This advantage is truly a double-edge sword, for while the professional prefers that the risk be with the customer, the customer prefers the exact opposite. The risks of unforeseen circumstances, scope creep, learning curve inefficiencies, and the like are all shifted to the customer with hourly billing. Professionals tend to be risk (and loss) adverse, and hourly billing places a comfortable floor on their profits. However, professionals have paid a high "reverse risk premium" to the customer for this floor. If the customer assumes the risk, the professional will only receive their hourly rate; no more, usually less. This is demonstrated by the fact that average realization rates in professional firms around the world are between 50 and 95 percent of the standard hourly rate.

Hourly Billing Has Served Us Well, Why Should We Change?

Rather than man being a completely rational calculator always trying to maximize his utility, similar to Mr. Spock of *Star Trek* fame, it seems in many areas of life we act more like Homer Simpson of *The Simpsons*. It is doubtful a Mr. Spock would need Alcoholics or Gamblers Anonymous, or the idea of a self-control credit card that, in advance, voluntarily limits one's spending in various categories automatically. Yet economists insist in being grounded in the assumption that people are rational, as economist David Friedman, in his book *Hidden Order*, defends:

> ... [T]he assumption describes our actions, not our thoughts. If you had to understand something intellectually in order to do it, none of us would be able to walk.

> Economics is based on the assumption that people have reasonably simple objectives and choose the correct means to achieve them. Both assumptions are false—but useful.

> Suppose someone is rational only half the time. Since there is generally one right way of doing things and many wrong ways, the rational behavior can be predicted but the irrational cannot. If we assume he is rational, we predict his behavior correctly about half the time—far from perfect, but a lot better than nothing. If I could do that well at the racetrack I would be a very rich man.

> ... [R]ationality is an assumption I make about other people. I know myself well enough to allow for the consequences of my own irrationality. But for the vast mass of my fellow humans, about whom I know very little, rationality is the best predictive assumption available (Friedman 1996: 3–5).

In short, I find both assumptions of rationality and irrationality useful. If Friedman is right, then we can predict 50 percent of human behavior with rationality, and perhaps some portion of the other 50 percent with irrationality. This goes a long way in explaining the endurance of hourly billing. This advantage is one of the most difficult to overcome. Far from being irrational, this attitude is actually quite rational and has been explained best by economist Herbert A. Simon's autobiography, *Models of My Life*. Among economists, Simon is best known for his theories of *bounded rationality* and *satisficing*.

Simon's bounded rationality and satisficing concepts are extremely explanatory, especially with respect to hourly billing. Bounded rationality posits that both elements of irrational and nonrational behavior bound the area of rational behavior. Satisficing posits that people search for good enough actions rather than optimal ones. Coupling the concept of satisficing to bounded rationality is how Simon explains how people really make decisions. Rather than attempting to maximize or optimize, people search for "good enough" actions. Simon writes:

Since my world picture approximates reality only crudely, I cannot aspire to optimize anything; at most, I can aim at satisficing. Searching for the best can only dissipate scarce cognitive resources; the best is the enemy of the good (Simon 1991: 361).

[Even Darwin's] natural selection only predicts that survivors will be fit enough, that is, fitter than their losing competitors; it postulates satisficing, not optimizing (Simon 1991: 166).

In sum, the assumption of rationality, coupled with Simon's bounded rationality and satisficing concepts, largely explain why so many professional firms cling to the billable hour and timesheets. It is simply good enough; neither requiring much cognitive resources. Like driving, it is an unconscious competence we do not have to think too hard about, which is definitely an advantage.

What about the Customer?

During the time when I practiced as a CPA, one day I entered the office to find my partner agitated. He had just finished a telephone conversation with a customer he had been auditing for several months. He had a fixed price agreement with this customer for the audit and other services, but the customer's accounting was not in the best of shape, audit adjustments were mounting, and the prepared by customer (PBC) schedules were not tying to the general ledger, all contributing to the audit taking longer than he had originally estimated.

He called one of the owners to discuss the situation and was trying to extract a few thousand dollars for the cost overruns. He explained to the customer that he had already spent the hours, and the customer replied, "Hours schmours." This did not make my partner happy—but the lesson is invaluable for anyone who cares to learn from the experience.

The customer was right not to equate hours spent with value. The firm had given him a fixed price and should stick with it, no matter the consequences. The fact that my partner underestimated the job is really not any of the customer's concern. The moral of the story is that when you and your customer see things differently, *you change.*

This conversation takes place every single day throughout professional firms, usually resulting in a write-down, a write-off, a reduction in trust within the relationship, or even a lost customer. In fact, in a lot of cases a conversation does not take place first, but rather the firm "bills and ducks," which results in an angry customer, then the conversation. Either way, the outcome is not pleasant, nor is it necessary. One of our colleagues says that hourly billing is the equivalent of "mail fraud" because the customer is usually unaware of the final price. We would not tolerate this behavior from any other business, so it is little wonder that so many customers are beginning to revolt against the billable hour. But we must deal with the *cause* of the problem, not simply its effect. The cause is hourly billing and the only cure is to provide a fixed price up front, *before the work begins*. Doing something dumb once is a mistake; doing it over and over and over is an ideology. The professions are clinging to hourly billing while ignoring basic laws of economics and customer psychology, which is causing the following deleterious effects of hourly billing.

The Disadvantages of Hourly Billing

Here, in no particular order, is a list of the deleterious effects of hourly billing for you to consider. It is by no means meant to be comprehensive.

Hourly Billing Misaligns the Interests of Professional and Customer

Even supporters of hourly billing, such as William G. Ross, will admit that there exists, right from the start, a conflict between the professional's interest and the customer's. In *The Honest Hour*, Ross writes:

> The first step toward more ethical billing practices is for both attorneys and clients to frankly admit the harsh truth that hourly billing creates an inherent conflict of interest between the client's needs for expeditious work and the attorney's desire to bill time. Only by recognizing that this tension tends to create abuse can attorneys begin to cultivate ethical standards for billing time (Ross 1996: 6).

When you make hours important, then the customer is bound to focus on hours, rather than on value. Those professionals caught "padding" their timesheets because they believe the value of what they created exceeded the price measured in hours will lose the respect of their customers.

This conflict of interest also exists because in a cost-plus pricing system one way to increase a firm's revenue is to increase its costs. Cost-plus is the antithesis not only to effectiveness, but even to the pursuit of efficiency. Customers are beginning to recognize this, which explains why many sophisticated customers—such as Coca-Cola, Procter & Gamble, Pfizer,

Cisco, among others—are innovating new pricing paradigms with their advertising agencies and law firms.

Incentives matter, as any good economist knows. No one washes a rental car and you should not ask your hairstylist if you need a haircut. While I am not arguing that hourly billing causes unethical behavior— although it certainly has—it is a system with a built-in conflict of incentives. Aligning incentives is difficult enough to achieve without the added burden of an inherent conflict in how your price your services.

One of the reasons why procurement and in-house counsel will audit their law firm's or advertising agency's overhead costs, labor rates, full-time equivalents, and so on is because they are ensuring compliance with their processes and procedures. Since they have no way to determine the results until after the fact, they obsess on the inputs. If you change the incentives, however, you make the processes and compliance obsolete.

No better example exists than the convict ships that took criminals from England to Australia during the eighteenth century, as told by Charles Bateson's *The Convict Ships*. At first, the captains were paid based upon how many prisoners boarded the ship in London. This gave the captain the incentive to pack as many prisoners onto the ship, regardless of the health or safety of the prisoners, for the six-month journey. In addition, the captains usually hoarded the food so they could sell it upon arrival in Australia. This created a mortality rate of nearly one-third for the prisoners. Those lucky enough to survive the journey arrived "lean and emaciated" and "full of filth and lice."

Now, there are many ways of dealing with this problem from a "process and compliance" point of view. One could pass a law, such as Sarbanes- Oxley, that forced captains to comply with procedures for limiting the number of convicts, assuring an adequate diet, competent medical care, sufficient exposure to sunlight, ample food and medicine on board, and so forth. In fact, you could even hire external auditors to attest to the compliance of these standards.

From an economists' perspective, all of this is quite bureaucratic, expensive, ineffective, and unnecessary. If a way can be found to align the incentives, the processes and compliance will take care of themselves, which is exactly what happened. Once the compensation was changed from paying for each convict *boarded* in London to paying for each one who *disembarked* alive and well in Australia, the "financial incentive to treat convicts humanely" dramatically improved. The first three ships to sail under this new compensation plan experienced only two deaths out of 322 prisoners." As Bateson concludes, "the gross abuses earlier practiced were almost entirely eliminated" (Bateson 1969: 20–21).

This type of thinking must be applied to the billable hour, which is vulnerable to thought. Firms need to stop dealing with the symptoms of the billable hour—penalizing partners and associates for write-downs and write-offs, appointing administrative people to hound customers for speedier collection, insisting that timesheets are submitted on time, and so on. All of these processes will amount to nothing because they do not deal with the cause, only the symptom, like plunging a thermometer into ice water to deal with a fever.

Hourly Billing Focuses on Hours, Not Value

Today's sophisticated customers understand the subjective theory of value; they simply do not automatically correlate value with billable hours. One of the reasons some in-house counsel and marketing departments are forcing their law firms and advertising agencies to change compensation is in recognition that the labor theory of value is deeply flawed. Today's corporate customers are also sellers who have to price their products and services, and more and more of them are turning away from cost-plus pricing, recognizing that it is suboptimal. Why would they want the same pricing paradigm from the professional firms they patronize?

Whenever professionals have to justify price to a customer, they inevitably resort to discussing hours spent. Marketers would never do this, as they always try to create value in the minds of the customer first, and talk price later. By having three-digit—and even four-digit in some law firms—hourly rates, you are putting customers in a psychological frame of mind to focus on how long things will take you. This is the wrong focus, for both parties.

Imagine learning from a doctor that you have a condition that is difficult to diagnose, possibly a rare disease, and saying, "Well, doc, please don't think about my case *too* long, and don't consult with your colleagues, since I want to keep the old billable hours down."

If the customers focus on hours, they are constantly trying to calculate a return on investment, or even whether they can continue to afford the service, with each hour logged, rather than focusing on the totality of what the firm is providing. The multidimensional value is turned into a one-dimensional, commoditized billing rate. You have to wonder how much of what is referred to as customers being price-sensitive is actually the customers simply doubting the value, because the professional has not discussed the value of their service.

If you do not discuss value, results, output, and alignment of incentives with your customer, expect to discuss inputs, activities, costs, efforts, hours, processes, and compliance. The latter will lead to frustration, mistrust, and unhappy relationships, while the former will lead to a better outcome for all.

Hourly Billing Places the Risk on the Customer

As discussed earlier, risk is where profits come from. If you offer customers fixed prices you will be able to charge a premium simply because you are reducing their risk. If this sounds counterintuitive, consider the mortgage market. Which commands a higher interest rate, a fixed rate or an adjustable rate mortgage? Surveys conducted by the American Bar Association Section of Litigation's Committee on Corporate Counsel repeatedly "indicate that most clients are willing to pay a premium in exchange for a predictable fee" (Reed 1996: 89).

Any strategy that can lower the customer's perceived risk should be able to command a price premium while providing a competitive differentiation. Strategies such as a service guarantee, risk-sharing, dealing with ownership in intellectual property rights—especially for advertising agencies—a price guarantee, and payment terms are just some of the ways a firm can command a premium price based upon real value created, not hours spent.

Hourly Billing Fosters a Production Mentality, Not an Entrepreneurial or Knowledge Worker Spirit

Over the decades of the billable hour's hegemony, the professions have lost sight of the all-important question "What did we accomplish?" It has been replaced with "How many hours did you bill?" Firms have rewarded production, measured in hours, and have been slow to recognize customer service, retention, loyalty, creativity, innovation, and other yardsticks of long-term profitability.

Hourly billing also has the pernicious effect of deemphasizing marketing, especially at the lower levels of a firm, because the professional does not want to forgo billable hours, since most compensation plans are based on them. Over time, the professional becomes production oriented, becoming adept at solving problems but lethargic at pursuing opportunities. This is a costly mediocrity, as the professional is simply living off existing skills and intellectual capital, not taking risks to become more valuable to customers.

Developing an entrepreneurial and knowledge worker culture is the responsibility of the firm's leadership, as team members do not automatically become outstanding professionals simply because they get promoted to partnership—moved up on the letterhead, as my friend Ric Payne likes to say. On the contrary, an entrepreneurial and knowledge worker mindset has to be part of a firm's culture, rather than just a focus on technical competence and, worse, efficiency.

A system that creates barriers to vision will not only lose visions, it will lose visionaries. This is one of the reasons people leave the professions— they do not feel they are operating or being rewarded for their potential, only their hours and efficiency rating.

Hourly Billing Creates a Nonsensical Subsidy System

If all customers are charged an hourly rate, it is a safe bet that some will be overcharged and others will be undercharged to meet hourly quotas.

An example of a nonsensical subsidy is a tax research project that is billed to the first customer for, say, $10,000. If a second customer appears the following week with the exact same issue, how much should the firm charge the second customer? Following the logic and ethics of hourly billing the answer is clear: You can only charge the second customer for the actual hours spent.

Under this method, one could argue that the first customer underwrote the R&D costs for the second customer. It would be as if a pharmaceutical company charged the first customer for all its R&D, while the following customers were charged just the marginal cost of producing the drug.

These types of issues arise with any pricing method. Economics deals with this issue by utilizing price discrimination, charging different customers different prices based upon their ability and willingness to pay. The problem with the billable hour's subsidy is it is based on *internal* costs, not *external* value, and is therefore disengaged from the true economic calculations of the buyer. If all customers were charged what they perceived as the value of the service, agreed upon up front, a strong argument can be made that no one customer is being subsidized at the expense of another. It also removes the ludicrous ethical questions that surround a scenario such as our tax research project.

Another point must be made here: Pricing intellectual capital based on hours is simply the wrong measuring device. Since intellectual capital is a nonrival asset, it can be distributed without being diminished. The tax project in our example may only be worth $5,000 to the first customer, but may be worth $100,000 to the second. This is why there is no standard price for intellectual capital—it is inextricably linked to the value you are creating. To believe the billable hour is the proper measure of this value is to believe that J. K. Rowling should be paid by the hour to write the *Harry Potter* novels.

Hourly Billing Cannot Price Risk

All professional firms take on varying levels of risk with each customer they serve. Completing a divorce for Brittany Spears is fraught with more risk than a couple with limited assets. These two divorces should not be priced the same simply based on the risk the firm is assuming, not to mention that the service will be of radically different value to Ms. Spears than another customer. Risk cannot be priced by the hour. Actuaries have an axiom that is useful to remember: There is no such thing as a bad risk; only bad premiums.

Hourly Billing Is Not Predictive of a True Professional

One of the most useless pieces of information we can gather as outsiders about a firm, or a professional who works in it, is billable hours. It transmits little information of value, though it does highlight the "finders" (rainmakers), the "minders" (managers), and the "grinders" (technicians)—billable hours are hardly necessary, though, to make this distinction. Far more meaning is discovered by *judging* a professional's customer service attitude, customer defection and retention rates, customer loyalty, profitability and collection speed, creativity and innovation, risk taking, willingness to delegate, teaching and learning skills, and practice development activities—in short, all the virtues necessary to become David Maister's definition of a true professional—a technician who cares. Billable hours, in and of themselves, shed no light in any of these areas. In fact, most *measurements* will shed no light in these virtues, as most need to be *judged*, not measured.

If an outside consultant can enter a firm and make a judgment of the performance of its professionals without ever looking at billable hours, then the question becomes, What kinds of decisions are being made internally by collecting hourly information? If it is not a necessary question to ask from an outside perspective, why is it so important on the inside?

Is it possible that this internal measurement is being made simply because that is the way it has always been done? Most of the decisions that are made in a professional firm regarding personnel, hiring, firing, effectiveness, promotions, and pay raises are based on judgments that are made long before it materializes on a timesheet or an annual performance review. How many major, profit-enhancing decisions have been made in your firm as a result of hourly information? It is considered sacrosanct simply because it is so closely correlated to how services are now priced. If you begin to price based upon external value, you will soon discover that hours are superfluous.

Hourly Billing Encourages Hoarding of Hours

Due to compensation, bonuses, and performance reviews being based on billable hours, professionals have a tendency to hoard work to fulfill their hourly quotas. This results in low-level work being performed by high-level associates, which is incredibly unprofitable, since it does not optimize the value of intellectual capital. Just as surgeons should not waste their time piercing ears, managers and partners should not spend their time on compliance work that could be more effectively completed by someone else.

How pervasive is this problem? David Maister and Patrick McKenna say, "Estimates given to us by our clients of the amount [of work they do] that could be done by someone more junior range up to 50 percent or more of each senior person's time" (McKenna and Maister 2002: 17). If true—and I suspect it is, although I know of no empirical study that confirms it—this is an astonishing statistic. Think of the intellectual capacity your firm could free up if the firm's senior team members were able—and willing—to delegate up to 50 percent of their work. Not only would it provide needed skills for junior team members, it would make available more capacity to service "A" and "B" customers with top of the value curve projects. Having the firm's executives become better at delegation would increase profitability many times more than an increase in efficiency could ever provide.

Another negative effect of hoarding deals with write-offs. Who decides when time should be written off? And whose time is inevitably discounted? Partners and managers unilaterally writing off team member time destroys the morale of those professionals—in effect signaling to them that the work they have created is not valued.

Hourly Billing Focuses on Effort, Not Results

Who buys efforts in the marketplace? One brilliant epiphany that occurs while in the shower or driving may be worth more to the customer than 1,000 plodding, ineffective hours spent researching and pondering an issue. Yet what do you record on your timesheet? How do you price the customer? Hourly billing simply does not reward creativity and ingenuity. On the contrary, it rewards inexperience, inefficiency, and even incompetence— the slowest horse wins the race.

In 1935, Edgar Kaufmann, the German-American businessman and philanthropist who owned Kaufmann's department store, asked Frank Lloyd Wright to design a small summer home for him near Mill Run (75 miles southeast of Pittsburgh). Wright surveyed the site but procrastinated on the design. When Kaufmann telephoned him one day saying he was nearby and would like to stop by to see the design, Wright replied, "Come on Edgar, we're ready."

Two of Wright's draftsmen who heard the call could not believe it, since no one had drawn a single line. In his book about Wright, draftsmen Edgar Tafel explains what happened next:

Wright hung up the phone, walked to the drafting room and started to draw, talking in a calm voice. "They will have tea on the balcony ... they'll cross the bridge to walk into the woods," Wright said. Pencils were used up as fast as we could sharpen them. He erased, overdrew, modified, flipping sheets back and forth. Then he titled it across the bottom: Fallingwater.

Two hours later, when Kaufmann arrived, Wright greeted him and showed him the front elevation. "We've been waiting for you," Wright said.

They went to lunch, and we drew up the other two elevations. When they came back, Wright showed Kaufmann the added elevations (Swartz and Swartz 2006: 39–40).

This is why intellectual capital, expertise, wisdom, judgment, and ability to synthesize information, along with all the other characteristics of knowledge work, cannot be denominated in hours. By focusing and pricing based upon efforts and hours, professionals are unwittingly fulfilling the prophetic vision of C. Northcote Parkinson, who developed Parkinson's Law: Work expands so as to fill the time available for its completion. This is the antithesis of creativity and effectiveness.

Hourly Billing Penalizes Technological Advances

Every year, professional firms make substantial investments in technology that allow any given task to be performed in less time. Perversely, under the billable hour, firm revenue will then decline, unless hourly rates keep pace with productivity increases—what economists call the *productivity paradox*. It is a double hit to income: First, you are penalized for your intellectual capital and creativity—as with the Wright story—then you suffer a decline based upon keeping up with technology.

If efforts were truly the sole determinant of value, then perhaps firms should scrap their computers and complete, say, tax returns with manual typewriters and carbon paper. Billable hours would soar. The only way to overcome the productivity paradox is not to stop investing in technology, but rather to price your services based on external value, not internal efforts.

Hourly Rates Are Set by Reverse Competition

When professionals are honest with themselves, they will admit that they actually established their hourly rates not by some elaborate cost-plus pricing formula, but instead a process known as *reverse competition*. This means you look at the rates of your fellow professionals operating in your geographical market, make a decision on where you want to fit in on the competitive spectrum, and set your rates accordingly. My partner and I did exactly this when we chose to locate our CPA firm in Marin County—just north of San Francisco, so we could command hourly rates comparable to those of the City by the Bay.

Be honest. Did you set your hourly billing rate by crunching the numbers? You know, the hourly rate equals overhead plus desired profit divided by expected billable hours. Less than 10 percent of the thousands of professionals I have asked admitted they did it in this manner, with the rest confessing they never performed any numerical analysis. This is an astonishing admission, especially from CPAs, the proverbial number crunchers. One of the ardent defenses of the hourly billing method is that it is an excellent cost-accounting tool. Yet, the overwhelming majority concedes that they have not even run the numbers. This makes the notion of a "standard" hourly rate a pure fiction.

Hourly Billing Prices the Service, Not the Customer

In a world where value is subjective, no two customers are alike, and professional firms have the enormous advantage of meeting personally with each and every customer, the mind-set of pricing services is obsolete. Instead, the *customer* needs to be priced.

Hourly billing tends to ignore these differences, dealing with them only through varying a one-dimensional, uninformed, hourly rate. But customers are multifaceted, and value cannot be determined by hours. *It is much easier to set a bad price than a good price.* Hourly billing by default establishes a price that bears little, if any, relationship to value created because its primary focus is on the scope of work, not the scope of value to the customer. One of the significant changes with value pricing is the firm's ability to price the customer, not the service.

Hourly Billing Creates Bureaucracy

A moderate-sized CPA firm recently calculated that it could save approximately $75,000 per year by eliminating timesheets, and that was only the direct, calculable cost of inputting, producing, and generating the reports. It did not include the incalculable hours spent by team members tracking every quarter hour, the morale problems of having to account for every single hour of every day, the negative effect of hourly quotas on marketing and practice development, and the other deleterious effects that have been discussed so far.

The next logical question is this: Does the time-and-billing program generate at least $75,000 worth of useful information? Does it enable the firm to become better at pricing? Project management? Is tracking hours the only way to achieve the end results we desire? Nobody could answer any of these questions. One point all the partners agreed upon was that the majority of important decisions that are made—hiring, firing, planning jobs, pay raises, promotions—are determined long before they even see the results of the time reports. If, for instance, a particular team member is not performing up to minimum standards, time reports could actually obfuscate this reality, whereas the grumbling from other team members, missed deadlines, and customer complaints are going to be leading indicators that there are problems. If the firm is operating at close to maximum capacity, the partners and managers will usually hire an additional person, not as a result of analyzing time reports but because the people who report to them can justify the extra need—the marginal revenue will exceed the marginal cost of the new person.

My colleague Ed Kless estimates that somewhere between 7 and 10 percent of a firm's gross revenue is spent tracking, reporting, compiling, reviewing, and billing time. This is an astonishing investment. Not only have firms not analyzed if it is worth the investment, they have not even questioned the premise that this needs to be done at all.

Hourly Billing Does Not Set the Price Up Front

The most absurd and economically illogical effect of hourly billing is how it denies the ability to quote a price before the work begins. Few products or services in the marketplace are purchased without the customer knowing the price in advance. In fact, many professional firms, when dealing with outside vendors, insist on knowing the price in advance for everything they purchase, despite how they deny this same reassurance to their own customers.

It is actually quite comic. If hourly billing is vulnerable to thought, it is also vulnerable to ridicule, which should not be underestimated as a warrior in changing the culture. The movie *Airplane!* ended, in one swoop, the era of 1970s copy-cat disaster films with its mocking parody. Karl Marx wrote, "The final phase of a historic political system is *comedy*," while George Orwell wrote, "Every joke is a tiny revolution." Sarcasm and mockery can be a rust that corrodes the infrastructure of everything it touches, and stories of the silliness of hourly billing no doubt help.

Source: John Chisholm, 2010.

INSURANCE COMPANIES ADOPT COST-PLUS BILLING   Maybe 140 years of economic theory, along with centuries of customer buying habits, are wrong. Customers really do like cost-plus pricing. In fact, I had an interesting conversation today with my homeowner insurance company. It certainly was an epiphany for me. I am now renouncing VeraSage's Quest to rid the professions of cost-plus billing.

Insurance Company Agent (ICA): "Good afternoon, CSAA, how may I help you?"

Ron: "Hello, this is Ron Baker and I am interested in earthquake coverage for my home."

ICA: "Excellent, Mr. Baker. I see you've been a customer with us for nearly 30 years. We will take excellent care of you, as we have in the past."

Ron: "Great. How much would the standard earthquake coverage premium be for my home?"

ICA: "Before I answer, Mr. Baker, I need to ask you if you are aware of the fact that our company was recently acquired by a consortium of lawyers and CPAs?"

Ron: "Uh, no, I wasn't aware of that. Congratulations, I think."

ICA: "Thank you. You see, at their recent partnership retreat they had what's known as a BFO (Blinding Flash of the Obvious). You see, Mr. Baker, we really don't know how much it is going to cost to insure your home against an earthquake. There are far too many risks and uncertainties in this line of business. We don't know how big the next quake will be, where it will hit, or what the damage will be to our policyholder's homes. How could we possibly give you a fixed price under these conditions, which is what our new owners asked themselves during the retreat. I think you agree that is certainly a conundrum, no?"

Ron: "I guess, but how I am suppose to know if I can even afford this extra coverage? How can I make a prudent and informed buying decision on the value of the coverage if I don't know the price?"

ICA: "I understand the question, Mr. Baker, and it's a good one. In fact, I've been getting it all week from our policyholders. Our new owners' answer is that it would not be fair to charge you a premium that exceeded the actual damages, plus a normal rate of profit of course, including the time value of money. Nor would it be fair to charge you a premium that did not cover the actual damages, plus a normal rate of profit, of course. So you see, we simply can't give you a price for your earthquake insurance. There are just too many variables. Does that answer your question?"

Ron: "Not really. I can't really make a decision about this until I know the price."

ICA: "Well, Mr. Baker, I understand your dilemma, but I don't think you're viewing this from our perspective. The new way it works is as follows: We put your name on the earthquake insurance list, along with the date you decided to opt for coverage. Heaven forbid, if an earthquake were to strike, and your home is damaged beyond the deductible, you will submit a claim. We will aggregate all the claims we receive, tally them up, then divide by the number of policyholders on the list, adjusted by a complicated algorithm for time. We will then simply send you a bill for the retroactive costs since you've been covered, adding a normal profit and the time value of money, of course."

Ron: "How do I know that your costs will be accurate?"

ICA: "Mr. Baker, I'm not sure I appreciate the tone of that question. We here at CSAA are very fastidious and ethical. Our costs accountants are excellent CPAs, who will carefully, and accurately, keep track of all outflows. I really think you must put yourself in our shoes. There is simply no other way to give you a fair price, wouldn't you agree?"

Ron: "But I know the price of everything else I purchase before I pay for it."

ICA: "Well that may be true for commodities like groceries and clothing, but it's certainly not true for law, accounting, and other professional services, is it now, Mr. Baker?"

Ron: "Touché."

ICA: "In fact, the new owners tell us they are consulting with the airline industry as well, and are transitioning them to an hourly model, since flying planes is also fraught with innumerable risks and uncertainties. Our new owners inform us that the airlines are unprofitable because they do not price like we do now. It makes imminent sense when you really stop and think about it, doesn't it?"

Ron: "All right, you've convinced me. Put me on the list for earthquake coverage."

ICA: "Consider it done, Mr. Baker. And thank you for selecting CSAA for this very important coverage. We look forward to continuing our relationship for at least another 30 years. You will be receiving your policies shortly, please read them carefully, sign them in triplicate, and return two copies to our offices. We appreciate your business. Good day."

The absurdity of hourly billing from the customer's vantage point should not be ignored. By not setting a price in advance, the customer has no control over the situation, which is not a good position to put your customer in. People like to feel they are in control, especially when they are spending their own money. With hourly billing, the only involvement the customers have is paying the bill, and that means they have to make a retroactive value judgment *after* the service has been rendered, which is not a good time to discover they do not agree with the price. Value cannot be managed retroactively, only proactively.

Hourly Billing Does Not Differentiate Your Firm

Converting their crown jewels of experience, expertise, culture, intellectual capital, and relationships into a commodity, codified in an hourly rate, is no way to differentiate your firm from the competition. Low pricing is not an effective competitive strategy, unless you enjoy price wars, since someone, somewhere, is always willing to do what you do for less money. Yet price is one of the most important signals a firm can transmit to the marketplace regarding its value proposition.

Because competition really means conformity, why not get out of the pack and offer fixed prices? If people call your firm, or send out a Request for Proposal, they will usually ask what your hourly rates are. If you respond that your firm does not charge by the hour, they will be intrigued, probably enough to come in and see you for an initial consultation, during which you can review their needs and wants and offer them a fixed price.

Hourly Billing Does Not Measure How Much Money Is Being Left on the Table

Even though one of the major defenses of hourly billing and timesheets is that they are essential cost-accounting tools to determine profitability, this method has a glaring weakness: It has no way to capture how much the price *could have been*. In other words, how much money is the firm leaving on the table by setting prices too low? No cost accounting, realization, or timesheet report can answer this question. When Google began its auction-based AdWords program, CEO Eric Schmidt was petrified it would not set prices as high as Google's salespeople were getting. In three short weeks Schmidt's fears were calmed when the new pricing strategy had doubled revenue (Brandt 2009: 98). It became obvious at that point that salespeople were underpricing ads, not overpricing them, which is the direction most pricing mistakes are made. Without the willingness to test this new pricing strategy, Google would have left untold millions on the table, and worse, if they had been using the billable hour, they would have never learned about it. This is one of the major consequences of hourly billing, and therefore deserving of its own exploration, in Chapter 20.

Hourly Billing Diminishes the Quality of Life

There is no doubt that morale in the professions is suffering, and one major cause is the relentless pursuit of the Almighty Billable Hour. In *The Honest Hour*, William Ross quotes an associate attorney at a Chicago law firm who billed more than 2,000 hours during the prior four years:

> One negative effect of hourly billing is the stressful impact on attorneys—particularly associates who in big firms have target hours of 2000 or more per year. It's not so much the fact that we must work hard but that we're slaves to the clock—almost like piecemeal workers. Perhaps that's why "sweatshop" well describes many firms. A young associate feels that an hour not billed is an hour wasted—an incredibly stressful state of mind. In short, hourly billing is a barrier to the quality of one's professional life (Ross 1996: 232).

This lessening in the quality of life results in a high cost to firms, measured in associate turnover, low morale, absenteeism, ineffectiveness, neglect of practice development, continuing education, and so on. These costs should be included in any cost/benefit analysis of maintaining hourly billing; these costs, in and of themselves, are likely to dwarf any benefits derived.

Hourly Billing Limits Your Income Potential

This is, without a doubt, the most egregious effect of the hourly billing regime. *There are only so many hours in a year.* On average, Bill Gates has just as much time on this mortal coil as the rest of us, so why does he make more money? The difference is he does not believe he sells time. The only way to make more money under the "We sell time" business model is to bill more hours, a tactic David Maister refers to as the *donkey strategy*—achieving more by pulling a heavier load.

Summary and Conclusions

Can there be any doubt the disadvantages of hourly billing outweigh the advantages, as catalogued in this chapter? Oscar Wilde's line sums up hourly billing with just the proper amount of irony: "He has no enemies, but is intensely disliked by his friends."

It is indeed difficult to defend the billable hour. The price being paid by the professions for continuing to utilize this antiquated method is enormously high. It has become, to borrow a term from the medical profession, an *iatrogenic* illness—that is, a disease caused by the doctor.

Time is indeed precious; it is what we are giving up when we are at work, and thus professionals have started to think their lives are bifurcated into *billable* and *nonbillable* hours. But this focus is far too narrow; professionals need to broaden their view of the value they add to their customers' lives. That value is not measured by time, but rather results. Hourly billing forces us to focus on the wrong measurement. Albert Einstein once wrote, "Our theories determine what we measure." Hourly billing is the wrong theory that measures the wrong things.

Professional firms are subject to the same laws of supply and demand and customer psychology as every other business. Hourly billing tries to evade these realities by placing the risk on the customer while misaligning the interest and incentives of the firm and the customer. It is an idea for which the French coined the perfect expression: *fausse idée claire*—a terrific idea that doesn't work.

It is up to the professionals—not their customers!—to change this business model. It is not so much a matter of what we must do, but rather what we have to *stop doing*. Have we lost the visionaries who are capable of changing the culture? I remain a paranoid optimist on this question.

There are certainly firms out there that have completely buried the billable hour and trashed the timesheet, proving, beyond doubt, it can be done. The only question that remains is how long will it take before the idea diffuses throughout a majority of firms. The pace of progress is only limited by the pace of our thinking. And we certainly should not look to the cynics to provide guidance. What is their alternative to the billable hour? To tweak it, and find more efficient ways to continue to do the wrong thing?

If you are a firm leader, you can remain a "We sell time" firm of the past, or you can transform into a firm of the future—where knowledge workers create extraordinary value for their customers.

Let us now examine what, exactly, replaces hourly billing and timesheets.

PART IV

What Replaces Hourly Billing and Timesheets

You can't keep on doing things the old way and still get the benefits of the new way.

—Thomas Sowell

CHAPTER 18

Why Carthage Must Be Destroyed

We shall not grow wiser before we learn that much that we have done was very foolish.

—F. A. Hayek (1899–1992)

Hourly billing and timesheets are inextricably linked; you cannot discuss one without the other. The reason is that both use a common measuring device: time. Most professionals exploring this topic for the first time—maybe even you—are usually persuaded of the logic between the labor and subjective theories of value, as we discussed in Chapter 4. They intuitively understand they have left much money on the table with the suboptimal strategy of hourly billing, yet when they turn their attention to the timesheet, their natural defenses begin to emerge.

There are four primary defenses of timesheets:

1. They are a pricing tool.
2. They are a cost accounting tool.
3. They are a project management tool.
4. They measure the productivity of our professionals.

We have falsified the first of these defenses with the subjective theory of value, price discrimination, and other value creating strategies discussed so far. Logic teaches us that if time is the incorrect measure of value, then timesheets are the wrong measuring device for knowledge workers. He who says *A* must also say *B*. Despite this impeccable logic, the most frequently asked question we receive at VeraSage Institute is "I agree with value pricing, but why must I discard my timesheets when they have so many useful purposes?" A creative example of such an inquiry is reproduced below, originally posted on the VeraSage Blog on October 23, 2008. I reproduce it here since it nicely summarizes the attitude of these four defenses and how they are so interconnected. At the request of the author, his name is not being disclosed. I have also included my responses, in italics, for clarity of presentation.

Ron,

Reading your books and the site materials I share your confidence that value-based pricing is the right thing for service selling. I feel, though, that your obsession to wipe out timesheets is akin to "delenda est Carthago" motto ("Carthage must be destroyed").

Maybe the evil is not in time-based pricing itself but in its mighty acceptance, which obscures the principle of value-based pricing making it the ultimate end instead of a means.

Indeed, you're fighting cost-based approach but what if one uses time as a driver of value? Airlines or tailors don't charge for time they spent because it's irrelevant. The scope is clear and predefined so the customer doesn't care how much time it would take or what internal cost would accrue. In the scope-defined engagements it makes sense, but I have two examples where I'm struggling to justify a Fixed Price Agreement (FPA).

I do not understand how you can reconcile the subjective theory of value while asking "but what if one uses time as a driver of value?" That is the whole point. Time is not value. You have simply asked if the labor theory of value is not true. It is not true; it was refuted in 1871 [see Chapter 4].

Time spent in Professional Knowledge Firms is just as irrelevant as with airlines and tailors. It is not because they have a more defined scope. It is because the labor theory of value is false across all human behavior.

I'm a "trusted adviser" and sell my brain-time to the customer via meeting attendance or calls. Say I have a retainer to spend one day a week with her and we sign a Fixed Price Agreement (FPA) for the advisory service for $2400 per week (read, 8 hours per day). Now the customer wants to change the scope to 2 days per week. What should I charge her? Something like $4800, right?

It's logical, clear, and simple. If the customer gives me some unusual "homework" and occasionally I need to spend between half to 2 days additionally on her projects, how should we agree on that? Regardless whether we shape it as a change order or a new FPA (taking into account the average extended time) the time will be the driver for the calculation. I'm not saying the customer buys my time—she buys my value—my advisory service, measured via the time we spent. I'm capable of charging $300 per hour not because I'm a commodity but certainly because I'm differentiated and the customer recognizes it. We use a timesheet here just as a measure of the scope and due to the lack of any project-finite scope. I see no other way to measure my services but to multiply the time I spend servicing her on the value the customer perceives to get from the service.

Again, you are not selling your "brain-time" since that is an input. What if you spend a long time thinking but creating no results for your customer? What you are selling is knowledge that creates wealth for your customer.

In your example of $2400 to $4800, you state the customer is not buying your time, but rather your value. But how can this be so? You priced this based on time, and that is not value. What if you come up with a million-dollar idea in an hour in that marginal second day? Under your method, it is worth the same $300 per hour as an hour in the first day. This is suboptimal pricing that has no relationship to your value. The fact that it is "logical, clear, and simple" does not mean it comports to reality—the subjective theory of value.

You are still locked into the $300 hourly rate mentality, which demonstrates you are still selling time. This is the exact problem with the timesheet. It is keeping you mired in the mentality that you sell time. You are not a day laborer or a union employee; you are a professional.

You ask how you should price another half or two additional days, and I would say up front, **before** *you do the work. Value is subjective, and contextual. It all depends on what you are doing.*

You then say that the timesheet is used "just as a measure of the scope and due to the lack of any project-finite scope." This is why you are still selling time, and not value pricing. Timesheets are backward looking, whereas project management, which always defines a scope no matter how limited it may be, forecasts the future.

You say you see no other way to measure your services, but there are, indeed, other ways to value your services when there is no project-finite scope [we will discuss this in Chapter 30]. You are letting a problem kill an opportunity to add value to your customers. As a result, you are suboptimally pricing yourself by the hour. Some would argue—I being chief among them—that this is the result of your timesheet.

Another example is about a typical project in high-tech consulting—solution integration. Timesheets make life easier when we do have a project scope but the customer has to develop (supply, prepare, deliver) additional tasks upon which my execution is dependent. If the dependency is very tight then often I won't be able to progress without the customer's delivery. Another pitfall is just so many unexpected things that may happen (which, honestly, may happen with an FPA too). So the whole project becomes a huge change order. In that case, the timesheet becomes a good protection for me since the customer knows that his inefficiency really costs him and I'm not its hostage. So should I drop such customers or just use the timesheet as a shield against his inefficiency?

No, you should quote a price for a defined scope of work, up front, with a covenant that the customer is responsible for providing certain tasks by a deadline. If they fail to deliver, you have a Change Order. Keeping your customer worried about the time you spend is exactly the wrong thing to have them focus on. It is not a shield to protect you, it is a shotgun pointed at their head.

You then say that so many unexpected things can happen that the whole project becomes a huge change order. That is usually the result of very poor planning and project management. It may also indicate incompetence. Face it, if things are that out of control, why are you doing the project in the first place?

But even allowing for your logic, so what? My insurance company provides me earthquake insurance, yet they do not know every contingency, nor do they even know what their costs are going to be. They still give me a fixed price because I, like all customers, demand it. No one would buy insurance being priced on a time and materials basis.

Your timesheet is preventing you from being a better project manager.

The last reasons for timesheets is it's much more accepted (I guess you've heard this one many times) in the industry, customers know how to measure and value my service, and I'm protected against inefficiency or unexpected things. On the other hand, when the scope is concrete and I can trust the customer, I'm all for using FPAs (and surely the time then is not the primary driver but the value the customer gets is).

Again, so what? Everyone used to think the world was flat, but that did not make it right. Customers accept the hourly rate, but they do not like it. Who wants uncertainty in the price of what they buy? You are far too focused on the internal machinations of your business. This is hindering you from focusing on external value.

Actually I'm negotiating now an offer to join a practice and I was re-reading your books thinking, maybe, to influence my new partners to switch to FPAs. The above is a result of "critical thinking" where playing the devil's advocate I wanted to reveal FPA weaknesses and exceptions.

*We love critical thinking. We love the fact that you are wrestling with this issue. We love it when people ask, "When will this theory **not** work?" since that is how you falsify a theory and come up with better ones.*

Critical thinking also means looking at empirical evidence, and the fact is there are over 1000 firms that have trashed timesheets. They have solved every one of the problems you point out. You have added nothing new here. That is not to belittle you; it is just to say firms have overcome these hurdles.

I think that the advantage of FPAs is in the value-based approach, but must I dig up timesheets completely to sell value? I think I can sell value and still use the timesheet for certain cases.

Yes, I believe you must ditch your timesheet if you are serious about becoming better at pricing. Your email is even an illustration of why this is so.

I used to not believe this. I used to say, "Keep your timesheets, but use them as they were originally intended, as a cost accounting tool only, but price on value." I no longer say this, because empirical evidence has changed my mind.

The best pricers across all PKF sectors—from accounting and law, to advertising and IT firms—all have one thing in common: None of them maintains timesheets.

I used to believe that this was because they became so good at pricing, timesheets became superfluous. But I now believe that they became good at pricing **precisely because** they got rid of the timesheet, which forced them out of the "we sell hours" mentality, causing them to become obsessed with value.

We are very reluctant at VeraSage to state a **causal** relationship. Too many confuse causation with correlation, as if to say wet streets cause rain.

But here is where I will state a **causal** relationship emphatically: If you want to become a better pricer, you have to trash timesheets. You have to do other things as well (project management, KPIs, AARs, leadership, etc.), but there is no doubt in my mind, if you are serious about creating and capturing value, the timesheet must be buried.

To borrow a phrase: **Ceterum censeo Carthaginem esse delendam** ("Furthermore, I think Carthage must be destroyed").

What, Exactly, Replaces Hourly Billing and Timesheets?

Without a doubt the most important characteristics to replace the status quo is purpose, vision, and leadership. Implementing any new idea, especially among professionals who consider themselves experts, is a daunting undertaking. Former longshoreman and self-educated philosopher Eric Hoffer has this incisive comment in his book _The Ordeal of Change_:

The plunge into the new is often an escape from an untenable situation and a maneuver to mask one's ineptness. To adopt the role of the pioneer and avant-garde is to place oneself in a situation where ineptness and awkwardness are acceptable and even unavoidable; for experience and know-how count for little in tackling the new, and we expect the wholly new to be ill-shapen and ugly (Hoffer 2006b: 109).

This is certainly true when it comes to replacing the decades-old practice of hourly billing and timesheets. For as much criticism as the billable hour has received in recent years, it is nonetheless the predominant method used for pricing in professional firms. One reason is professionals—experts—tend to be risk-adverse. Whenever the concepts discussed in this book are introduced into a firm, certain individuals always act like an organism's immune system and try to fight off anything that is foreign. That is fine, as it prevents firms from wasting time and resources pursuing panaceas that probably would never work anyway. Rigidity is what most organizations manifest when faced with either superior competition or outdated processes. They blindly cling to "that is the way we have always done it" in defense of the evidence that this way is no longer relevant to success.

However, if every possible objection had to be overcome before we tried something new, we would still be rubbing rocks together to create fire while gazing up at the sky wondering if we will ever be able to fly. So let us list, exactly, what replaces hourly billing and timesheets:

1. Price-led costing (Chapter 19)
2. Value council and Chief Value Officer (CVO) (Chapter 21)
3. Fixed Price Agreements and Change Orders (Chapter 32 and 34)
4. Project Management (Chapter 33)
5. Key Predictive Indicators—Firm-wide (Chapter 23)
6. Key Predictive Indicators—For Knowledge Workers (Chapter 24)
7. After Action Reviews (Chapter 25)

When professionals see this list for the first time they object that it cannot be this simple—only seven things replace the way we have been doing things for decades? But *simple* should not be confused with *easy*. Echoing the teaching of Leonardo da Vinci that "Simplicity is the ultimate sophistication," the strategies in the list above are far more sophisticated for a professional knowledge firm, because they will enhance the intellectual capital of the firm. There are simple answers; they just are not easy.

Others will argue that the devil resides in the details, and this is no doubt true. Before we proceed, however, I would only ask that you keep in mind the following: The devil may be in the details—but so is the angel.

CHAPTER 19

Price-Led Costing Replaces Hourly Billing

Innovation requires builders not bean-counters, and the last person who should be running something is the man who controls the costs. Sure, you need that man in there somewhere to keep a rein on things, but he shouldn't be at the top.

—James Dyson, *Against the Odds*, 2003

Andrew Carnegie was fond of saying, "Cut the prices; scoop the market; run the mills full. … Watch the costs and the profits will take care of themselves." Of course, Carnegie made steel in mass quantities, and greatly reduced its price so use could be expanded. In today's intellectual capital economy, there does not exist as strong a correlation between inputs and outputs, costs and value. The value of the book you are now holding is not the sum of the paper, ink, glue, and binding costs, but rather the value of the knowledge it contains. To believe otherwise is to fall prey to the materialist fallacy. George Gilder once said this worldview is similar to believing that Canada will produce the world's greatest literature since it has the largest trees.

For all of the economic evidence assembled on why costs do not "add up" to equate to value, it is amazing how many firms still cling to the cost-plus pricing method, a direct cousin to the labor theory of value. The mirror image of a bad idea is rarely a good one. In their outstanding book *The Strategy and Tactics of Pricing* (third edition), Thomas T. Nagle and Reed K. Holden offer the following indictment of cost-plus pricing:

The problem with cost-driven pricing is fundamental: In most industries it is impossible to determine a product's unit cost before determining its price. Why? Because unit costs change with volume. This cost change occurs because a significant portion of costs are "fixed" and must somehow be "allocated" to determine the full unit cost. Unfortunately, since these allocations depend on volume, which changes with changes in price, unit cost is a moving target (Nagle and Holden 2002: 2).

... [P]ricing affects sales volume, and that volume affects costs. Cost-plus pricing leads to overpricing in weak markets and underpricing in strong ones—exactly the opposite direction of a prudent strategy. The financial questions that should drive proactive pricing are "How much more sales volume must we achieve to earn additional profit from a lower price?" and "How much sales volume can we lose and still earn additional profit from a higher price?" (Nagle and Holden 2002: 3).

If one were to lay the two theories of value—labor and subjective—side by side, it would look like this (adapted from Nagle and Holden 2002: 4):

Cost-Plus Pricing—Labor Theory of Value

Services » Cost » Price » Value » Customers

Value Pricing—Subjective Theory of Value

Customers » Value » Price » Cost » Services

Notice how value pricing turns the order of cost-plus pricing inside out, by starting with the ultimate arbiter of value—the customer. Services do not magically become more valuable as they move through the firm and have hours allocated to them by cost accountants. The *costs do not determine the price*, let alone the value. It is precisely the opposite, as the Austrian economists pointed out; that is, the *price determines the costs* that can be profitably invested in to deliver a service desirable to the customer, at an acceptable profit for the seller. This subtle reordering of the value/service chain—referred to as *price-led costing*—has a dramatic impact on value, price, and profit.

Being restricted by the final price focuses the firm like a laser beam on incurring only costs that will add value to the customer. What separates this method from cost-plus pricing is *when* costs are considered. As Henry Ford said, "No one knows what a cost ought to be." It is *planned* costs, not *past* costs, that are critical since all pricing decisions deal with the future. Cost accounting and activity-based costing only deal with past costs, yet those are often quite irrelevant to pricing decisions made in a world of risk and uncertainty. As Nagle and Holden point out, "The job of financial management is not to insist that prices recover costs. It is to insist that costs are incurred only to make products that can be priced profitably given their value to customers" (Nagle and Holden 2002: 4).

There is a long history of firms that became obsessively focused on cost at the expense of providing a service of value to the customer. The fact of the matter is you can make a pizza so cheap no one is willing to eat it. The obsession with cost cutting can be counterproductive to fulfilling the real mission of any business: to create wealth for the customer.

Firms that use price-led costing will soon realize that perceptions of value can often be raised in the minds of customers. Cost is not the starting point for price; it is the final stage in the process. It does no good to know your costs to the penny if the customer does not agree with your value/ price proposition.

Toyota is so good at this—they call it target costing—it does not even maintain a standard cost accounting system. See *Profit Beyond Measure* (Johnson and Bröms). Another auto giant understood this value pricing chain as well.

Wisdom Is Timeless

If you follow the price-led costing strategy, what would your firm have to do differently in terms of creating value, setting prices, and planning costs than it does now? History is a good teacher, for even Henry Ford understood price-led costing—long before it was diagrammed, as in the above illustration—recognizing that no cost is truly fixed and that value drives price. While price may be taught in business schools as the last of the four Ps of marketing, Ford knew value had to be understood first. Oscar Wilde's famous quip about "A man who knows the price of everything and the value of nothing" was his definition of a cynic, not a businessman—and certainly not Henry Ford.

With respect to the pricing revolution taking place in businesses around the world, Ford's understanding of this topic is truly prescient, as demonstrated in his autobiography *My Life and Work*, published in 1922. It is worth quoting at length for the historical lessons it teaches since putting the customer first is just as relevant to the professional firm of today as it was in Ford's day. The idea that cost determines price was not foreign to Ford, but here is how he refutes this thinking:

> If the prices of goods are above the incomes of the people, then get the prices down to the incomes. Ordinarily, business is conceived as starting with a manufacturing process and ending with a consumer. If that consumer does not want to buy what the manufacturer has to sell him and has not the money to buy it, then the manufacturer blames the consumer and says that business is bad, and thus, hitching the cart before the horse, he goes on his way lamenting. Isn't that nonsense?

But what business ever started with the manufacturer and ended with the consumer? Where does the money to make the wheels go round come from? From the consumer, of course. And success in manufacturer is based solely upon an ability to serve that consumer to his liking (Ford 1922: 135–36).

Keep in mind Ford's primary objective was the mass consumption of the automobile, so he focused more on driving the price down to increase volume. In a growing industry this is a viable strategy. In mature markets in which professional firms are more likely to be operating, it is more strategic to increase value, thus allowing higher prices. Nevertheless, with Ford's objective in mind, consider his views on the importance of cost accounting and prices, which are profound (perhaps Ford was influenced by the Austrian economists?):

Our policy is to reduce the price, extend the operations, and improve the article. You will notice that the reduction of price comes first. We have never considered any costs as fixed. Therefore we first reduce the price to the point where we believe more sales will result. Then we go ahead and try to make the prices. We do not bother about the costs. The new price forces the costs down. The more usual way is to take the costs and then determine the price; and although that method may be scientific in the narrow sense, it is not scientific in the broad sense, because what earthly use is it to know the cost if it tells you that you cannot manufacture at a price at which the article can be sold? (Ford 1922: 146–47).

Notice Ford "never considered any costs as fixed." He understood, in the long run, all costs are avoidable, and by subjecting every cost to the test—does it add value to the customer?—he was able to lower the costs in the factory:

But more to the point is the fact that, although one may calculate what a cost is, and of course all of our costs are carefully calculated, no one knows what a cost ought to be. One of the ways of discovering what a cost ought to be is to name a price so low as to force everybody in the place to the highest point of efficiency. The low price makes everybody dig for profits. We make more discoveries concerning manufacturing and selling under this forced method than by any method of leisurely investigation (Ford 1922: 146–47).

If you were to draw a diagram of the following statement, it would mirror the price-led costing chain above:

Standardization, then, is the final stage of the process. We start with [the] consumer, work back through the design, and finally arrive at manufacturing. The manufacturing becomes a means to the end of service. It is important to bear this order in mind. As yet, the order is not understood. The notion persists that prices ought to be kept up. On the contrary, good business—large consumption—depends on their going down (Ford 1922: 148).

Again, notice Ford's emphasis on driving prices down to achieve large consumption. As is argued throughout this book, however, focusing on value can drive prices up.

Summary and Conclusions

Another reason for the popularity and widespread use of cost-plus pricing is the rule of the bean counters. Cost accountants have had a significant impact on pricing decisions in firms, and it is time to bring their tyrannical rule to an end. Cost accountants focus on the _inside_ of an organization, yet all value takes place in the _external_ world, beyond the four walls of the firm. By and large, accountants are not well equipped to judge and measure value, despite all the recent blather about activity-based pricing. Listening to cost accountants discuss pricing is like hearing eunuchs lecture on sex. Our next task must be to put the cost accountants back where they belong, in allocating _internal_ historical costs, not making _external_ pricing decisions to capture value in a world of risk and uncertainty.

It is time we lay to rest cost-plus pricing, and for the firm of the future to embrace the price-led costing chain explained in this chapter. Tradition is nothing but the democracy of the dead, but pricing is far too important to be left to the worldview of the bean counters, since they are prone to making too many wrong mistakes.

CHAPTER 20

The Wrong Mistakes

Accounting statements are like bikinis: what they show is interesting but what they conceal is significant.

—Abraham Briloff, Emanuel Saxe Distinguished Professor of
Accountancy emeritus at Baruch College

I write this chapter, indeed this entire book, as a reformed sinner. To be sure, when I started my career as a CPA with one of the then Big Eight accounting firms, I might just as well have believed a business existed to keep fastidious books rather than creating wealth for its customers. An accounting education will foster the worldview that a business exists to close books, provide quarterly and annual financial statements, and allocate costs to every single product to ensure it is making a profit—like the mythological Greek King Midas—on everything it touches.

Part of the blame lies with management accounting, a thoroughly *inward*-looking discipline, from cost accounting to the DuPont return on investment (ROI) formula. It was not until I began seriously studying economics, with an emphasis on price theory, when I started to show contrition for my past cost accounting ways, and finally understood a comprehensive theory of value. It was a difficult road to travel, because as the Roman statesman and philosopher Seneca once said, "The mind is slow in unlearning what it has been long in learning." Working with customers in my accounting firm illustrated just how irrelevant the financial statements were in running a business in a world of risk and uncertainty. One customer said something I will always remember: "To use the financial statements you provide me once a year to run my business is the equivalent of timing my cookies with a smoke alarm."

I was a historian with a bad memory, coming in after the battles my entrepreneur customers were engaged in daily and bayoneting the wounded with my casualty reports (i.e., financial statements). And the biggest offense of all: I charged an hourly rate to do the work, falling prey to Marx's labor theory of value. I would even justify my billings to my customers by saying, "I only sell my time." What nonsense, since *no customer buys time*. In fact, let us see how wrongheaded the mind-set of the accountant's view of the world really is.

The Almighty Hourly Rate

Let us analyze how the *standard hourly rate* in a professional firm is calculated, since it is no different than cost-plus pricing in any other industry:

$$Houryly\ Rate = \frac{Overhead + Desired\ Net\ Income}{Expected\ Billable\ Hours}$$

The first fact to note is that the above equation is not cost accounting; it is *profit forecasting*. There is no cost accounting theory that allocates desired profit—or a return on investment—among its costs. The desired net income in the equation above is an *opportunity cost* concept, and while economists may use that theory, cost accountants do not. Hence, the more relevant question firms need to be asking is not "Did we make money on this customer?" but rather, "Did we *optimize* the profit from this customer?" The equation—or cost accounting in particular—cannot answer this more relevant question.

There are two essential problems with this cost-accounting formula. First, one way to increase revenue is to expand your overhead, a prescription for failure unless the firm increases value to the customer concomitantly. The second problem is far more insidious, but quite prevalent among firms: the desired net income. There is no customer of a firm who lays awake at night wondering if her lawyer is making enough money. It is not the customer's job to provide a business with a profit. It is the firm's job to provide a service experience so good that customers willingly pay a profit in recognition of what is being done for them. Cost accounting and cost-plus pricing confuse cause and effect, putting the inputs and activities before the result and value. The customer simply does not care about any of the numbers in the above formula. Furthermore, if this formula actually modeled the real world, no business would ever lose money, or go bankrupt, since all businesses have overhead and desired net income. So what? What counts is value to the customer, which is conspicuously absent from the equation.

Professionals defend this practice by arguing that since they cannot fully anticipate every contingency in serving the customer, charging by the hour is fair since the customer is then only paying for what she uses. What they do not seem to understand is that the customer is hiring them precisely for their expertise and intellectual capital, and the fact that they have done the work before and can point out all of the possible scenarios and contingencies. The last thing one wants to hear upon being wheeled into the operating room is the surgeon saying, "Wow, I've never seen that before."

While the argument is not being made to eliminate cost accounting, it is strongly suggested cost accountants not have a dominant influence in strategic pricing decisions. The fact of the matter is, no cost accounting method can capture pricing mistakes or lost pricing opportunities; they simply do not show up in the analysis or on a firm's financial statements. An example will illustrate this point.

Making the Wrong Mistakes

In 1997, Tim was the managing partner of a top accounting firm, and his best, long-term customer (of 20 years) had come to him wanting to sell his $250 million closely held business. He told Tim (and I am paraphrasing here), "You've been my CPA for 20 years and I trust you with my life. It is time for me to sell my business and enjoy my golden years. Here is what I want you to do:

- Update our business valuation to maximize the sales price.
- Fly with me anywhere we have to go to meet with potential buyers.
- Be actively involved at every stage of the sales negotiation.
- Perform the due diligence, along with the attorneys, of the qualified buyers.
- Work with the attorneys on the sales contract to make sure my interests are protected.
- Perform tax planning and structure the deal in such a manner as to maximize my wealth retention."

Obviously, this was a very sophisticated customer and it is true Tim had no idea, at the outset of this engagement, how long it would take to close the deal and how much firm capacity (his and his team members) it would require. But he did know more than an average salesman would know, which is one of the enormous advantages professionals possess when it comes to pricing the customer, not the service. He knew the customer's business was well niched, profitable, and growing. This would indicate a very high probability of success. He also knew this customer was an audit customer of the firm's and therefore he would not be able to charge a contingency price based upon a financial outcome (such as a percentage of the sales price, or of any tax savings), since that would impair independence, which is illegal for an auditor.

When I asked Tim how he priced this engagement, he proudly proclaimed that every hour charged to this project was at his highest consulting rate of $400 per hour, indicating, right from the start, Tim knew there was more value on this project than he would ever be able to pad on a timesheet. He further explained how he had updated the business valuation, negotiated with two buyers, and did all of the other tasks requested by the customer. As a result of Tim's work, the customer received (and saved in taxes) an additional $15 million, and acknowledged that Tim was directly responsible for this outcome. In Tim's own words, the customer was "elated."

Tim then told how he priced the engagement. He reviewed all of the hours from the work-in-progress time and billing system, believed it did not adequately reflect the value he provided, and marked it up an additional 25 percent over the $400 hourly rate. He then sent out an invoice for $38,000, which the customer promptly—and happily—paid. He believed he was value pricing. He was not—he was *value guessing*, since the customer had absolutely no input into the price up front, and only a customer can determine value.

I asked Tim what he thought the customer would have paid if he had utilized a TIP clause (also referred to as the *retrospective price*, or *success price*), such as the following:

> In the event that we are able to satisfy your needs in a timely and professional manner, you have agreed to review the situation and decide whether, in the sole discretion of XYZ [company], some additional payment to ABC [CPAs] is appropriate in view of your overall satisfaction with the services rendered by ABC.

The TIP is being based on the "overall satisfaction with the services rendered," and not any financial contingency, which is the origin of the acronym TIP—to insure performance. This TIP clause would be discussed with the customer *before* any work began. If needed, you could put a minimum price on the engagement (such as $40,000) to cover immediate firm capacity. But in this case, given the 20-year relationship with the customer, even a price *solely* determined by a TIP would have been acceptable, since the customer was not likely to take advantage of Tim after the services he rendered and the long-term relationship they had.

In answer to my question, Tim said his customer would most likely have paid him $500,000, a sum I believe to this day is below the real number—but at least better than the $38,000 he finally charged. Nevertheless, since Tim knows the customer better than I do, let us take his number as correct.

I informed Tim he had made the Ultimate Accounting Entry:

	Debit	Credit
Experience	$462,000	
Cash		$462,000

Tim was providing extraordinary value to this customer—he was at the top of the Value Curve shown in Chapter 10—yet his cost-plus pricing theory prevented him from capturing a fair portion of it. Are we not ruled by our theories? This is why it is imperative to extinguish the cost-plus mentality from your firm. No one in any seminar I have shared this story with believed Tim would have received less than $38,000 for his services on this engagement. In effect, Tim paid a *reverse risk premium*—he was assured he would not go below his hourly rate, but in return he gave up the added value the customer already believed he had created. This is not a risk worth taking if you want to maximize your firm's profitability.

The deleterious effects of this are deeper than just being deprived the value from the work you provided on any one engagement. The problem lies at the very core of a firm's measurement system and points out how it does not offer the opportunity to learn from lost pricing opportunities, or pricing mistakes.

In his inimitable way, Yogi Berra explains this situation with his quip, "We made too many wrong mistakes."

When it comes to pricing, the wisdom from Yogi is profound. Tim made the *wrong mistake*, and here is why: He will not learn anything from it because the firm's primary assessment is billable hours—once again the billable hour is the incorrect measuring device for value. When the partners review the realization report on this engagement, they will see 125 percent, which is excellent when you consider most firms realize between 50 and 95 percent overall on each hour. Most likely, Tim will get nothing but accolades and praise from his fellow partners. No one will ask where the $462,000 is because the billable hour metrics do not have a way to capture that type of information, which is precisely why pricing is more of an *art* than a science.

This is an excellent example of a wrong mistake for another reason: Tim (or the firm) will not learn anything from this lost pricing opportunity. The $462,000 simply vanishes into thin air (or, more precisely, the consumer surplus remains on the customer's income statement). No knowledge was gained by the firm on how to price the next similar engagement in accordance with value—it will simply perpetuate the same mistake, over and over. Being a more accurate activity-based cost-accountant, or even excellent project manager, would also not have helped Tim to capture the value.

This is not meant to imply with value pricing you will never make mistakes. You certainly will. The difference is they will be the *right mistakes*, because with value pricing, as opposed to cost-plus pricing, you are forced to receive input from the customer as to your value, and have in place pricing strategies that will capture more of that value (like the TIP clause). If you engage in After Action Reviews (AARs), which perform value assessments on each engagement, and elicit feedback from your customers, you will learn from your mistakes and become better at pricing in the future (AARs will be illustrated in Chapter 25).

Most feedback that firms receive on pricing is negative: "Your price was too high." Or it is ambivalent: "Your price was just right." No customer ever discloses how much money your firm left on the table. Since humans emerged from the cave and began to barter, it is the customer's job to do everything in his or her power to push down prices. There is nothing new about this, and it should not surprise any executive. Your firm's job, however, is to push back. The only effective way to accomplish this is by emphasizing value.

Innovative pricing strategies, such as the TIP clause, that are outward focused and attempt to measure value have allowed more and more firms around the world to capture more of the value they provide, as Case Study 20.1 illustrates.

Case Study 20.1: The Million-Dollar TIP

This story comes from Gus Stearns, a partner in an accounting firm, whom I met on September 25, 2000, at a conference in Las Vegas. Gus tracked me down at the dinner party, walked me over to the bar, and over a glass of wine told me his amazing TIP story. Here are the two e-mails I received from Gus explaining his success, the first one prior to our meeting in Las Vegas and the second one after:

April 20, 2000
Hello Ron,

I hope the tax season finds you well. I was fortunate enough to be at the Atlanta conference [January 2000] when you spoke and picked up an autographed copy of your book [*Professional's Guide to Value Pricing*], which I devoured on the plane trip back.

The engagement which I refer to had already started a month or two before and I had used the old standard rate-time-hours routine and billed about $2,000 at a standard rate of $180/hour. After listening to you and reading the book, I was determined to reevaluate the price structure and simply went back to my customer and said, "Guys, this is what I am bringing to the table. It brings a lot of value which is etc., etc. I don't believe hourly rates based upon time is appropriate. I am unable to place a value on this. I need your help. You tell me what the value of all this is to you. You are the customer and only you can truly establish the value. I know I'll be happy with what ever you come up with." This is almost an exact quote.

I left it at that two months ago. I was handed a check for the first installment of $50,000 on the way out at the end of the engagement. I guess this is what you call "outside-in pricing." I like it.

Gus Stearns, CPA

It gets better, since this engagement was in two phases. Here is the follow-up e-mail from Gus explaining the final result after the job was done:

Hello Ron,

Basically the large engagement was for a previous client that I had hired a controller for. He took over the tax work, at my suggestion, as he was a CPA. The engagement was an exit and management succession strategy, which involved some fairly hefty income tax savings as well. The total time expended was about 100 hours, although a lot of the time was on unrelated things that I did not want to charge for due to the magnitude of the price (we quit using timesheets some time ago).

I used a flip chart in the presentation, pointing out the value of what they were getting. At the end of the presentation, I asked how much they thought it was worth, and suggested $300,000, $500,000, a million? I wanted them to think in big numbers. The CEO was rather excited and said a million. Knowing that this would be difficult to obtain in one fell swoop I suggested $400,000 down and a retainer of $4,000 per month. They agreed but asked that I serve on the board of directors and attend quarterly meetings through 2008, when the note to the previous owners would be paid off. They were also kind enough to put me on salary so I could participate in their pension plan, which is a 25 percent direct

Continued

contribution from the company. This all adds up to a little bit over $1 million.

Never once was the word "time" used or referred to by myself, or my client. They could have cared less about time. In all of our engagements, I never use the word. By concentrating on value and encouraging the client to participate in the valuation of the engagement our prices have skyrocketed. You were absolutely on-target when you said that accountants are terrible at valuing our services (myself included).

Keep up the wonderful work,
Gus

These types of engagements are certainly not the *rule* in any firm; they are the *exception*. Nonetheless, they do arise, and when they do, it is critical to recognize the value you are creating and to utilize innovative pricing strategies to capture it. This also demonstrates why pricing is the most potent lever you have in terms of increasing your firm's profitability, much more than cutting costs or increasing efficiency.

I include these stories not because I believe you will earn a $1 million TIP but rather to illustrate how the cost-plus pricing mentality has placed a self-imposed artificial ceiling over the heads of firms. Never in his wildest dreams would Gus have placed a $1 million value on his work; but the customer did. Does he not deserve it?

But who is in charge of value? Who in the firm is keeping their focus on the outside in an attempt to understand and continuously enhance value for customers? It is time to appoint a chief value officer, along with a value council, the functions of each to be explored next.

CHAPTER 21

Who Is in Charge of Value?

The greatest improvement in the productive powers of labour, and the greater part of the skill, dexterity, and judgment with which it is anywhere directed, or applied, seem to have been the effects of the division of labour.

—Adam Smith, *An Inquiry into the Nature and Causes of the Wealth of Nations*, 1776

My VeraSage Institute colleagues and I have had the privilege of posing the question "Who's in charge of value in your firm?" to thousands of professionals around the world. We are usually met with a momentary *staring ovation*, and then someone will inevitably shout out, "Everyone!"

Really? I live in California, where I'm told everyone "owns" the Golden Gate Bridge. I would like to sell my portion; unfortunately I encounter what economists call the *tragedy of the commons*. If everyone owns something, no one does. No one has an incentive to protect and maintain the value of the asset in question. Think *public toilet*. Species become extinct because no one owns them, such as the American Buffalo; species thrive— such as dogs, cats, cattle, and even elephants—because they are privately owned.

Not everyone can be good at everything. Nonetheless, it is rare to encounter a partner who does not believe he is quite competent at pricing, even though the empirical evidence is overwhelming that this is not the case. Furthermore, everyone in the firm already knows who the best and weakest pricers are, and in many firms there exist no clear lines of authority for this function. This is not pricing strategically, and it is a serious violation of the division and specialization of labor, not to mention a barrier to profitability. In golf, the less skilled players receive a handicap; with respect to poor-performing pricers, the handicap is less profit.

Pricing is far too important to the viability of the firm to be left to mediocre pricers. As we have seen, no other area—not cost cutting, efficiency increases, or rainmaking—can have as large an impact on profitability as does pricing. It is time for firms to recognize that if they are serious about pricing commensurate with the value they create, they need to establish a core group of enthusiastic pricers to make pricing a core competency within the firm. Pricing needs to become a *function* within the firm, delegated to a chief value officer (CVO) and a value council, who will develop an intellectual capital base of skills in this vitally important area, while developing pricing policies in alignment with the firm's overall purpose and strategy.

The World's First CVO

Do not go where the path may lead; go instead where there is no path and leave a trail.

—Ralph Waldo Emerson

The CVO role grew out of an experiment we conducted with professional knowledge firms. We initially established a pricing committee—sometimes called a pricing panel—a group of people who would have ultimate responsibility for pricing all engagements above a certain dollar threshold, in several firms around the world.

As in any company, pricing exists at the crossroads of almost every other discipline, such as marketing, sales, finance, project management, and even research and development. Yet these various functions sometimes have conflicting objectives and priorities. Marketing tends to focus on brand awareness and market share, while finance may insist on maintaining certain margins, and sales is interested in making the next sale. Pricing tends to become an afterthought, taking a backseat to these other functions that normally can secure executive attention and clout.

What we learned with our pricing committee experiment was enlightening. While every firm that implemented the idea became better pricers, and were more effective on focusing on the customer, some of the committees degenerated into what Paul Kennedy, partner at O'Byrne & Kennedy, Chartered Accountants in the UK, described as "an auction house." He said (I am paraphrasing here):

We'd sit around and discuss a particular contract for a client and when we finished with scope and an obligatory nod to value, we started throwing out prices. One member would say £10,000, the next £12,500, on up to £20,000. It dawned on me after this scenario was repeated several times we were becoming as *inward* focused as cost accountants. Yes, we had moved up from costing the job to placing a more strategic price upon it, but we were still not giving proper attention to the *outward* value we were creating, or should have been creating, for the customer. This was an epiphany for us. Soon thereafter, we created a *value council*, whereby the focus is, first and foremost on value, then price. This has been much more effective, and has resulted in happier customers and greater profits for the firm.

In this particular firm, the value council has become the eyes, ears, and throat for the customer. Rather than merely setting prices, they have begun to think strategically about value—we have become "obsessed with value" as Paul now says—which should be the basis for how prices are set.

Brendon Harrex, at age 31, was the world's first CVO, appointed in March 2005 by his former chartered accounting firm in New Zealand. In May 2007, he launched his own firm, The Harrex Group, which has embraced the business model of the firm of the future, described in Chapter 2. Brendon described what he learned as CVO in his prior firm, in Case Study 21.1.

The CVOs that have been appointed in firms to date have also learned that the hardest task of the job is determining value. After all, cost is relatively easy to determine, since most firm's costs are fixed. In determining value, cost accounting provides little help, since customers purchase value, not a bundle of allocated costs. This turns cost accounting into a relatively low-value activity.

Establishing a price above cost is also not difficult—even the most inept professional should be able to accomplish this, as the billable hour demonstrates. For all its faults, it has proven to be a profitable pricing strategy, just not an optimal one.

Yet to understand value, we have to understand the customer. This is not accomplished with more accurate cost accounting, better project management, or any other internal initiative. Firms have a wealth of information on how long things take and what they cost; they have a paucity of metrics on the value they create for customers.

Since the CVO position is relatively new, we are learning more and more everyday about this responsibility within professional firms. It is an unusual position, to say the least. The firms that have implemented it so far have reported favorable results, so much so that the idea warrants further testing. One question that continually comes up is what are the traits of a successful CVO, or value council member? The acronym LACEY is a useful framework for identifying what characteristics are essential for a successful CVO:

Leadership
Attitude
Commitment
Experimentation
Youth

Case Study 21.1: What Brendon Learned as CVO

I am learning so much in the CVO role. It is like climbing a mountain—just when you think you are nearing the top, you find it merely another ridgeline and the horizon still is a distant vision.

I am coming to realize what a wimpy pricer I really am. I think sometimes we price for the 80 percent of the job that everyone else can do and forget to capture the real value that being focused and fanatical brings to a customer.

I am learning very quickly that as an individual and a business you cannot be all things to all people and you have to say no quite a lot more than I am used to.

I am learning how scared many of us are of change, even if there is no logical or illogical argument supporting the status quo.

I am learning that business value is maximized when we realize that the customer owns the shop.

I am learning that fun is maximized when we realize the customer owns the shop and start acting like it.

I am learning that as in life, control in business is just an illusion. Yet we allocate valuable resources into sustaining the illusion.

I am learning that vision drives the structure and sometimes the structure needs changing to assist fulfillment of the vision.

I am learning the value of a decision and the high cost of indecision.

I am learning that the less we focus on our own importance, the more important we become.

I am learning that one wrong doesn't overcome another.

I am learning the importance of laying the foundation before beginning to build.

—Brendon Harrex, Founder, The Harrex Group, Invercargill, New Zealand

Let us briefly examine each of these attributes, and discuss the functions required for each one.

Leadership

A firm will never rise above its leadership. CVOs implicitly and explicitly understand that the firm's prices are the language in which they strategically communicate value to customers.

Perhaps the first important characteristic of a successful CVO is high self-esteem, as discussed in Chapter 14; they believe that their firm's services are worth every penny they charge.

In addition to high self-esteem, a CVO must have demonstrable leadership skills, while commanding respect and creditability across multiple functions within the firm. She will be responsible for communicating the importance of pricing and value to the media, thereby negating price wars within the industry. Since competitors tend to judge a firm's pricing behavior based upon its most ruthless actions, think of the message appointing a CVO would send to others in your profession about how committed you are to price for value and not engaging in self-destructive price wars.

The CVO is also responsible for establishing the value council, a group of motivated team members who look upon pricing as an enormous opportunity, not a limitation. The council will have final authority to set prices to maximize profits across the entire firm, while also acting as an educational unit and resource to assist all employees in capturing prices commensurate with value.

The size of the council will vary by firm size, sector, and customer segments, but it has been our experience that smaller is better (usually four, with no more than ten). It should not consist of all partners, but should have a cross-selection of disciplines, from finance, marketing, sales, and so forth. Some firms have made one-third or one-half of the positions rotate, perhaps on a two- or three-year basis, to bring in fresh perspectives, while spreading the value message throughout the organization.

Leadership is essential, and leadership demands tough decisions (the word *decision* comes from Latin *decidere*, meaning "to cut off"), and sometimes individual opinions have to be sacrificed for the good of the firm. Too many firms operating under the partnership model find it hard to introduce innovations because it requires a consensus. If any one or two partners object, the entire initiative can be killed. This is another reason why professional firms have not abandoned the billable hour—the partnership model is simply not conducive to innovation. Margaret Thatcher, former prime minister of Britain, was fond of pointing out: "Consensus is the negation of leadership."

Attitude

The CVO and members of the value council have to view pricing as an enormous opportunity for the firm to create and capture value, rather than a limitation imposed on them in which they have no control, like the weather. Pricing is far too important to assign to narrow minds. Pricers have to be intellectually curious, constantly learning, reading, and studying why humans behave the way they do.

Look for a CVO who is constantly learning and who is moving through the five levels of learning: awareness, awkwardness, application, assimilation, and art. Pricing is an iterative process of the mind and it will always require human judgment. Pricing strategy, ultimately, is a human endeavor in a professional firm. As Professor Ernest Rutherford, the man who split the atom, said, "It's true we don't have much money so what we have to do is think."

Commitment

A CVO and value council that does not have the support of the CEO are destined to be feckless. Effective centralized pricing has to have total authority, which we believe needs to be vested in one individual so there is one throat to choke. Taking it a step further, if value creation is truly the purpose of a firm, the CVO should report directly to the CEO. This will send a powerful message throughout the organization that the leaders are serious about value and pricing, as well as to competitors, thereby possibly reducing the threat of price wars.

The commitment to a CVO also provides a competitive advantage, since competitors can only monitor historical pricing, not value. Value creation and pricing competence create a sense of self-worth among team members, and although nearly impossible to measure quantitatively, can certainly be observed in morale. Why should your firm not be paid what it is worth?

Perhaps the largest commitment required will be in the area of pricing talent. Since this is a relatively new skill in the marketplace, talent is presently hard to find and firms will have to develop it internally. If resources are limited, the best advice is: read, read, read. There are many more books out there on pricing than there were even ten years ago, which is why there is a bibliography in the back of this one, and a Suggested Reading list on the Web site offering some of my favorites and must reads. Assign the council a reading list, and make every member teach what they learned, and what they think the firm should do differently as a result, to their colleagues. There are also graduate level courses on pricing taught at many universities' executive education divisions, which are worth the price of admission. Be sure to join one of the pricing associations, which provide seminars, workshops, and a chance to share intellectual capital with other pricers.

Also, as with any new initiative there are bound to be mistakes, failures, and setbacks. The CVO must be committed to the process. A pro golfer does not give up the game after hitting a drive into the lake. Pricing is hard, but so is training for the Olympics, or anything else worth doing. Obtaining a competitive advantage is never free. Determination and commitment defeats diffidence.

Experimentation

The CVO has to take a stand for the customer, constantly asking how the firm can provide more value. They have to be willing to experiment and cannot be prisoners of the past. "That is the way we have always done it" should inspire nothing but contempt from CVOs, since they have little respect for the status quo. They are not simply seeking change for change sake, but rather to fulfill the purpose of the firm.

After observing Brendon institute some changes in his firm—along with the normal amount of resistance—I recalled the late economist Julian Simon's struggle with airlines. If you have ever been bribed off an oversold airplane—with a free flight voucher, upgrade, or airline money equivalent—you have Mr. Simon to thank. Until 1978, travelers were bumped off overbooked planes rather capriciously—the airlines preferred to bump old people and military personnel on the theory they would be least likely to complain—and this caused enormous amounts of customer complaints and ill will. Sometimes an entire flight would be canceled and rebooked at proper capacity, causing even greater outrage. Worse yet, the problem fed upon itself, because passengers began to expect being bumped and so would book several flights under various names to ensure a seat on at least one; this caused the airlines to increase bookings even more to ensure decent load factors. A flight attendant friend who worked for United Air Lines told Simon of this problem:

> The next day when shaving it occurred to me that there must be a better way; indeed, an auction market could solve the problem by finding those people who least mind waiting for the next flight. The practical details fell into place before the shave was complete.

> In 1966 and 1967 I wrote to all the airlines suggesting the scheme. The responses ranged from polite brushoffs, to denials that they overbooked, to assertions that the scheme could not work, to derision.

... I was unable to persuade any airline (or the Civil Aeronautics Board) to conduct an experiment for even one day on a single airline at a single airport at a single boarding gate—an experiment that I believed would be sufficient, even with the inevitable breakdowns in any new activity (Simon 2002: 289–94).

Incidentally, what was the value of Simon's idea? Every single airline eventually adopted it, with great effect. If he billed by the hour, he would have either have had to track his time shaving, or pad his timesheet. Far better to price based on results.

Had the airlines had a CVO, Simon's idea would have been tested much sooner, to the benefit of both the airlines and its customers.

Soren Kierkegaard wrote, "Purity of soul is to will one thing." What is more important than to champion the cause of value creation within today's firms? A CVO is never satisfied with the status quo because they will constantly be on the search for new ways of doing things, all the while eliminating procedures and processes that do not add value to the customer. This is the CVO mandate.

Youth

Out of all of the characteristics in LACEY, I will admit a certain amount of uncertainty as to the implications of this last one. I am not suggesting you cannot teach an old dog new tricks. Instead, research on age and innovation suggests you should not expect an old dog to *innovate* a new trick to add to the repertoire. If firms want innovation and dynamism, they will have to give more authority and responsibilities to their youthful team members. At the least, some people in their twenties or thirties should be on the value council. Organizations, like people, tend to calcify with age, and youth can keep the blood pumping at a more vigorous pace. No doubt they will make more mistakes and incur more failure, yet risk is where profits come from. What is the alternative? Ossification is not an option.

Not Final Thoughts

One executive in charge of strategic pricing noted, "You're messing with a company's DNA when you change how you do prices." No doubt this is true, which is precisely why it needs to be accomplished if firms are truly serious about changing their business model from "We sell time" to "We sell intellectual capital." Pricing is not simply a *decision* to be determined for each project; it is a *process* that deserves the intellectual capital needed to carry it out.

It is often said we get what we measure. If this is true, isn't it time we measure what we want to become? Who in your firm is measuring value? Unless someone in your organization owns the value function, it will not get the proper executive attention, respect, and resources it deserves.

If you are competing against a firm with a CVO—either for customers or talent—you may well be at a severe competitive disadvantage. The Roman god Janus had two faces, one to see what lay behind and the other to see what lay ahead. A CVO is an outward-looking position, with duties carried out in a world of risk, uncertainty, innovation, and faith in the future, where value is solely arbitrated by the customers your firm is privileged to serve. If the only set of eyes you possess look behind you—at historical costs, hours, activities, and efforts—you are destined for a perilous future.

So, who is in charge of value in your firm?

CHAPTER 22

Measure What Matters to Customers

Grown-ups love figures. When you tell them that you have made a new friend, they never ask you any questions about essential matters. They never say to you "What does his voice sound like? What games does he love best? Does he collect butterflies?" Instead they demand "How old is he? How many brothers has he? How much does he weigh? How much money does his father make?" Only from these figures do they think they have learned anything about him.

—Antoine de Saint-Exupéry, *The Little Prince*, 1943

In the sixteenth century, a new word appeared in English dictionaries— *pantometry*, which means universal measurement. Ever since, humans have been obsessed with counting things, from people and sheep to the number of cars imported and the number of McDonald's hamburgers served. Being able to count and measure is one of the traits separating man from animals. The thoughts of Scottish mathematician and physicist Lord Kelvin (1824–1907), are inscribed—slightly inaccurately—in the stones of the Social Science Building at the University of Chicago:

When you cannot measure it, when you cannot express it in numbers, your knowledge is of a meagre and unsatisfactory kind. ... It may be the beginning of knowledge, but you have scarcely in your thoughts advanced to the stage of science (McCloskey 2000: 80).

The problem for the pantometrists is the same one facing business-people today: What should be measured? Facts and figures do not provide a context, or reveal truth; we still need our imaginations and creativity. If we focus only on what we can measure, we will become prisoners of our past, because it would be impossible to create a future that would be different than an extrapolated past. Even Lord Kelvin's statement cannot be expressed in numbers, but that does not automatically make it "meagre and unsatisfactory." If everything important has to be quantified to be comprehended, how are we to understand art, music, poetry, literature—indeed, our own human feelings? One could persuasively argue that the more valuable something is, the more likely it *cannot* be quantified.

Numbers give the illusion of presenting more truth and precision than they are capable of providing. Human's genetic code is 98 percent identical to our chimpanzee cousins. We share even more DNA with whales. So what? Should we marry whales and chimps? That 2 percent is an enormous difference, so obviously the accuracy of the measurement misses the reality.

Much of what is measured in today's firms suffers from the same fatal flaw.

The McKinsey Maxim

We have all heard the famous saying, often referred to as the McKinsey Maxim, named after the famed consulting firm: "What you can measure you can manage." This bromide has become such a cliché in the business world that it is either specious or meaningless. Specious since companies have been counting and measuring things ever since accounting was invented, and meaningless because it does not tell us what ought to be measured. Besides, has the effectiveness of management itself ever been measured? How about the performance of measurement? Measurement for measurement sake's is senseless, as quality pioneer Philip Crosby understood when he uttered, "Building a better scale doesn't change your weight."

This is not to imply we need to eliminate "hard data," but rather that we do not allow measurement mania to crowd out "soft" judgment. Since management itself cannot be measured, we have to rely on judgment. We can certainly use hard data to vouch for soft intuition, but we can also do the opposite—use soft judgments to check hard facts.

A lot of information is soft—gossip, hearsay, and intuition. The partner who learns his largest customer was golfing with a major competitor is not going to be served well by the time the lost revenue shows up on his profit and loss statement. As one manager quipped, "I would be in trouble if the accounting reports held information I did not already have" (Mintzberg 2009: 27). Accounting reports, cost accounting, realization and utilization rates, and timesheets—the matrix of measurements in most firms—are, by their nature, *lagging* indicators. Yet what is needed in firms today, similar to the canary in the coal mines of the last century, are *leading* indicators—

early detection systems that allow companies to perform their ultimate function of creating wealth for the customers they serve.

Blindly relying on this metric mania can obscure many oblique realities. The ultimate problem with numbers and measurements is what they *don't* tell us, and how they provide a false sense of security and the illusion of control—that we know everything that is going on. In fact, one could put forth the argument, running counter to the McKinsey Maxim, that the most important things in life *cannot* be measured. How do you measure happiness? How do you measure love, joy, respect, or trust? How do you measure the success of your marriage?

Even the not-for-profit world is infected with this mentality. Consider the one measure that most people believe establishes the "efficiency" of a charity: What percentage of my donation goes to the cause? This metric explicitly assumes that a lower administrative and overhead structure leads to a more effective charity. Yet the empirical evidence does not warrant this false belief. This efficiency measurement, in and of itself, provides no information on the effectiveness of the charity. If Jonas Salk had spent 50 percent on overhead and administration but developed the polio vaccine— saving countless millions of lives—should we conclude that his charity was "inefficient" because the ratio was only 50 percent spent on the cause? To ask the question is to answer it. Measurements can crowd out judgment.

As Albert Einstein said, "Sometimes what counts can't be counted, and what can be counted doesn't count." If this is true in a scientific discipline such as physics, it is certainly true in business, which is not a science, but rather an art.

Perhaps we need a corollary to the McKinsey Maxim: What is really important cannot be measured. This is what author David Boyle calls the *McKinsey Fallacy.* This will no doubt be met with tremendous resistance. It goes against the very grain of the MBA mind-set, the modern-day pant-ometrists, who are taught that everything needs to be quantified and counted, and decisions should be based on the numbers. In other words, don't think, count. This is not to suggest that no measurements are relevant or useful. Rather, that anything we measure that is meaningful needs to be guided by a theory.

Developing a Theory

The only way to look into the future is use theories since conclusive data is only available about the past.

—Clayton Christensen et al., *Seeing What's Next,* 2004

When the late Milton Friedman taught his graduate courses in economics at the University of Chicago, he used to ask what his students came to call his two terrifying questions:

- How do you know?
- So what?

In terms of building a theory, these questions are profound; the first making us observe the world, the second forcing us to say what the effect is. To answer the latter, we need theory—a statement of cause and effect. Philosophers of science, such as Karl Popper and Thomas Kuhn, have explained how to build a theory, which is done in a cyclical pattern as follows:

- Observation
- Categorization
- Prediction
- Confirmation

This is why all scientific theories are formulated in a manner exposing them to being disproved. Scientists always ask, "What would it take to admit your theory is wrong?" If you answer nothing, you are arguing an assertion—a matter of faith—not reason. If you cannot be wrong, you cannot be right either. This is why scientists are constantly looking for anomalies. It is an iterative process, a never-ending quest of improvement, since only a better theory can replace an inferior theory. Nassim Taleb, author of *The Black Swan*, describes this as "Subtractive epistemology: the sucker thinks Truth is search for knowledge; the nonsucker knows Truth is search for ignorance." This is what the Scottish philosopher David Hume meant when he wrote "Knowledge is only ignorance postponed."

Pantometry versus Theory

Unlike management accountants and auditors, who tend to focus on lagging indicators—such as a business's financial statements—economists developed not only *lagging indicators*, but also *leading* and *coincident indicators*.

- *Leading indicators* anticipate the direction in which the economy is headed.
- *Coincident indicators* provide information about the current status of the economy.

- *Lagging indicators* change months after a downturn or upturn in the economy.

This is not to claim economists can predict the future; far from it. There is a tremendous amount of history that supports the observation that no one can predict the future. That said, the indicators have no doubt expanded our knowledge of how an economy operates, and may even provide a clue as to where it is heading, but they are still a compendium of averages, and averages can be very misleading—you can drown in a lake that is, on average, four feet deep. Nonetheless, the indicators can be useful.

Your individual FICO—Fair Isaac Corporation—score is comprised of five weighted components that have been tested to have *predictive* capabilities about your future credit worthiness:

- Payment history (35 percent)
- Amounts owed (30 percent)
- Length of credit history (15 percent)
- New credit (10 percent)
- Types of credit used (10 percent)

Notice the FICO score is not simply a measurement. It certainly contains measurements, but it is driven by a theory of which characteristics can predict future behavior. This is the essential difference between measuring for the sake of measuring and a measure that is enlightened by a theory.

The social networking Web site Facebook discovered that the best predictor of whether members would contribute to the site was if they saw their friends contributing content, which is why most sites list updates on what their friends are doing online.

This is a critical distinction being made between a key *performance* indicator and a key *predictive* indicator. A performance indicator is merely a measurement, such as the number of patents filed, or new revenue, but lacks a falsifiable theory. A predictive indicator, by contrast, *is a measurement supported by a theory*, which can be tested and refined, in order to explain, prescribe, or predict behavior. Utilizing Einstein's method of a *gedanken*—thought experiment—is a good place to start.

A Gedanken

Engage in this thought experiment. You are the CEO of Continental Airlines. Which leading indicators would you want to look at on a daily—or even hourly or shorter—basis to determine whether Continental was fulfilling its mission of flying passengers around the world profitability? It is relatively easy to develop *lagging* indicators, such as profit, revenue per passenger mile, cost per passenger mile, repeat customer bookings, frequent flyer miles earned, and so on. But they are lagging indicators; all of the employees would not be able to influence those results on a day-to-day basis. How would the baggage handler's behavior change as a result of learning last month's load factor? We need some canaries in the airline that are leading indicators of performance.

You could certainly develop *coincident* indicators, by tracking in real time all of the lagging indicators mentioned; and no doubt the airlines do this internally to some extent. But that still does not necessarily help the pilots, flight crews, baggage handlers, or food service caterers fulfill the goals and objectives of the airline on an hour-by-hour timeline. What are needed are leading indicators—theories—that have some *predictive* power; in other words, they predict the financial results of Continental by predicting future customer behavior.

In his book *From Worst to First*, Gordon Bethune details how he was able to turn around the failed airline (which had filed for Chapter 7 bankruptcy twice in the preceding decade) between February 1994 and 1997, transforming it into one of the best and most profitable airlines in the sky. It is a remarkable story, and it illustrates the importance of utilizing leading key predictive indicators (KPIs) to focus the entire organization on its purpose and mission. Bethune basically tracked three leading KPIs:

- On-time arrival
- Lost luggage
- Customer complaints

When Bethune became CEO, Continental ranked dead last in all of these indicators, which are also measured by the Department of Transportation (known as the "Triple Crown Criteria"). Bethune analyzed the problems—and there were many—and discovered the culture of the airline was focused on driving down cost per available seat mile (the standard measure of cost in the airline industry). It cut costs at every opportunity, by packing the planes with more seats, reducing the food and drink portions, paying its people poorly, and so forth. It believed its mission was to cut costs; but as Bethune constantly pointed out, "We aren't in business to save money, we are in business to put out a good product. ... You can make a pizza so cheap nobody wants to eat it. And you can make an airline so cheap nobody wants to fly it" (Bethune 1998: 123, 50). There is an enormous difference between controlling costs and being cheap. A firm must make investments that deliver value to the customer.

What makes the three indicators just listed leading is that they measure success the same way the customer does. And that is critical because, ultimately, the success of any business is a result of loyal customers who return. None of the three indicators would ever show up on a financial statement, but, as the airlines have learned over the years—by testing the theory—they have a predictive correlation with profits.

Now that we have a solid understanding of the difference between a Key Performance Indicator and a Key Predictive Indicator, we will view the approach various professional firms have used to develop their own KPIs.

CHAPTER 23

Firm-wide Key Predictive Indicators

Everything should be made as simple as possible, but not simpler.

—Albert Einstein

Developing KPIs is a metastrategy—that is, a strategy for defining strategies. They need to be intimately linked with the firm's value proposition, as well as quantitative measurements, or—and this is even more important in knowledge firms—qualitative judgments. They should have a common definition and be understood across the entire firm, with no ambiguity, similar to the Continental example from Chapter 22.

Having your entire team focused on KPIs not only gets the right job done daily, it also gives them a sense of commitment to the process of improving *how* that job gets done. Since the front lines are at the coal face observing actual customer behavior, they know which processes work and which cause frustration, and can readily suggest improvements to make the customer experience more enjoyable. This process must be based on observed reality, and it must make sense in explaining *actual* customer behavior, not illusions or specious conclusions.

KPIs for a Professional Knowledge Firm

According to an article in the *Journal of Accountancy*, CPA firms lose customers for the following reasons (Aquila and Koltin 1992: 67–70):

1. "My accountant just doesn't treat me right" [Two-thirds of the responses].
2. CPAs ignore clients.
3. CPAs fail to cooperate.
4. CPAs let partner contact lapse.

5. CPAs do not keep clients informed.
6. CPAs assume clients are technicians.
7. CPAs use clients as a training ground [for new team members].

Turn the coin over, and this is why people select accountants:

- Interpersonal skills
- Aggressiveness
- Interest in the customer
- Ability to explain procedures in terms the customer can understand
- Willingness to give advice
- Perceived honesty
  (Winston 1995: 170)

David Maister, Charles H. Green, and Robert M. Galford, in *The Trusted Advisor*, offer the most commonly expressed customer suggestions regarding what they want from their professional relationship (Maister et. al. 2000: 180):

1. Make an impact on our business, don't just be visible.
2. Do more things "on spec" (i.e., invest your time on preliminary work in new areas).
3. Spend more time helping us think, and helping us develop strategies.
4. Lead our thinking. Tell us what our business is going to look like five or ten years from now.
5. *Jump* on any new pieces of information we have, so you can stay up to date on what's going on in our business. Use our data to give us an extra level of analysis. Ask for it; don't wait for us to give it to you.
6. Schedule some offsite meetings together. Join us for brainstorming sessions about our business.
7. Make an extra effort to understand how our business works: sit in on our meetings.
8. Help us see how we compare to others, both within and outside our industry.
9. Tell me why our competitors are doing what they're doing.
10. Discuss with us other things we should be doing; we welcome any and all ideas!

Despite all this evidence, the average professional firm will track the hours its team members spend working on various assignments. There are many problems with this, the first being that no customer defines the success of their professionals by how many hours they spend on their work. It also focuses the team on efforts, activities, and inputs—not to mention ways to inflate their personal charge hours—at the expense of results, output, Total Quality Service, and value to the customer. Another problem with this metric is it is not a theory; and to add insult to injury, it is a lagging indicator. Perhaps this explains why the surveys mentioned above on losing and gaining customers have not materially changed in the past half-century. The right measures, and judgments, are simply not on the dashboard of most professional firms. The canaries are hacking and wheezing.

If a firm wanted to develop leading KPIs, it should study the preceding factors to determine how it can create KPIs that would either discourage—or encourage—the behavior described. This requires modeling a theory of factors important to measure and reward, no small task for the professions. And in our experience with thousands of firms around the world, very few have taken the time to do this, let alone think about it.

Fortunately, this is beginning to change in some of the more enlightened firms. Our VeraSage Institute fellows have been fortunate enough to conduct hundreds of workshops around the world on this very issue and have had professionals from all sectors brainstorm to come up with some KPIs for a professional firm. We believe the following KPIs allow firms to eliminate timesheets, as they attempt to define success the same way the customer does. This provides the firm with a competitive advantage, which translates to enhanced pricing power.

Here are some firm-wide KPIs selected by those firms that have quit using timesheets for a more customer-focused set of predictive indicators.

Firm-Wide KPIs—Velocity	Turnaround time
Firm Wide KPIs—Financial	Innovation revenue
Firm Wide KPIs—Customer	Customer loyalty
	Value gap
	Customer referrals
	Number and quality of customer contacts per week

It is important to note there is ample evidence that between *three* to *five* KPIs should be enough for *any* firm to have predictive value for customer behavior. Though I wanted to provide enough so you can at least begin to think in this direction—and perhaps develop even better KPIs for your particular firm—it is important to keep in mind I am emphatically not suggesting you adopt *all* of the preceding KPIs. *Do not boil the ocean.* If you try to track too many KPIs, you end up knowing nothing.

Another caution: When choosing your firm's KPIs, do not overintel-lectualize the process. Selecting KPIs is not merely a matter of left-brain analysis; your firm's right brain is important, too. You are testing a theory, which will greatly influence what you are measuring and observing. You are looking for KPIs that will measure and reward results over activities, output over input, performance over methodology, responsibilities over procedures, and effectiveness over efficiency.

Let us analyze each of the firm-wide KPIs given, explain their logic, the results they are trying to measure, the behavior they are trying to encourage, how some professional firms have implemented them, and even improved upon how they can be used to enhance a customer's experience in dealing with their professional. It should be noted that not all of the following KPIs are leading, some are coincident, and some may even be lagging, depending on how often they are disseminated throughout the organization.

Turnaround Time

Michael Dell likes to refer to the time lag between a customer placing an order and the company assembling and shipping the finished product as *velocity*. We believe professional firms should also be diligent about track-ing when each project comes in, establishing a desired completion date, and measuring the percentage of on-time delivery. This prevents procras-tination, missed deadlines, and projects lingering in the firm while the customer is kept in the dark. Proper project management, as discussed in Chapter 33, is instrumental in achieving these objectives.

Imagine installing 360-degree webcams everywhere in a firm. Also imagine customers being able to log onto a secure Web site, type in their names and passwords, and the appropriate camera would find their project and give them a real-time picture of it, probably lying on a manager's floor or credenza awaiting review. Would this change the way work moved through a firm? Would this hold the firm accountable for results, not merely efforts? FedEx and UPS do exactly this; and in fact some law firms utilize intranets that provide their customers with real-time access to the work being performed on their behalf. Even day care facilities have installed webcams so parents can watch their children over the Internet while at work. The kennel where I board my dog does the same. This one metric would go a long way toward mitigating most of the reasons customers defect from firms (not kept informed, feel ignored, and so on).

The turnaround KPI also implements Peter Drucker's recipe for avoid-ing the pitfalls of procrastination, by implementing the following alliterative triad of steps:

Definition, delegation, and deadline. The executive needed to define the problem or the task, delegate accountability to a specific person along with responsibility for the specific thing to be accomplished, and establish a firm deadline for completion. The definition ensured a sense of purpose, the delegation identified who was going to do the actual work, and the deadline substituted action for inertia (Flaherty 1999: 328).

Turnaround time can be tracked at the firm-wide level as well as the team member level (we will deal with team member KPIs in the next chapter). If a particular team member is missing deadlines, it is a good indication that person has been given too much work, does not have adequate education to do what has been assigned, is unclear on the assignment responsibilities, is simply not up to the job, or perhaps is having a personal problem. Whatever the reason, the turnaround time provides a leading indicator to firm executives to intervene and correct any problems in real time. The timesheet does not provide this advantage, because once it has been discovered, the problems are history.

Innovation Revenue

This metric measures revenue from services introduced in recent years, and measures the firm's innovation in offering additional services to its customers. It is an essential measurement to determine the lifetime value of the firm to the customer. For example, Hewlett-Packard wants 50 percent of its revenue from products that did not exist two years ago. Intel achieves 100 percent of its revenues from products developed within the last three years.

Firms spend an enormous amount of resources measuring billable hours, realization rates, and other internal metrics, but we have found very few that measure innovation revenue and make it a key component of its strategic vision. This is not to say firms are anti-innovation; it is more a matter of not being proinnovation, by not having measurements and reward systems in place to encourage this behavior. Innovation is essential to creating new wealth; as Gary Hamel asks, "What does it matter to an investor if a company is earning its cost of capital if its rivals are capturing the lion's share of new wealth in an industry?" (Hamel 2000: 285).

Customer Loyalty and Referrals

Frederick Reichheld, in his work with Bain & Company, estimated that fewer than 20 percent of corporate leaders rigorously track customer retention. For professional firms, who derive anywhere from 80 to 95 percent of their revenue from existing customers, this is a major oversight. Also, when you consider it costs an average of 4 to 11 times more to *acquire* a customer than to *retain* one, this metric must become part of the firm's value system.

Because word of mouth is the most effective way to acquire the right kind of customers, referrals from existing customers are a leading indicator that the firm is delighting its current customers. A firm has no business taking on new customers if its existing customers are not completely happy. Also, if the firm's leaders are interested in promoting rainmaking activities at all levels within the firm—and rewarding them commensurately—referrals can also demonstrate the firm is asking its existing customers for colleagues they believe could derive the same benefits as they do from doing business with the firm. A lot of firms do not get the referrals they could simply because they do not ask on a regular basis.

One theory being tested in some companies to measure customer loyalty is Fred Reichheld's Net Promoter® Score (NPS) from his book *The Ultimate Question.* The hypothesis is as follows: You only need to ask your customers one question:

How likely is it that you would recommend this company to a friend or colleague?

The scores, on a one-to-ten scale, are then divided into three categories:

1. *Promoters (P)*—loyal enthusiasts (score 9–10)
2. *Passives*—satisfied but unenthusiastic, easily wooed by the competition (score 7–8)
3. *Detractors (D)*—unhappy customers trapped in a bad relationship (score 0–6)

The NPS calculation is then computed with the percentages from above, as follows (Reichheld 2006: 19):

$$NPS = P - D$$

Reichheld concludes most companies have an NPS score of only 5 to 10 percent, while those companies with the highest growth—due to higher customer loyalty—have NSP scores of 50 to 80 percent, such as Harley-Davidson, Costco, Amazon.com, eBay, Apple, and FedEx (Reichheld 2006: 19–20).

A caveat: This is merely a theory, which still needs to be tested. For instance, Dell and Electronic Arts had high NPS scores but encountered difficult times due to outdated business models. One reason is that the NPS score is based on what people *say* in surveys, not what they *do*. I received a card upon check-in to a resort in Hamilton Island, Australia, that asked me the ultimate question. I answered yes, but I have never been back. Examples abound of companies that score high on satisfaction surveys but still have customers defect, since they are not taking account the economist's concept of *revealed preference*—watch what people do, not what they say. That said, we have seen firms that use NPS report higher levels of customer loyalty and profit, and it is one method to gauge customer loyalty.

Value Gap

This measurement attempts to expose the gap between how much the firm *could* be yielding from its customers and how much it actually is yielding. It is an excellent way to reward cross-selling additional services, increase the lifetime value of the firm to the customer, and gain a larger percentage of the customer's wallet. One CPA firm made this calculation part of its partner compensation model. What actions can your firm take to close the value gap?

Number and Quality of Customer Contacts per Week or Month

Since two-thirds of customers defect from firms because of perceived indifference, why not encourage all of the firm's team members to meet regularly with the customers they serve? This keeps the firm visible and in front of the customer; will lead to a narrower value gap, more referrals, and increased loyalty; and aid in the development of communication and listening skills of team members.

However, this KPI cannot be gamed just to achieve some arbitrary quota of contacts per week or month; it must also consist of *subjective* evaluations of the quality of each contact: what was discussed, the body language of the customer, additional services discovered, and a host of other *judgments* that are simply too oblique to be measured quantitatively but that are the true characteristics of providing a good experience for customers while demonstrating you care about them.

Remember, as a general rule, any KPI that requires information from financial statements—income statement, balance sheet, or statement of cash flows—is usually a lagging or, at most, a coincident indicator. *All leading indicators are theories derived from information not found on financial statements.*

KPIs Equal Customer Accountability

There ain't no rules around here! We're trying to accomplish something!

—Thomas Edison

There is little doubt that what you measure defines how people work, especially if those measurements determine pay, promotions, and other career advancements. Most firms, when they are guided at all by indicators, do not formulate a set of coherent KPIs focused on the real-time, day-to-day, customer experience. Most performance measures are simply abstracted from lagging accounting data, and while they may be able to report the score of the game, they provide no insight or guidance on how to improve performance.

The firms that have gotten rid of their timesheets and replaced them with some (usually between two and three) of the firm-wide KPIs above have also implemented this change in a very rational manner. That is, they involved the team members in the change. Although it is widely believed that people do not like change, we believe there is a difference between change *imposed* and change *adopted*. As Michael Basch reminds us: "People don't mind change. They mind being changed."

Let the team members decide for which KPIs they want to be held accountable. These are smart, bright, motivated, and professional people who want to do an outstanding job not only for the customers and the firm, but also for themselves. They know what the key drivers of success are. The debate about organizational control is not whether it is needed—it certainly is—but about how it is best achieved. Imposing controls such as billable hours, which do not have a palpable or predictive relationship with customer success, might cause obedience and the minimum level of effort to obtain the standards, but it will not drive firm excellence.

All of the firms that have let the team decide on the KPIs discovered, usually to their pleasant surprise, the team chose KPIs that were tougher on themselves than the partners would have been. People who select their own goals are usually more demanding of themselves than when those goals are selected for them.

Social controls are far more effective than financial controls for influencing your team member's behavior. This explains why most professional firms that have trashed timesheets tend to hold frequent meetings—both on marketing and work-in-process—in which everyone is held accountable for the selected KPIs. If you know your peers are holding you responsible and answerable for your results, you are more likely to act in a manner consistent with the wishes of the group.

Jim Casey, founder of UPS, said in 1947, "A man's worth to an organization can be measured by the amount of supervision he requires." Is it not time firms recognize they are dealing with knowledge workers, not Frederick Taylor's factory workers? Knowledge work is not subject to the same rhythms and cadences of an assembly line; it is an iterative process of the mind, and the traditional time-and-motion studies are out of place in the knowledge firm. It is time for the firms of the future to remove the Sword of Damocles—the timesheet—hanging over the head of their professionals, and unleash them from a theory that is not applicable to the Intellectual Capital economy of the modern firm.

We have examined creating KPIs at a firm-wide level, those with predictive capability to peer into the future of customer behavior. It is time to cascade these firm-wide KPIs down deeper into the organization, at the individual knowledge worker level to align their day-to-day activities with the firm's overall strategy, value, and purpose.

CHAPTER 24

Knowledge Worker Key Predictive Indicators

For the "knowledge workers" the question is less how much they produce than whether they direct their attentions to the right "product." It is effectiveness rather than efficiency that characterizes their economic contribution. And efficiency itself in the knowledge worker is much less a matter of the individual doing more, as it is a matter of the group doing better. These are new things. So far none of us, whether we be Americans or Russians or Europeans or Japanese, know how to do this.

—Peter Drucker, *People and Performance*, 2007

Engage in this gedanken: You want to build the world's finest automobile. You decide to use individual parts with a reputation for excellence from various cars around the world—the engine from a Ferrari, brakes of a Porsche, suspension of a BMW, and so on. What you would end up with is not the world's greatest automobile, but rather a really expensive piece of junk.

This, in a nutshell, is the problem with the way we attempt to measure the "efficiency" of knowledge workers—we measure each task in six-minute units in the false belief that maximizing the efficiency of each one will maximize the efficiency of the entire firm. This metric is redolent of the days of Frederick Taylor, no longer applicable to the product of the intellect. Knowledge work is not repetitive; it is *iterative* and *reiterative*. That is, it is a process of the mind, a difficult place for metrics to have any meaning. Not many people would want a time-and-motion surgeon, who equated efficiency with quality medical care. The old joke among physicians applies here, where the surgeon is admiring his competence: "The operation was a complete success! Although the patient died, we kept him in perfect electrolyte balance throughout!"

The task at hand is formidable, since the relationship between inputs and outputs is not as well defined in the knowledge era as it was in the agricultural or industrial revolutions. Increasing the effectiveness of knowledge workers is one of the new frontiers. In his Nobel Prize lecture, the economist Friedrich von Hayek urged policymakers to emulate gardeners, not engineers, by creating the environment for growth rather than trying to bring it about directly through command and control. This applies to knowledge workers as well. It does no good to admonish your team members to work *smarter*, not *harder*. It is not bad advice; it is just not very helpful—like telling people to be healthy, wealthy, and wise. We need to apply the same ingenuity and creativity management thinkers did with manual workers to increase the effectiveness of knowledge workers.

A Model for Knowledge Worker Effectiveness

What made the traditional workforce productive was the system— whether it was Frederick Winslow Taylor's "one best way," Henry Ford's assembly line, or Ed Demming's Total Quality Management. The system embodies the knowledge. The system is productive because it enables individual workers to perform without much knowledge or skill. … In a knowledge-based organization, however, it is the individual worker's productivity that makes the system productive. In a traditional workforce, the worker serves the system; in a knowledge workforce the system must serve the worker.

—Peter Drucker, *Managing in the Next Society,* 2002

Knowledge work is not defined by *quantity* but by *quality.* It is also not defined by its *costs* but by its *results.* Frederick Taylor started with the assumption that there was "one best way" to achieve productivity and it was not necessarily determined by the physical—or even mental— characteristics of the job. But in knowledge work, the traditional tools of measurement need to be replaced by *judgment,* and there is a difference between a measurement and a judgment: a measurement requires only a stick; a judgment requires knowledge.

Frederick Taylor did not attempt to measure the productivity of knowledge workers because there were not very many in his day. He did not focus attention on how to educate the workers to do the job better next time because he developed systems and procedures that removed the need for workers to use their imaginations. He substituted rules for thinking. Yet he is the man who inspired Reginald Heber Smith to introduce timesheets into his law firm in 1919 (see Chapter 16), and his outdated ideas still hold sway over the professions. This is a classic example of a thinker of whom

Justice Oliver Wendell Holmes wrote, "a hundred years after he is dead and forgotten, men who never heard of him will be moving to the measure of his thought." In this case, the thought was a bad one.

It took approximately half a century before companies began to learn this made their organizations complacent and stupid—not the traits you want in an auto factory, let alone among knowledge workers. Knowledge work can only be designed _by_ the knowledge worker, not _for_ the worker. In a factory, the worker _serves_ the system. The same is true in a _service_ environment; but in a knowledge environment, the system should _serve_ the worker. Only the most mundane, routine, and low-value work can be systematized. The more complicated work requires judgment, experience, wisdom, and tacit knowledge, which is next to impossible to put into a standardized checklist, let alone believe there is "one best way" to achieve results. (Tacit and explicit knowledge will be discussed in Chapter 25.)

We need new thinking and new models to _judge_ the effectiveness of knowledge workers. Fortunately, Peter Drucker blazed the trail in this area, drawing an enormous distinction between _efficiency_—always a ratio of outputs to inputs—and _effectiveness_, which is the extent to which the desired result is realized:

> Efficiency means focus on costs. But the optimizing approach should focus on effectiveness. Effectiveness focuses on opportunities to produce revenue, to create markets, and to change the economic characteristics of existing products and markets. It asks not, How do we do this or that better? It asks, Which of the products really produce extraordinary economic results or are capable of producing them? ... It then asks, To what results should, therefore, the resources and efforts of the business be allocated so as to produce extraordinary results rather than the "ordinary" ones which is all efficiency can possibly produce?
>
> This does not deprecate efficiency. Even the healthiest business, the business with the greatest effectiveness, can well die of poor efficiency. But even the most efficient business cannot survive, let alone succeed, if it is efficient in doing the wrong things, that is, if it lacks effectiveness. No amount of efficiency would have enabled the manufacturer of buggy whips to survive.
>
> Effectiveness is the foundation of success—efficiency is a minimum condition for survival _after_ success has been achieved. (Drucker 2007: 34–35).

Wise firm leaders will build on this wisdom to usher in the new era of the knowledge worker. Drucker believed the main focus of the knowledge worker needs to be on the task to be done—with all other distractions eliminated as much as possible—and this is defined by the worker him- or herself. Asking knowledge workers the following questions (these are adapted from Peter Drucker and other sources) about their jobs is a rich source for learning a great deal about any firm:

What is your task?
What should it be?
What should you be expected to contribute?
How fair are those expectations?
What hampers you in doing your task and should be eliminated?
How could *you* make the greatest *contribution* with your strengths, your way of performing, your values, to what needs to be done?
What *results* have to be achieved to make a difference?
What hinders you in doing your task and should be eliminated?
What progress are you making in your career?
How is the firm helping you to achieve your professional goals and aspirations?
What does the firm do right and what should it continue doing?
What are the firm's weaknesses and what should it stop doing?
What critical things should the firm start doing?

These are excellent questions for leaders to ask the team members periodically. Between the firm-wide KPIs and these questions, the firm will be able to focus its resources and attention on external opportunities, rather than internal bureaucratic procedures, rules, and systems that probably do not add much value to the customer experience.

Recall that a business does not exist to be efficient—it exists to create wealth for its customers. Efficiency can be taken to ludicrous extremes. For instance, I doubt any efficiency expert would have suggested to the Nordstrom brothers to place pianos and hire piano players in their department stores. What could this possibly add to efficiency? Indeed, it reduces the efficiency as traditionally measured by retailers—sales and margins per square foot. Yet how *effective* is it in providing a competitive differentiation that Nordstrom can leverage to create a more valuable experience for its team members and customers?

It is easy to cite examples of where efficiency is sacrificed for greater effectiveness—from Walt Disney's *Snow White and the Seven* (not *Three*) *Dwarfs* to Google's 20 percent time for knowledge workers to innovate pet projects. But I cannot think of any examples that run in the opposite direction—that is, where an increase in efficiency leads to greater effectiveness. Why, then, do so many firms worship on the altar of efficiency, confusing being busy with being profitable?

Even the word *technical* comes from the Greek word *techne*, which means "art." The word *art* is an old word for "skill." According to the *Oxford English Dictionary* art is "skill in doing anything as the result of knowledge and practice." Aristotle pointed out that art is about making, and the question of *what* one should make is always more important than the question of *how* to make it—or effectiveness over efficiency. We can have artists paint by the numbers to become more efficient, but it leads to lousy art.[1]

It should be obvious at this juncture that leaders who are responsible for knowledge workers are going to have to become much more comfortable with intuition, judgment, and discernment over measurements, as well as verbal, visual, and visceral forms of information. You simply cannot manage people by numbers. Professor Henry Mintzberg tells the story of one student who asked him, "How can you select for intuition when you can't even measure it?" (Mintzberg 1989: 83). This is a sad commentary on the state of current MBA education. We seem to be turning out greyhounds in counting but ignoramuses in dealing with human beings.

Emotions are essential to good decisions, since "most people reason dramatically, not quantitatively," as Oliver Wendell Holmes once wrote. This is why people are inspired more by stories than spreadsheets. Martin Luther King did not proclaim, "I have quarterly objectives," but spoke of having a dream.

So many firm leaders appear to subscribe to Lenin's maxim "Trust is good. Control is better." They worry that if they get rid of objective measures they will introduce subjective bias into the decision-making process. So what? That is exactly what needs to happen. We simply cannot measure the most important things in life. To get rid of bias we would have to give up judgment, which is too high a price to pay. Neurologist Antonio Damasio has studied brain-damaged patients, demonstrating that without emotion it is impossible to make decisions. Why would we want to disregard our human emotions? For as accurate or scientific as you can make any measurement, judgment and intuition are more important. In the final analysis, any measurement a firm makes is only as valuable as the decisions it improves, leading to greater overall organizational effectiveness. Do we really believe the timesheet satisfies this criteria in a knowledge organization?

---

[1] After writing this chapter, James Caruso, CPA, sent me a provocative tweet from Nassim Nicholas Taleb, author of *The Black Swan*: "Only in recent history has working hard signaled pride rather than shame for lack of talent, finesse, and, mostly, sprezzatura" (sprezzatura [plural sprezzaturas]). From the Italian Sprezzatura, meaning nonchalance. 1. (art) The art of doing a difficult task so gracefully that it looks effortless.

We need KPIs for knowledge workers that create an environment of responsible autonomy, where workers will decide for themselves what and how to perform their jobs, while taking full responsibility and accountability for the outcome. For this to happen, leaders of the future are going to have to fend off the ghost of Frederick Taylor, since it is they who are ultimately responsible for creating conducive organizations that maximize the contribution of their knowledge workers.

Key Predictive Indicators for Knowledge Workers

Many managers agree that the effectiveness of their organizations would be at least doubled if they could discover how to tap the unrealized potential present in their human [capital].

—Douglas McGregor, *The Human Side of Enterprise*, 1960

Many of the "hard" and "objective" measures we do use can be gotten around by the average worker with a modicum of intelligence. It is actually the "soft," "fuzzy," and "subjective" measures that are harder for leaders to deal with, because they require judgment and discernment. Measurements only require a scale, and it is much easier to be precisely irrelevant than it is to be approximately relevant. Measures also provide us with the illusion of control, as if you can manage people by managing numbers.

The following knowledge worker KPIs are offered in the spirit of flouting bureaucratic command-and-control rules and direct performance from an externally guided standard, all the while maintaining a sense of pride in helping others, which is one of the most important intrinsic rewards people earn from their profession.

Customer Feedback

What are the customers saying—good and bad—about the team member? Would you trade some efficiency for a team member who was absolutely loved by your customers? How does the firm solicit feedback from its customers on team member performance? Does the firm reward team members for delivering outstanding customer service or going above and beyond the call of duty for a customer? Are these stories shared with the rest of the firm so they can become part of its culture, as they are at Nordstrom, Southwest, FedEx, and Disney? Or is the firm simply rewarding billable hours while preaching customer service, creativity, and innovation—what leadership expert Steven Kerr described in his famous 1975 essay "On the Folly of Rewarding A, While Hoping for B."

Effective Listening and Communication Skills

If reading and writing go together, so too do speaking and listening. Yet is anyone really ever taught to listen? It is well known that speaking and listening are harder to teach than reading and writing; and if we lament the low level of reading and writing being taught in the schools, just think how much less developed speaking and listening skills must be. Unlike reading and writing, which are solitary undertakings, listening and speaking always involve human interactions.

Aristotle's book *Rhetoric* explained the art of persuasion by using three Greek words: *ethos, pathos*, and *logos*. Ethos signifies a person's character, the sense that you can be trusted and know what you are talking about. Pathos is arousing the passions of the listeners, getting their emotions running in the direction you are trying to take them. It is the motivating factor. Logos is the intellectual reason—and note the Greeks put it last. Think of the old saying "People do not care how much you know until they know how much you care." Reasons and arguments can be used to reinforce your position, but it is the passion that will move the listeners in your direction. I once saw these three words written on the whiteboard in the office of a lawyer. I asked him about them, and he replied: "They remind me how to write a good brief."

But how do you measure listening and communication skills? It is truly a soft measure, but is it not a critical skill for the development of a true knowledge worker, especially in an era where teamwork and wide collaboration with others is essential to perform their tasks? I observed a panel discussion at the American Institute of Certified Public Accountants' Group 100 meeting of executives in corporations and government agencies that hire CPAs, lawyers, and consultants. The number-one capability they look for—and it influences their decision to hire one firm over another, even before price or quality—is communication skills. These skills must be *judged*; they cannot be measured. Firms—and knowledge workers themselves—need to invest in the education necessary to make their team members exceptional in these skills.

Risk Taking, Innovation, and Creativity

These are other soft measures (actually, judgments), but critical skills for any knowledge worker. How often do they take risks or innovate new ways of doing things for customers or the firm? Do they engage in creative thinking in approaching their work? Most leaders say they want their people to "think out of the box," but when you look at what they measure and reward there is an enormous gap between what they say and what they do.

Innovation and creativity need not be thought of as separate from the rest of the firm, but rather an integral part of it. Shouldn't firms work to make innovation ordinary? This is why 3M implemented the "15 percent rule," which encourages technical people to spend up to 15 percent of their time on projects of their own choosing and initiative.

Yet I am met with *staring ovations* when I suggest knowledge firms adopt a similar policy, where at least the knowledge workers are given time to dream up better ways to innovate, improve systems, or add value to customers. A survey conducted by the Net Future Institute found that most people do their best thinking not at the office but during their commute, or while at home. Some people do it in the shower. Why? Because you are not distracted by other things in these environments—you actually have time to think. But in today's frenetic firms, contemplating, cogitating, daydreaming, and thinking lower efficiency, do not look good on your timesheet (there are no codes for these activities), and hence are underinvested in by most firms.

Knowledge Elicitation

Ross Dawson, in his book *Developing Knowledge-Based Client Relationships,* describes knowledge elicitation as "the process of assisting others to generate their own knowledge." Note that this encompasses more than simply learning new things; it involves educating others so they are able to generate their own knowledge. One of the most effective techniques for knowledge workers to learn any subject—especially at a very deep level—is to teach it. As they say, to teach is to learn twice. How often do the team members facilitate a lunch-and-learn on an article or book they have read or seminar they have attended? How good are they at educating their customers?

Effective Knowledge Producer and Consumer

This is designed to judge how well the team members draw from—and contribute to—the firm's intellectual capital. Are they simply consumers of IC or do they also produce IC? How many After Action Reviews have they performed? How many times were those AARs accessed by other members of the firm? How well do they convert their *tacit* knowledge into *explicit* knowledge the firm can reuse and make part of its structural capital? (AARs and tacit and explicit knowledge are explained in Chapter 25). Do they look for the most effective way to leverage knowledge, or do they merely reinvent the wheel? This type of evaluation will help ensure the firm is leveraging what really counts—its IC—and developing more of it.

Ability to Deal with Change

How well do the team members adapt to discontinuity, ambiguity, and tumultuous change? How do they assist others—colleagues and customers alike—in dealing with change? Sure, this is another soft skill, but it is a critical one in developing the type of temperament required to become a successful knowledge worker.

Continuous Learning

What do team members know this year that they did not know last year that makes them more valuable to the firm and its customers? This is more than simply logging time in educational courses; it would actually require an attempt to judge what they learned. Are they constantly enhancing their skills to become more effective workers? How many books have they read this year? More important, what did they learn from them? Does the firm adequately invest in its people's education to fulfill this mission?

Effective Delegator

Peter Drucker wrote: "I have yet to see a knowledge worker, regardless of rank or station, who could not consign something like a quarter of the demands on his time to the wastepaper basket without anybody's noticing their disappearance" (Drucker 2006: 17). If true, this is an astonishing statistic. Think of the additional capacity your firm would gain if its senior team members were to avoid up to 25 percent of their work, while delegating another 25 to 50 percent that could probably be more effectively done somewhere else in the firm. Not only would it provide needed skills for junior team members, it would make available greater capacity to service first-class and business-class customers with more valuable services, the true specialization advantage of the knowledge worker. If the firm's knowledge workers were to become better at delegation, it would increase profitability many times more than an increase in efficiency could ever provide. Does your firm encourage its knowledge workers to become effective delegators, as opposed to hoarding work to meet irrelevant billable hour quotas?

Coaching Skills

How well does the firm develop team members who can coach those who are less experienced? Are adequate resources being invested in this area? Knowledge workers cannot be managed. They can, though, be coached, directed, focused, and inspired to perform based upon their strengths.

Personal Development

What inspires knowledge workers? Why did they enter their chosen profession in the first place? What is their preferred vision of the future? How is the firm helping—or hindering—their professional development? Is it giving them the feedback they need to direct themselves? Ultimately, all development is self-development, and nowhere is this more true than with knowledge workers. These are all vital areas to address if you intend to develop your human capital investors, who are, ultimately, volunteers.

Pride

I agree with Jon Katzenbach, co-author of *The Wisdom of Teams*:

> Pride is a more effective motivator of professional's talent than money. And you can motivate that talent with pride in more than just belonging. There is pride in the specific work product that you deliver to clients, pride in the kinds of clients that you serve, pride in the expertise that you can apply, pride in the values of your firm (McKenna and Maister 2002: 147–48).

If you thought some of these other KPIs were hard to measure, how would you measure pride? But pride in one's work, customers, colleagues, employer, and values are critical to operate with passion and commitment, the next KPI.

Passion, Attitude, and Commitment

These might be the three most subjective criteria, none of which is a substitute for actual talent, but can there can be any doubt that passion, attitude, and commitment are important to the effectiveness of a knowledge worker?

The glass can be either half empty or half full, depending on your disposition. Mathematically, these are the exact same positions, but in the arena of human decisions and actions, they lead to radically different consequences. For example, if you wanted to predict the risk of low birth rate among newborns, there are several factors you could posit, including the income of the mother, access to health care, or possessing health insurance. It turns out that none of these factors has explanatory power. The one that does is the mother's *attitude* toward her pregnancy, and that requires a *subjective* evaluation, not a measurement. As Homer Simpson explains to his daughter Lisa, "If adults don't like their jobs, they don't go on strike.

They just go in every day and do it really half-assed." This is easier to do in a knowledge office than a nuclear power plant.

High Satisfaction Day™

I am indebted to John Heymann, CEO, and his Team at NewLevel Group, a consulting firm located in Napa, California (www.newlevelgroup.com), for this KPI, which is trademarked. When John's firm held a retreat for the purpose of developing their KPIs, the suggestion of High Satisfaction Day (HSD™) was made. An HSD™ is one of those days that convinces you, beyond doubt, why you do what you do. It could mean landing a new customer, achieving a breakthrough on an existing project, receiving a heartfelt thank-you from a customer, or any other emotion of exhilaration that makes you happy you got out of bed in the morning. Sound touchy-feely? John admits it is; but he also says the number of HSDs logged into the firm's calendar is a leading indicator—and a barometer—of his firm's morale.

Here is how John defines the effectiveness of this KPI in an e-mail to me on February 21, 2006:

> As for the HSD, it's really meant as a check for more than just "happiness." We have a well-defined culture and values that we believe, if nurtured, will yield exceptional results (we already have some bottom-line evidence of the effect). Our core values include commitment, collaboration and, especially, a focus on results. We find that the things that trigger an HSD generally stem from paying attention to those values. Therefore, the greater number of HSDs experienced, the stronger our culture becomes, leading to increased performance (results).

> Also, the commitment/collaboration values demand (and engender) a high-trust culture, and an HSD-type of metric draws attention to the individual's own drive and success without requiring a subjective management judgment, so it removes a lot of the frustration professionals often feel at having their performance judged by others. Smart people don't need to be controlled, they need to be in an environment where they feel valued and respected so they can make a difference while being successful. What's the old saw? If you have smart employees, your job is not to motivate them—it's to not de-motivate them.

> I hope that helps clarify a bit more—I could go on! HSDs are touchy-feely, but I'm ok with that. Perhaps we need more insights into humanistic management practices instead of just the science. At [my old firm] people joked that my title stood for Chief Emotional Officer.

In a survey of 254 employers, titled "Job Outlook 2005," by the National Association of Colleges and Employers of Bethlehem, Pennsylvania, prospective employers rated the most important qualities they look for are, on a scale 1 to 5, from not important to extremely important:

Communication skills	4.7
Honesty and integrity	4.7
Relating and working well with others	4.5
Strong work ethic	4.5
Teamwork skills	4.5
Analytical skills	4.4
Motivation and initiative	4.4
Flexibility and adaptability	4.3
Computer skills	4.2
Detail-oriented	4.1
Leadership	4.0
Organizational skills	4.0

Source: www.naceweb.org.

With the possible exceptions of analytical and computer skills, I defy anyone to *objectively* measure the above criteria. This is why hiring a knowledge worker is fraught with so much more risk than other types of employees. Once someone is assessed to have the above traits, they are thrown into an environment where metric mania takes over and tries to quantify, count, and objectify everything they do. Formulas just cannot adequately deal with these critical characteristics of knowledge workers. To be sure, these criteria raise more questions than they answer, but at least they are the right questions.

The Manager Letter

Another practical suggestion to hold people accountable for their contribution, when combined with the KPIs given here, is what Peter Drucker called *the manager's letter.*

> This [setting objectives] is so important that some of the most effective managers I know go one step further. They have each of their subordinates write a "manager's letter" twice a year. In this letter to his superior, each manager first defines the objectives of his superior's job and of his own job as he sees them. He then sets down the performance standards that he believes are being applied to him. Next, he lists the things he must do himself to attain these goals—and the things

within his own unit he considers the major obstacles. He lists the things his superior and the company do that help him and the things that hamper him. Finally, he outlines what he proposes to do during the next year to reach his goals. If his superior accepts this statement, the "manager's letter" becomes the charter under which the manager operates (Flaherty 1999: 93).

Implementing KPIs and the manager's letter suggested by Drucker requires enlightened leadership that understands knowledge workers must contribute based on their strengths, be given autonomy over how they do their work, and be convinced more than controlled because they are colleagues, not subordinates. This attitude does not fit well with the Taylorite command-and-control hierarchies, but it will become an essential mind-shift if firms are to reap the rewards of knowledge workers.

CHAPTER 25

After Actions Reviews

The only irreplaceable capital an organization possesses is the knowledge and ability of its people. The productivity of that capital depends on how effectively people share their competence with those who can use it.

—Andrew Carnegie

Between 1644 and 1737, in the small northern Italian town of Cremona, lived Antonio Stradivari, who made over 1,000 violins, violas, and cellos; a harp; and a couple of lutes that bear his famous name. These instruments are the most sought-after and expensive in the world, regularly selling in the millions of dollars.

Today, even with all the advances in modern technology—with our precision equipment, lasers, computer-aided design, and analytical machinery—and notwithstanding gallant attempts by researchers for over a century, we still cannot replicate the musical quality of an instrument handcrafted over 300 years ago. The knowledge—known as "the Stradivarius secret"—has been lost.

This process of creating and losing knowledge is nothing new, with the lost Library of Alexandria by A.D. 300 perhaps being the greatest example in history of lost intellectual and cultural capital. With the so-called Graybe Boom, the average age of the workforce in the rich world is increasing at the same time many of the Boomers are anticipating retirement, making them the first wave of knowledge workers to do so.

Companies lose knowledge from people leaving, forgetting, retiring, and so on. Knowledge also becomes obsolete and must be constantly replenished. Given the coming demographic trends, how can knowledge organizations capture some of that valuable knowledge before it is lost, like the lost Library of Alexandria? No one knows what the cost of this lost knowledge might be. Furthermore, how can firms leverage the knowledge they do have?

Before we can leverage this knowledge, we must first understand how knowledge is possessed.

We Know More Than We Can Tell

A teacher tells one of his pupils to write a letter to his parents, but the student complains, "It is hard for me to write a letter." "Why! You are now a year older, and ought to be better able to do it." "Yes, but a year ago I could say everything I knew, but now I know more than I can say" (Gregory 1995: 59).

Albert Einstein's research assistant-turned-philosopher Michael Polanyi drew a distinction between *tacit* and *explicit* knowledge. To illustrate tacit knowledge, he said, try explaining how to ride a bike or swim. You know more than you tell. Tacit knowledge is "sticky," in that it is not easily articulated and exists in people's minds. It is complex and rich, whereas explicit knowledge tends to be thin and low bandwidth, like the difference between looking at a map and taking a journey of a certain terrain. It is the difference between reading the employee manual and spending one hour chatting with a coworker about the true nature of the job and culture of the firm. For tacit knowledge to become explicit knowledge—that is, stored somewhere where it can be viewed, reviewed, and used by others—it must first be converted from the mind to another medium (a database, white paper, report, manual, video, podcast, picture, etc.). Tacit knowledge tends to be dynamic, while explicit knowledge is static; both are required for innovation and leverage to take place.

Explicit is from the Latin meaning "to unfold"—to be open, to arrange, to explain. *Tacit* from the Latin means "silent or secret." Try describing, in words, Marilyn Monroe's face to someone, an almost impossible task, yet you would be able to pick her out among photographs of hundreds of faces in a moment. Germans say *Fingerspitzengefühl*, "a feeling in the fingertips," which is similar to tacit knowledge (Stewart 2001: 123). The French say *je ne sais quoi* ("I don't know what"), a pleasant way of describing tacit knowledge. The highest levels of knowledge and competence are inherently tacit, being difficult and expensive to transmit, which is why the concept of master and journeyman still exist, albeit in different forms in a knowledge economy. It also why the fad of "free" is nonsense, confusing data and information—which does move toward free, especially over the Internet—with knowledge and wisdom, which is incredibly expensive to transmit.

This type of knowledge transfer is a "social" process between individuals, and is especially important in knowledge organizations where so much of the intellectual capital (IC) is "sticky" tacit knowledge. Studies have shown that managers receive two-thirds of their information through face-to-face meetings and phone calls, and during the physical meetings, body language can convey up to three times as much meaning as the words spoken for some types of interactions. Ikujiro Nonaka and Hirotaka Takeuchi postulate four different modes of knowledge conversion in their book *The Knowledge-Creating Company.*

1. From tacit knowledge to tacit knowledge, which we call socialization
2. From tacit knowledge to explicit knowledge, or externalization
3. From explicit knowledge to explicit knowledge, or combination
4. From explicit knowledge to tacit knowledge, or internalization (Nonaka and Takeuchi 1995: 62)

All four are important to capture in a firm, but how much time does the average firm spend in documenting and sharing what it knows when its primary metric is how many hours did you bill last week? How often do firms take the time to coach their colleagues on the importance of learning and sharing knowledge? No doubt this gets done in most firms, but it is on an ad hoc and as-needed basis, rather than as a systemized, assessed part of the performance criteria of team members. But it is not "efficient" according to the existing Taylorite metrics, which is one of the reasons knowledge management in most firms have failed—it clashes with the business model of "We sell time."

Managing explicit knowledge is certainly easier than managing tacit knowledge, since the latter exists in the heads of knowledge workers who are difficult to manage, to say the least. Nor is it possible to capture 100 percent of the tacit knowledge that exists in each team member's head, but that is not the goal. The goal is to capture as much of it as we can and place it somewhere (e.g., a file, intranet, Web portal, blog, social media site, etc.) where anyone else in the firm can get it when they need it. This way we are not constantly reinventing the wheel.

The Economics of Structural Capital

One of the most important distinctions between the three types of intellectual capital—human, structural, and social—is that structural capital is the only one that is wholly owned by the firm. Thus, it becomes critically important to capture and leverage as much tacit knowledge as possible from the human and social sources of IC. Think of structural capital as the infrastructure within the firm responsible for converting human capital into wealth for the organization. Economist Sidney Winter describes businesses as "organizations that know how to do things," while Karl Weick called institutions "compressed expertise" (Davenport and Prusak 1998: xiii, 11). Structural capital is what remains with the firm after the human capital goes home at night:

- Organization structure
- Recruitment and remuneration policies
- Management information systems
- Intellectual property (patents, copyrights, trademarks, etc.)
- Documented systems, processes, performance management systems
- Management contracts
- Employee development and education
- Proprietary systems
- Customer lists and contracts
- Supplier contracts

Knowledge, like physical and human capital itself, is subject to obsolescence—people change industries, leave companies, forget, and so on. Alvin Toffler has coined the creative, if awkward, term *obsoledge* to describe this phenomenon, pointing out that no one can calculate the costs of degraded decision making as a result.

Make no mistake, knowledge management (KM) is not simply a new technological tool that can simply be installed into an organization; it is a *cultural*—and I might add, business model—change in the way IC is perceived, created, shared, and sold. Adding a sophisticated KM software program to any organization, in and of itself, is not going to create any long-term sustainable advantage unless the firm also conveys the importance and expectation of sharing and reusing knowledge. Yet many KM initiatives are controlled by the information technology (IT) function in many firms and are measured by inputs rather than outputs, while many others degrade into nothing more than "document management" systems, which have nothing to do with tacit knowledge capture. This is probably due to the fact that IT spending can be measured more easily than knowledge codification, and the return on investment (ROI) is therefore more apparent.

My late VeraSage Institute colleague Paul O'Byrne was a partner in O'Byrne & Kennedy, a chartered accounting firm in Goffs Oak, Hertfordshire, just to the north of London. Along with his partner, Paul Kennedy, the firm has taken to heart the message of leveraging IC, creating a "knowledge bank" within their firm, wherein everyone is expected to make deposits and withdrawals. Paul O'Byrne called this "building our invisible balance sheet," making the firm more valuable. Here is what he had to say on the subject of converting tacit to explicit knowledge:

A knowledge worker carries the means of production around in his own neck-top computer. Many professional firms have a black hole in their income statement where the IT department spends money on knowledge management. Now whether knowledge can indeed be managed is a matter of debate. We are presently on our sixth iteration of a software solution to capturing, categorizing, and accessing knowledge which we call KnowledgeBank. One thing we have definitely learned over the years of trying to develop our own system of knowledge management is that it is a cultural, not an IT, issue.

A variation we have found effective is to make recordings of ideas and store those in the KnowledgeBank. For example, we may be with a customer and discussing pricing. It's all very well for any of our accountants to assert to customers they should put their prices up, but what to say? What analogies to bring? What insights to share? We have over the past four years been video recording our seminars, stories, and interviews that encapsulate some point in a memorable (if only a voyeuristic) way.

The greatest challenge in knowledge management seems to us to be tacit knowledge. Everyone understands the need for procedures, checklists, and precedents and these should indeed be formalized and shared. But what competitive advantage is there in that? Indeed, many of us buy these from the same sources, so there can be no competitive advantage. As many of the public think: many accountants *are* all the same.

A firm of knowledge workers worthy of the name is inevitably differentiated in the application of knowledge and the delivery of personalized service. This is a challenge for firms: can you only be good by recruiting brilliant people? Or can you recruit able people and leverage their skills by recognizing the tacit knowledge of the most effective practitioners and transferring it to them? But we don't know how to do this, or at least we never have. It's generally not wise to do so, since the normal insecurity of professionals means you guard your knowledge in the hope you will be thought indispensable.

Even if you can overcome the self-interest aspect and get buy-in to the idea of sharing knowledge, you have to form new habits of recognizing when we are applying things we "just know," synthesizing different experiences, insights from our wider reading or conversations, and thinking skills that are all examples of tacit knowledge we need to share, but don't know how to.

"Red Polo Syndrome" is the name I gave to the phenomenon that struck me when my wife bought a Volkswagen Polo. Suddenly, from nothing, the number of cars of that type on the road—painted the exact same shade of red—exploded. My wife can be something of a trend-setter, but I had to know that those red cars had been there all the time, but I never noticed. I wasn't attuned to seeing them. I wasn't sensitized to seeing red Polos until I had an interest in them.

So it is with knowledge. It's there, floating around all the time, but until we had an interest and were desirous of seeing it, we didn't notice it, and it passed us by. Now, varying by individual and how we feel that day, we see knowledge all the time. Sometimes it's too routine to mention, sometimes not exciting in itself, but perhaps valuable nevertheless.

Like Paul said, valuable knowledge can exist all around us that has the potential to create great wealth. One of the most effective ways to capture it is by utilizing an After Action Review.

Knowledge Lessons from the U.S. Army

The Army's After Action Review (AAR) is arguably one of the most successful organizational learning methods yet devised.

—Peter Senge

The Army's use of AARs began in 1973, not as a knowledge management tool but as a method to restore the values, integrity, and accountability that had diminished during the Vietnam War. Thinking back on my own career in public accounting, I became convinced the AAR is a practice that would have many salutary effects in a knowledge organization. I began to think about how well my firm learned from past mistakes, or how often we would reflect on what we did, rather than just moving onto the next project. Being generous, I can say there was plenty of room for improvement. We were not taught how the *evaluation* is ultimately more important than the *experience*. The average knowledge worker is so busy *doing* they do not have the time to *reflect* on what they have done, let alone discover major breakthroughs. But action without reflection is meaningless. In Latin, *reflect* comes from the verb meaning *refold*, implying the action of turning things inward to see them in a different way. Reflection without action is passivity, but action without reflection is thoughtlessness. Combine experience with reflection, and learning that lasts is the result.

Perhaps we ignore innovations in the military because its mission— to break things and kill people—is so divergent from that of a civilian organization. But this is far too parochial an attitude; and once again we discover a useful practice from another sector. In fact, because the AAR is such a useful method for turning tacit knowledge into explicit knowledge, not to mention to foster learning and sharing of knowledge throughout the organization, I highly recommend you read *Hope Is Not a Method: What Business Leaders Can Learn from America's Army*, by Gordon R. Sullivan and Michael V. Harper.

Here are the questions you need to ask in each AAR:

- What was supposed to happen?
- What actually happened (the "ground truth")?
- What were the positive and negative factors here?
- What have we learned and how can we do better next time? (from the Center for Army Lessons Learned [CALL]: http://call.army.mil, accessed March 22, 2010).

The Army suggests you divide your time in answering the AAR's questions into 25-25-50—that is, 25 percent reviewing what happened, 25 percent reviewing why it happened, and the remaining 50 percent on what to do about it and how can you learn from it to improve. The objective is not just to correct *things*, but rather to correct *thinking*, as the Army has learned that flawed assumptions are the largest factor in flawed execution—another way of saying there is no good way to execute a bad idea. An AAR is more of a verb than a noun. It does not have to be a formal written report; it can be a conversation held among the team. If the project is large and important enough, a facilitator is recommended to get the most from the process. The AAR could be videotaped, audio recorded, or summarized later in a formal report, any of which could be deposited into the organization's knowledge bank. The Army also recommends answering the following summary questions to wrap up the AAR:

- What should the organization learn from this experience of what worked and did not work?
- What should be done differently in the future?
- Who needs to know these lessons and conclusions?
- Who will enter these lessons in the knowledge management system, or write the case up for future use?
- Who will bring these lessons into the leadership process for decision making and planning? (from the Center for Army Lessons Learned [CALL]: http://call.army.mil, accessed March 22, 2010)

In their *Harvard Business Review* article, "Learning in the Thick of It," Marilyn Darling, Charles Parry, and Joseph Moore discussed the After Action Review process. They added to it an interesting tool, the Before Action

Review (BAR), which they say "requires teams to answer four questions before embarking on an important action":

1. What are our intended results and measures?
2. What challenges can we anticipate?
3. What have we or others learned from similar situations?
4. What will make us successful this time?" (Darling et al. 2005: 92).

Imagine the benefits of having a library of AARs for almost any type of project, process, or method the company may encounter. Imagine further creating a culture that rewards knowledge workers for taking the time to contribute to this stock of knowledge, and perhaps even determines its utility by tracking how many times particular AARs are accessed by others. Imagine further a culture that understands AARs are real work, where time is spent on not just *doing* the work but also *improving* the way work is done. Perfectionist cultures, however, resist this type of candid reflection, as they tend to be intolerant of errors, and mistakes are associated with career risk, not continuous learning. Confucius said, "being ashamed of our mistakes turns them into crimes." The medical world has an appropriate axiom for mistakes made: forgive and remember.

Fear is another reason for learning not taking place. AARs mitigate fear, if they are used not as a method to place blame but to learn from mistakes so they do not happen again, and identify best practices so they can be spread throughout the organization. AARs should not be used for promotions, salary increases, or performance appraisals. This is an enormous advantage of AARs compared to the annual performance appraisal. AARs provide instant feedback, where in their absence a supervisor may delay feedback—and hence learning—to a once-a-year review ritual.

Once again, let us hear from Paul O'Byrne and how his accounting firm, O'Byrne & Kennedy, utilizes AARs:

> We were introduced to the concept of After Action Reviews (AARs) by Ron when he wrote about them in his book *The Firm of the Future*. The concept of reviewing what has taken place with a view to learning from it makes total sense. Funny that it is so little practiced. From the moment we read about it, we decided to embrace this and set about designing a process to capture our AARs. The idea is to note what happened, consider what clues there was to it happening (things rarely come out of a clear blue sky), what we could have done about it, what implications there are for product or service design or learning, and— often most valuable—what other things might be like this where we can apply the lessons learned.

Admittedly, the early days after introducing this were like a contest for "foul-up of the week." This was probably inevitable, as we all tend to focus on things that go wrong, but we wanted to learn from success too, and introduced a system whereby for each "failure" AAR a team member would have to bring in a "success" AAR as well.

The significance of the AAR process for a firm of knowledge workers is blindingly obvious. In many organizations it is not healthy to confess your sins in public, better to hope they are not spotted. Fortunate for us, the partners in our firm made—and willingly reported—more foul-ups than everyone else put together. This leadership showed it was okay to admit fault, with the overriding objective one of learning so we can perform better next time. The sharing of knowledge, whether by means of AARs or in some other way, is a cultural process. If you believe in your knowledge workers, why wouldn't you want them to share their knowledge? As economists say, knowledge is a nonrival asset: If I give you my pen you have it but I don't; but if I give you knowledge, you have it and I still have it. Interestingly, we have discovered that when we exchange knowledge, not only do we still have it, we often gain a new perspective that enhances it and makes it more valuable.

One innovative idea that came out of our AAR process was the concept of "badges." You remember, from Brownies or Boy Scouts? Visible recognition of knowledge and skills learned and tested, lovingly sewn on to your uniform. Part of the context of knowledge is the ability of the user to use it. Our newest team member has needs that are significantly different from our most senior tax planner. They have different prior knowledge, different technological abilities, different people skills, and they'll be doing different work. Our junior recruit cannot possibly do complex tax planning, and our senior tax planner should not be doing basic tax returns. But they do (the latter case, I mean). As the team thought about it, there were lots of instances where this applied, so we set about mapping work to the knowledge and skills required to perform it. The point being, until you've got your personal tax return badge, you couldn't do all of a tax return unsupervised. Perhaps more significantly, if you've got your advanced tax planner badge, you have to turn in your personal tax return badge—your human capital is too valuable to be doing work that could be done by someone else. We see this concept of badges linking back into our methods for categorizing our knowledge and to our work and resource planning.

Once again, we can hear the objections from some partners on this note, who are myopically focused on efficiency rather than effectiveness and learning. Your firm's IC is the most important source of its long-term wealth-creating capacity. It must be constantly replenished and created to build the firm's invisible balance sheet. Constantly focusing on *doing* rather than learning, creativity, innovation, and knowledge sharing is the equivalent of eating the firm's seed corn.

Capturing the tacit knowledge that exists in the heads of your human capital and making it part of your organization's structural capital will insure that your firm knows what it knows, and can deploy it more quickly and at a greater value than the competition. It is IC that is the ultimate lever in the firm of the future, and firms have to begin to understand this fundamental economic truth of wealth creation.

Summary and Conclusions

We have explored the necessity of capturing your firm's tacit human capital and creating structural capital as a result, which will stay with your firm even if your human capital should depart. We also discussed why it is so important to leverage your structural capital to create wealth both for the company's customers and itself.

Is it not tragic that there are more knowledge workers today in the labor force than ever before, yet they are not really rewarded for thinking and reflecting because they are too busy tracking and billing hours? It should not be considered a waste of time to read a business book at work, or write on a blog—let alone conducting an AAR or BAR—but these tasks require us to shift our focus from efficiency to effectiveness, learning, and adding to our IC. Part of the problem is that our traditional metrics and business models focus on precisely the wrong things, and many firms have not taken the necessary time to study the success of other IC organizations. In fact, I posit the following argument: Most firm's legacy systems of measurements and reward systems—from productivity, efficiency, time accounting, and other production-oriented metrics—have actually become embedded negative structural capital, hindering firm's ability to becoming a firm of the future. As with negative human capital, these types of antiquated capital must be extricated from the organization to achieve its latent potential.

Let us read the story of one firm that has put all of the ideas of the firm of the future into practice.

CHAPTER 26

O'Byrne & Kennedy:
A Firm of the Future

At the beginning of Part IV, Chapter 18, four common defenses for timesheets were laid out:

1. Pricing
2. Cost accounting
3. Project management
4. Measuring productivity

Then in the following chapters of Part IV, the replacements for both the billable hour and timesheets were explained: price-led costing; appointing a Chief Value Officer and Value Council; Key Predictive Indicators; and After Action Reviews.

This chapter will bring it all together through the words of the partners of O'Byrne & Kennedy (OBK), a chartered accounting firm we met in the previous chapter on sharing knowledge and performing After Action Reviews, and in Chapter 13 on firing the wrong customers. Now allow them to tell their story of how they made the last step of their transition from a firm of the past to a firm of the future by trashing their timesheets.

Tragically, Paul O'Byrne passed away in November 2008, but his legacy lives on through the work of his partner, Paul Kennedy, and the firm they founded. This is their story, in their own words.

Case Study: Getting Rid of the Timesheets

By Paul O'Byrne

We were frightened of trashing our timesheets. As a general practice working for owner-managed businesses, everyone in our practice had grown up with them; it was what people in practice did. Over the years, we had developed very good patter explaining how time-cost billing worked, why it was best, and—we were very good at this—why fixed prices were bad. I had often told other accountants the single best investment we had made was our time and fees software. We even persuaded certain customers that they needed to record time, otherwise how could they know what the profitable jobs were, and who was and wasn't pulling their weight?

So when first introduced to Ron Baker in March 2000, initially by reading his book (*Professional's Guide to Value Pricing*) and shortly afterward hearing him speak at an event, I was deeply unsettled. He was very persuasive and made sense as he talked and described a world of fixed prices, guarantees, and—horror of horrors—no timesheets. I read his book again and had the opportunity to discuss (argue, really) many of the points with him over the next couple of years (he is indubitably the world's best replier to e-mails).

We didn't see why we had to adopt everything he advocated. He seemed to be right about fixing prices in advance. We had long noticed customers' resentment to the blank cheque approach of professional pricing, and started to introduce fixed prices and adapted his example Fixed Price Agreement (FPA). However, we still had timesheets, and so could track the success of this experiment. It took us time to even try FPAs, initially just using them on new customers or on one-off assignments. But once we committed to having them firm-wide, we had all but a handful of customers on them within a year. Some customers were somewhat suspicious of FPAs, partly as a result of our training them as to the benefits of time-cost billing. The overwhelming majority welcomed fixed prices for agreed assignments—and turnaround times. "About time, too" was the single most common reaction when we told them we were going to fix all these things in advance.

We had been using FPAs for around 18 months before we decided to discard timesheets. We had some successes but several failures—or losses—on jobs with FPAs. Being accountants and never wanting to take a loss on anything, we, of course, scrutinised the losses. We found three causes:

- Outrageous optimism/myopia on our part
- Not holding clients to what they said they would do
- Scope creep, being of two types:
  - Misunderstanding the customer expectations of what we were to do and then being made to do it
  - Blithely doing more than we contracted to perform

Of course, the way we recognised our losses (especially the blithe ones) was by looking at our time records and wondering how on earth so much cost was on a job. The big revelation ("epiphany" in Baker-speak) was our abject disappointment that one particular "good job," a £25,000 management advisory, training and accounts job, made a £2,000 loss.

Our post-mortem analysis here showed that willful scope creep ("This is such a profitable job. I'll just do this one more thing," what Alan Weiss calls "scope seep") poured time on to the job needlessly. This extra work did add value to the customer, but we did not capture any of the value created by utilising "Extra Work Orders," our name for Change Orders. But even that did not cause the loss; it just stopped us making a profit. The root problem was that a qualified manager did work that a junior could and should have done. (This may never happen in your firm, but sometimes we mis-schedule, have insufficient resources of the right type available, etc.). Thirty or forty hours were recorded on this job at £96 (don't ask me why £96!) per hour that should have been less. Fact is, we do not actually pay our managers £96 per hour. The whole "loss" was spurious, just as Baker argues, because it included a "Desired Net Income" factor. We made money on the job—of course we did—but the timesheets led us to believe otherwise.

Holding on to timesheets after introducing FPAs had led us to recognise scope creep—albeit after the fact—and to be attentive to customers' expectations and their obligations to provide us with information. But it finally dawned on us that all of those things should be dealt with *before* the work was done. Timesheets were a crutch, but one that was holding us back.

We understood we should price independently of timesheets. What surprised us was that timesheets did not help us with our profit forecasting or profit recognition. Maybe we were too analytical about this, but once FPAs were in place firm-wide we realised just how inadequate a measure of value timesheets were. They were also inadequate measures of costs. Professional firms have fixed costs. Our task is to

Continued

consider how to allocate the resources bought by those fixed costs. The introduction of FPAs taught us how to discuss value with customers for a given outcome. We recognised that it was our task to design the cost structure to meet the price—the opposite of the "blank cheque" approach of hitherto.

The last possible reason for holding on to timesheets (odd that we so desperately wanted to hold on to them: Nature abhors a vacuum?) was for work-in-progress valuation. Timesheets and time recording had given us something to fix on as the amount of value created in a given period, be it a day or a year. They gave a way of assessing work-in-progress at the month end, which we then adjusted for known write-downs (never write-ups, of course; timesheets don't help capture the extra value you create).

We realised that we had to talk with our team as to what work was going to be done, by whom, and when we could expect to complete it—in other words, proper project management. Otherwise how could we be sure when to recognise profit? We went so far as to suggest that if we wanted to make life easy for ourselves, wouldn't it be best if we could start and finish any given assignment within a calendar month, thus assisting profit recognition? This, serendipitously, gives customers exactly what they want: predictable and (compared with the past) quicker turnaround times. So our firm decided to track the following Key Predictive Indicators (KPIs):

- Value *expected* to be created in the month
- Total FPAs at start and end of month
- Average turnaround time of jobs

Now we do the timesheets *in advance*. We learned from experience and mistakes somewhat slowly, but now are so confident that we can plan our work and capacity sufficiently in advance, that we could abandon timesheets. In effect, we complete the timesheet *before* we do the work, and then use the turnaround time KPI to track—on a real-time and leading basis—our firm's velocity. Thus from 1 July 2002, we became a firm of accountants not using timesheets for pricing, nor for project or team evaluation (not that we ever did, but we always thought we could).

We are now in a position where "no timesheets" attracts customers, and prospective recruits (think about it!), and the partners, team members, and bank manager love it. Our customers welcomed fixed prices so much that we arranged the payment terms so that we are paid almost entirely in advance. We now have negative lock up [accounts receivable] (20 percent, or 73 days, of our annual income is prepaid) and at the start of the month the team agrees what jobs will be completed in the month and thus what income earned.

I know what you've read in this book sounds unsettling, even scary. I've been there, gone through it, and have now emerged on the other side. I had the benefit of Ron Baker constantly berating me for holding on to the antiquated timesheet, and we had some major arguments over this issue. Once he developed the KPIs presented in this book, we decided to take the leap of faith and abandon timesheets.

You now have the same opportunity. I have yet to meet a professional who likes completing their timesheet. And since no customer buys time, and does not measure the success of their professional based on time, why do we all continue to hold onto a practice that is not relevant to our success—and injurious to our relationships with our customers? I commend Ron Baker and his ideas to you. He has helped our firm with his insights, logic, and passion. We could not be sure, in advance, that we were right to abandon timesheets, so to some extent we took a leap of faith. Not a very big leap, because we could always bring them back, but it was uncomfortable abandoning something everyone else was doing. Now we scoff at timesheet-padding scandals, we tell customers and referral sources that we don't do timesheets, and we certainly tell recruitment agents and potential recruits.

We love not having timesheets and will never look back!

Case Study: An Essay on Timesheets

By Paul Kennedy

I write as reformed sinner.

Once, not only did I believe that a firm could not be managed without timesheets but thought our profession privileged to have such important information!

I now write with all the passion of a reformed sinner. My conversion probably went through various stages, not unlike the development of mankind from Neanderthal to modern man.

The Five Stages of an Accountant

The development of the thought process of an accountant regarding pricing can be broken down into five stages:

Continued

1. "We need timesheets to price and to monitor team performance otherwise we wouldn't make any money."
2. "Timesheets are not relevant to pricing but they are an essential tool to monitor job and customer profitability and team performance."
3. "Timesheets are not the only way of monitoring customer, job and team performance, *but are still relevant* and they don't do any harm."
4. "Timesheets are not the only way of monitoring customer, job, and team performance, they are **not** relevant, but they don't do any harm."
5. "Timesheets are dangerous and lead to massive sub-optimisation but how do I run a business without them?"

I now run an accounting practice without timesheets and I am so glad I found a way to do it. Any reader who thinks that value is in any way related to time needs to find a more basic article to read. This essay addresses readers who are at stage two or beyond.

Our Focus Determines Our Destiny

If timesheet measurements were a small part of an overall Management Information System (MIS), their impact would not be so insidious. The fact is they are the main (only?) tool for managing accounting practices. The problem with this is that they focus our attention on the wrong things—and what we focus on is what we get.

Take the true story of the supermarket cashier: A customer at a supermarket asked the cashier if he could help him pack his purchases into the bags. The cashier just shook his head and kept on scanning the goods and passing them along the conveyor. Only after scanning the last item and ringing up the till did the cashier turn to help the customer, who by this time was swamped with the purchased items. The cashier apologised for not helping before and explained that the management measured his scanning speed against benchmarks. This story illustrates the dangers of measuring the wrong things. What the supermarket really wanted was happy customers who kept coming back. By measuring efficiency they unwittingly cultivated a behaviour that was inconsistent with this main aim. Timesheet metrics do the same thing in the professions.

Metrics must be aligned with our main objective. If professionals typically pursued a cost leadership strategy or a operational excellence model, then cost-related, short-term resource allocation KPIs like yield and productivity may be more important metrics in an overall MIS dashboard (although only partly, since every organisation exists to create value outside of itself, to quote Drucker). Yet professionals are not these sort of businesses, or shouldn't be!

Most professionals are in a mature, fragmented industry and a more appropriate strategy involves differentiation through customer intimacy. Management and management metrics therefore need to focus on the customer's view of the business.

Profits come from our ability to create value for our clients and from our ability to capture some of that value (and of course risk). We create value by delivering benefits by satisfying their needs. We capture that value by pricing those benefits over the resource costs of creating those benefits. Our long-term profitability therefore depend on:

1. Our ability to understand our target customers' needs
2. Our ability to target those customers most likely to value those things we can do well (customer segment selection and selection criteria within segment)
3. Product/service design and mix
4. Our ability to develop our customers needs in their minds (selling)
5. Our ability to generate and convert leads of the type we want
6. Our ability to value-price our services
7. Our ability to select and manage appropriate intellectual capital (mainly people)

If timesheets were part of a range of feedback metrics covering all the points above, and the information was properly put in context of the main aim of the firm, then arguably the data could contribute to the overall view. However, in many firms timesheets are the dominant (sometimes only) feedback system and are not put into any proper context. As a result, they lead to behaviours that contradict the firm's main objective (not that many firms have a consensus as to what their main objective is!).

For the purposes of this discussion, let's assume the firm's main aim is long-term profitability with a wish to pursue a customer intimacy strategy.

Ironically, the first problem lies with the profession's failure to understand all the dimensions of profitability. You cannot maximise profits without asking the question "Over what period of time?" If you wanted to maximise profits during the current hour, you should probably not be reading this essay. The fact is that long-term profitability

Continued

requires investment. It requires investment in fixed and current assets but also intangible assets including social capital, structural capital, and human capital. These intellectual capital investments are particularly significant to the knowledge economy and to professional firms.

Timesheet data gives us crude (some would say inaccurate) data about efficiency, yields, and recovery rates. Problems with timesheets include:

1. They measure quantity of time spent, not quality.
2. They assume time spent is a cost not an investment.
3. They do not consider longer-term profitability issues, such as life-time value of a customer.

Not All Hours Are Equal

Take the example of accountant A and accountant B in Table 26.1. In Job 1, Accountant A performed well using the traditional way of measuring performance. The average yield per hour was above target with a recovery rate in excess of 1 (1.05).

Accountant B, by contrast, wasn't watching the timesheet reports. He was thinking about the customer. He recognized customer expectations could be greatly exceeded if he put some additional thought (and, in this case, some extra hours) into the job. As a result, the job added value to the customer in such a way that the customer became a "raving fan." The customer's trust was enhanced, his price sensitivity eased, and he was more willing to spend more money with his accountant. Job 2 is meant to represent the long-term numbers for this customer.

In this example, Accountant B put additional work into delighting the customer when he spotted the opportunity. The question is, had he been looking at his timesheets, would he have done so? Would he have done so if he had to explain the recovery rate to his boss?

Adding additional value doesn't always mean doing more hours. Indeed, the *quality* of the hours is what counts, not the *quantity*. However customer relationships do need investment especially in the early days of the relationship when trust is being established. Timesheets militate against such investments because time is seen as a cost, not an investment. The long-term benefits of such investments are represented in Job 2 (in Table 26.1). By focusing on customer value and not on short-term profitability metrics, Accountant B became more profitable in the long term. Long-term profits will *only* come from focusing on customer value.

TABLE 26.1 The Recovery Trap

Job 1 for Client Alpha

Accountant	Maximum Available Hours	Price	Hours	Target Hourly Rate	Productivity	Yield per Hour	Recovery	Client Value Index**
A	150	10000	100	95	67%	100	1.05	73
B	150	10000	130*	95	87%	76.92	0.81	94

Job 2 for Client Alpha

Accountant	Maximum Available Hours	Price	Hours	Target Hourly Rate	Productivity	Yield per Hour	Recovery	Client value Index**
A	150	10000	100	95	67%	100	1.05	73
B	150	18000	70	95	47%	257.14	2.71	94

Traditional P&L

	Accountant		Difference
	A	B	
Income	20000	28000	8000
Costs	same	Same	n/a
Profits			8000

Intangible balance sheet

	Accountant	
	A	B
Relationship capital index	73	94

*Not all hours are equal; the last 30 hours relate to adding value the customer really wants. These hours would not have been worked if looking at recovery rates. We see hours worked as costs when really they are, at least in part, investments.
**Impacting on customer trust, price sensitivity, and willingness to invest more with accountant.
Source: Paul Kennedy.

In Table 26.1, the additional work is reflected in a higher rate of productivity. If productivity was already very high, this could not have happened, which is why we should always leave capacity for first-class customers.

Also, the example in Figure 26.1 should not be confused with discounting, scope creep, or being cheap. If you have selected the right

Continued

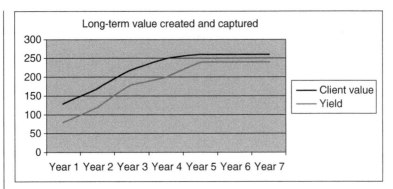

Client Alpha	Year 1	Year 2	Year 3	Year 4	Year 5	Year 6	Year 7
Client value	130	170	220	250	260	260	260
Yield	80	120	180	200	240	240	240

FIGURE 26.1 Impact of Investments of Time (quality rather than quantity) on Long-Term Value Captured
Source: Paul Kennedy.

sort of customer who recognises that he or she is paying a price premium in the first instance, then you have all the more reason to do whatever it takes to delight the customer and keep them for the long term. It amazes me that firms are prepared to budget for "lost time" to win new customers and then think the marketing and selling to that customer finishes once the lead becomes a customer.

Strategy/Positioning Is Everything

Delighting the customer must be our aim. In the long term, this is what will lead to profitability. Timesheets do not measure relationship capital or consider any long-term issues, however. They focus our attention on short-term profitability and force us to behave in a way that contradicts our long-term aim.

As I have illustrated, Figure 26.2 represents the variability of the value customers receive over time compared to the relatively invariable nature of a typical customer's prices. Area *x* represents the additional value the customer received, some of which could have been captured through higher prices. Area *y* represents the work from which the customer did not perceive any value and for which the customer resents paying (whether articulated or not).

A number of observations on this diagram.

Do customers tolerate *y* because of *x*? In other words, do customers console themselves that in the long-term they get value, if not from

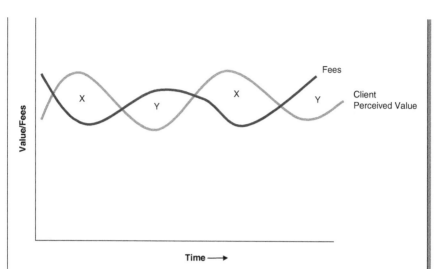

FIGURE 26.2 Hourly Billing Misaligns Value and Fees
Source: Paul Kennedy.

every job? Or does *y* make the client very cautious about using the accountant? Does it make him query the price (which in reality is value) of future work? Does *y* erode the trusted status of the accountant?

Also, we must not ignore the impact of pricing on the perception of value, effectively taking the perceived value line higher.

As I have also illustrated, Figure 26.3 assumes that the firm's pricing policy is aligned to the customer's perception of value received. By pricing to value in this way the firm and the customer can choose whether the work in area *y* is done or not. If the price at which the customer would value it is too low for the accountant to want to do it, other options can be explored. It may be that doing the work at a loss is better than doing it at a profit because of the impact on long-term relationship capital. By constantly ensuring the customer receives value—by understanding the customer's needs *whatever the cost*—the firm builds trust, which translates into premium pricing, value-added work, and a bigger share of the customer's wallet.

Once again, we cannot ignore the importance of good strategy. Good positioning, customer selection, and value-added product design all make the difference. If a firm takes the "whatever the cost" approach to a mixed bag of customers, some of whom are never going to value what their accountant does, then they are going to have problems. The fact is most accounting firms are overservicing some customers (those

Continued

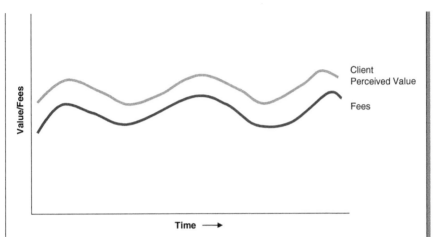

FIGURE 26.3 Value Pricing Aligns Value and Fees
Source: Paul Kennedy.

they should not have) and underservicing others. The cost of under-servicing our better customers is huge and the rewards of addressing this are similarly large. By focusing on short-term profitability, timesheets systemically prevent us from tapping this potential.

Mismanaging with Timesheets

Take a typical write-off report. For example, a write-off report tells you that you have worked 10 hours at an average hourly rate of £100 and your work in progress is £1,000. Let's say your fixed fee was £800. What does this mean? Does it mean that £200 was lost on this job? How would you use this information to manage the business? The answer in most cases is that the accountant would charge a higher price to this customer next time (maybe). But price has nothing to do with cost! If the customer would pay the higher price next time, shouldn't the higher price have been charged in the first place? Even firms that have made the intellectual leap of fixing prices in advance and believe they are not using timesheets to price still are. Only now they are making pricing adjustments on future contracts based on historical timesheet records. Accountants even use it for customer self-selection: "We will put our price up on this job so that we will make a profit (as defined by them) and if the customer won't pay then they can go somewhere else." In this way, the customer is given the choice, which is better than not offering the choice by after-the-event billing. Customers must always be given the choice; however, this form of marginal pricing is an abdication of our responsibility to choose our market in the first place. And maybe the price wasn't wrong. Maybe the problem was our cost. Or maybe the price wasn't wrong, the customer was. But timesheet data looks at the *effect* of cost, not the *cause*. To control cost at the source, you need to consider:

- Product/service selection and scope
- Target market selection and scope
- Customer selection criteria
- Internal process design
- Recruitment and education

What if the write off report shows time costs at £800 and the price at £1,000? How would this information be used? Is the inclination to pat ourselves on the back and say "well done"? But what if the price could be £3,000, not £1,000, based on customer perception of value? In short, timesheet feedback tends to punish professionals who think about long-term relationships and reward those who are failing to capture real value. Truly we are a profession intent on not making job losses and not making (too much) job profit. The argument given is often, "Yes, but how do you know whether you are making money on a job/customer?" Timesheet data doesn't tell you. The problem is that accountants think it does and this is why timesheets are so dangerous. The truth is that the typical job cost report does not measure profit (see "Not All Hours Are Equal," earlier) but focusing on this false information we make decisions that take us further away from our objectives of higher real profitability.

Firms spend huge amounts on maintaining this irrelevant and misleading information. Software, time taken to do time recording, write-offs, report production, and erroneous decision making are just a few of the costs. That said, the real costs are performance sub-optimisation, degraded team morale, and loss of strategic focus.

How to Run a Firm without Timesheets and Live Happily Ever After

The practical issues surrounding ditching timesheets include:

- How do we measure revenue, WIP, and prepaid income for the purposes of our monthly and annual practice accounts?
- How do we know how well our team members are performing?
- How do we plan and monitor jobs?

Continued

Our firm has designed its own systems for doing these things. Our system also gives us a forward view of value creation and pricing and allows us to plan capacity looking ahead, rather than looking backward with timesheets. The benefits of working this way include:

- We have become a value-obsessed firm.
- We price based on customer perceptions of value (we have no choice!).
- We fix all prices and arrange standing order payments for invoices (utilising Electronic Fund Transfer, credit card authorization, or other payment mechanisms).
- We no longer have damaging and time-consuming price disputes.
- We have prepaid income in excess of our work in progress.
- We have no credit control or administrative collections function.
- We have no timesheet management processes including:
  - No Timesheet completion and input
  - No write-off processes
  - No after date invoicing processes (we do all our invoices at the outset of the FPA)
- We have no timesheet software (we have our own value and job tracking software)
- We have happier team members, which makes it easier to attract better talent.
- We have happier, less price-resistant clients.

Fear of Change

Having moved from a timesheet/cost culture to a value culture I now wonder what stopped us from taking this step before. I think the answer, I now confess, was fear. Winning the intellectual argument may do it for some. But change is usually about emotion. To paraphrase Anthony Robbins, "You intellectually know chocolate cake is not good if you are trying to lose weight, but you will only stop eating it when you mix it with tuna casserole in your gut." Ron Baker has started a true revolution. The value-based professional firm has been born—a true renaissance. The marketplace has been destabilised, the dominant business model challenged. If you fear change, be afraid. Be very afraid.

PART V

Eight Steps to Implementing Value Pricing

The man who grasps principles can successfully select his own methods. The man who tries methods, ignoring principles, is sure to have trouble.

—Ralph Waldo Emerson

CHAPTER 27

The Eight Steps at a Glance

We have been disappointed before, swindled by promises that it seemed—and were—too good to be true. ... Our worries are our safe boundaries; over time we have learned to identify with our limits. Now, leery of trusting the promise of an oasis, we defend the merits of the desert.

—Marilyn Ferguson, *The Aquarian Conspiracy*, 1987

I offer no oasis in this section of the book—just hard work, and a more optimal pricing model along with the challenge to focus on what the customer is really purchasing from your firm: value.

The criticisms leveled against hourly billing in this book have centered on it being a suboptimal pricing strategy. Value pricing is a more optimal model as it comports to the economic and behavioral laws of customer value. Recall the word *optimal* to a management scientist or engineer means: *the best solution relative to a stated set of objectives, constraints, and assumptions.*

Since hours spent on a engagement do not relate to the value created, if the objective of the firm is to maximize—or even optimize—profits, then value pricing needs to become a core competency so firms are better able to align price commensurate with the value they create. Pricing is one of the most important, and convincing, forms of communication and positioning for firms. Price is also the start of a relationship with new customers, and cutting price is the equivalent of giving up respect, akin to being a supplicant to your customer rather than their equal.

Unfortunately, most firms' pricing mistakes are the result of underpricing, not overpricing. According to a 2003 McKinsey & Company study, 80–90 percent of poor pricing decisions were the result of underpricing. This is mostly because pricing authority and decisions are not vested in one area that can focus on increasing this skill over time.

Pricing is an *art*, not a science. This is especially true in a professional firm that has the ability to price one customer at a time at a very low marginal cost. This is an enormous advantage most other businesses are envious of, as they must set a few prices over thousands or millions of customers.

Yet pricing, like any art, is also a *skill*—the more you do it, the better you get. Pricing is also complicated, even complex, since all value is subjective. In that spirit, it is beneficial to understand the *science of complexity*.

Three Different Kinds of Problems

Professors Brenda Zimmerman of York University and Sholom Glouberman of the University of Toronto distinguish among three kinds of problems:

1. **Simple.** If, for example, you are baking a cake, there is a recipe to follow. After making a few cakes, this process can be mastered and successfully replicated.
2. **Complicated.** Sending a man to the moon is complicated because there is no recipe, there are uncertain factors, and unanticipated problems. These types of problems require coordination among many teams of experts. However, once you do it, it can be replicated relatively easily.
3. **Complex.** This is similar to raising a child. Unlike rockets, one child is not like another. Expertise may be necessary, but it is not sufficient. Complex problems have highly uncertain outcomes. Yet it is possible to raise a child well. (Gawande 2009: 48–49).

Pricing is both a complicated and a complex problem. There are no simple recipes. It requires judgment, discernment, wisdom, conjecture, and intuition, along with the willingness to experiment and take risks. It requires comfort with being approximately right, rather than striving to be precisely wrong. As Nobel Laureate economist Douglass North remarked in 1994, "The price you pay for precision is inability to deal with real-world questions."

Part V offers an eight-step checklist to implementing value pricing. But it does it in the spirit—and with the understanding—that pricing is complicated and complex, and no one single checklist could possibly cover all of the factors that are important in pricing for value. Nor are the eight steps meant to imply that the world is linear, where you can only move onto the next step after completing the previous one. The world is messy, but since we cannot deal with everything at once, we must break things down into understandable components.

My objective with this eight-step checklist is to inspire thought; to engage your brain, not shut it down with a mindless meandering through the steps. The checklist merely covers the basics, just as surgical teams ask people their names before beginning an operation. A checklist needs to be concise and precise, so your brain can focus on the higher-order job at hand that requires judgment. A checklist cannot price a customer—but a model can assist in this complex process.

Eight Steps to Implementing Value Pricing

The word *value* has a specific meaning in economics: "The maximum amount that a consumer would be willing to pay for an item." Therefore, value pricing can be defined as *the maximum amount a given customer is willing to pay for a particular service, before the work begins*. This is not to suggest we can capture one hundred percent of maximum value, but rather that we have the potential to access some of it utilizing strategic pricing.

By employing the following eight steps for every customer, your firm will be on its way to pricing on purpose (the chapter where each step is discussed is shown at the conclusion of each step):

1. **Conversation.** Have a conversation with your customer to determine their needs and wants on the engagement. This is your opportunity to *comprehend* and *communicate* the value you can add, establishing the scope of value and then the scope of the work to be performed. Sometimes a member from the value council attends this meeting, especially if the relationship partner is not a member of the value council, or is uncomfortable with pricing (Chapter 28).
2. **Pricing the customer: Questions for the value council.** The information gleaned from Step 1 is then presented to the value council, with the objective of pricing the customer, not the services. The value council goes through the "Questions to Ask before Establishing a Price" to assess a price driven by value, not hours and costs. The council conjectures three internal prices—Reservation, Hope For, and Pump Fist—based upon their assessment of the customer's subjective value and price sensitivity (Chapter 29).
3. **Developing and pricing options.** Firms have to get over the idea that there exists one optimal price. There are many optimal prices, depending on the customer's perception of value. Think of American Express's Green, Gold, Platinum, and Black cards. Each are varied in

price based upon the value and services they deliver. Firms should offer the customer various pricing options, not a take-it-or-leave-it single price. This allows customers to convince themselves of value, while revealing their individual price sensitivity, which the firm can use in future pricing decisions. It also helps the firm answer the question: Did we leave money on the table? In tough economic times, this tiered pricing model is an excellent opportunity for firms to offer less expensive options for struggling customers. When economic conditions improve, many customers will often upgrade to a more expensive option (Chapter 30).

4. **Presenting options to the customer.** Sometimes, a member of the value council would attend this presentation, especially if the partner in charge of the customer is not a member of the value council, or is uncomfortable discussing price. Handling price objections is discussed in this step (Chapter 31).

5. **Customer selection codified into the Fixed Price Agreement (FPA).** The option selected by the customer is then codified into an FPA, such as the sample provided. The firm can include as much detail as required as to the scope of work, customer responsibility to provide information, timelines for delivery of work, etc. (Chapter 32).

6. **Proper project management.** The firm would perform proper project management on the scope of work, detailing who will perform the work, timelines for delivery to the customer, and other planning details (Chapter 33).

7. **Scope creep, and change orders.** If the firm—or the customer— encounters *scope creep* while performing the work, the customer is informed, given the option to decide how to proceed, and a Change Order will be issued if the firm is to perform any additional work. This policy also applies to any new services the firm provides not specified in the FPA (Chapter 34).

8. **Pricing After Action Reviews.** The U.S. Army has a policy of doing After Action Reviews (AAR), which take place *after* every mission (see Chapter 25). After assisting many firms in implementing AARs, we are convinced it is a practice that would have numerous salutary effects for firms, especially as it relates to the roles of the CVO and value council, helping them evolve pricing into a core competency (Chapter 35).

Do not skip any of these steps; all are necessary for developing a core competency in pricing. If these eight steps are followed on every customer, is there any doubt your firm will begin its journey to pricing on purpose? Let us now examine each of these eight steps in more detail.

CHAPTER 28

Step One: Conversation

Language was invented to ask questions. Answers may be given by grunts and gestures, but questions must be spoken. Humanness came of age when man asked the first question. Social stagnation results not from a lack of answers but from the absence of the impulse to ask questions.

—Eric Hoffer, *Reflections on the Human Condition*, 2006a

After returning from the seminar I attended in June 1989, "Increasing CPA Firm Profitability" (as explained in the preface), I enthusiastically began implementing fixed-fee engagement letters (what I called them at the time). I selected a few good customers (based on my relationship with them, not necessarily the size of their revenues), and offered to enter into a fixed-fee arrangement with them. They were very receptive to the idea, as it allowed them to budget exactly their accounting and tax costs. I had no idea *why* I was doing this (e.g., provide a better experience, remove risk from the customer, etc.) so I did not engage in any price discrimination or charge a premium for the risk I was assuming.

Worse yet, I drafted these agreements in a vacuum, without any customer involvement. This was my biggest mistake, and it caused most of my early attempts at value pricing to fail dismally. I would meet with the customer, explain the concept, and say something to the effect of "I'll go back to my office and draft the agreement with what I believe your accounting and tax needs will be in the forthcoming year, price it out, and send it to you for approval"—treating it like a request for proposal rather than a collaborative undertaking. For every five agreements drafted in this manner, four were rejected. I did so many things wrong that recounting my errors would be of little benefit. I want to share what I have since learned is a more effective way to prepare the Fixed Price Agreement (FPA) *with* the customer's involvement.

The Conversation

Any firm that value prices will agree that the conversation with the customer is the most important step in the process. Skipping this step is similar to a contractor attempting to build a customer's dream home without any architectural plans. The better your firm *comprehends* the customer's value drivers, the more likely you will be able to *create* maximum value, *convince* the customer they must pay for that value, and *capture* that value with an effective strategy custom tailored to the customer.

The major benefit of an FPA meeting (or several, if that is what it takes) is that the focus is on providing exactly what customers want and expect. This is an opportunity for you and the customer to create a shared vision of the future, to analyze where the customer is at this point, and to develop the necessary action plan to move them to where they want to be—providing the highest value of transformations (see Chapter 8).

This focus is crucial, because if you do not discuss value with the customer, you will be forced into a discussion of hours, efforts, activities, deliverables, and costs, usually by procurement, in-house counsel, or some other professional buyer within the customer's organization. Remember that the customer is trying to *maximize* the value they receive while attempting to *minimize* your price. It is far more strategic to engage in a discussion over what the customer is trying to maximize rather than what they are trying to minimize. If all you focus on is price, it can never be low enough. If the customer says your price is too high, what they are really saying is, "I don't see the value in your offering." It is not a question of money; rather, it is lack of belief.

Naïve Listening

> When I am getting ready to reason with a man I spend one-third of my time thinking about myself and what I am going to say, and two-thirds thinking about him and what he is going to say.
>
> —Abraham Lincoln

An excellent story about the difference between talking and listening is illustrated by Calvin Coolidge, said to be one of the country's most laconic presidents. When his successor as governor of Massachusetts met him in the White House he is said to have asked the president how it was that he sometimes stayed in the governor's office until 11:00 P.M. working and meeting with his designated appointments. Yet his aides informed him that when Coolidge was governor he used to leave the office each day no later than 5:00 P.M. The successor asked Coolidge, "What's the difference?" Coolidge responded: "You talk back."

Questions require doubt, something educated professionals are not comfortable with. After all, we are paid to have the answers, not express doubt; and if you already know the answers there appears to be no need to gather any more information from the customer, chaining ourselves to the limits of our existing knowledge.

For this reason, during the conversation the customer should talk at least twice as much as the professional. This is incredibly difficult because it requires self-restraint. Naïve listening is difficult because you think much faster than people talk. While someone is talking, you are usually listening with one-half of your brain and formulating your answer with the other. Active listening is a skill that needs to be developed. Professionals are fairly good at this, at least when it comes to the technical requirements of their profession. But we can all get better through practice.

Talkers may *dominate* a conversation but the listener *controls* it. Also, taking notes conveys to the customer that what they are saying is important and that you care enough to record it. It also helps you remember exactly what they said. But most of all—and this is precisely why psychiatrists and psychologists take notes—is the person will provide much more detail. The more you know, the more value drivers you will be able to uncover, and the higher the prices you will command.

Ideally, you want to hold this conversation away from your office or the customer's, if possible. By getting out of your respective environments, you are less susceptible to distractions and interference. Avoid holding the meeting in the customer's office, where the customer will feel in control. Another disadvantage of meeting in the customer's office is that he or she may be less candid—the walls have ears—than in neutral territory.

You also want to deal with the *economic buyer*—the person who can hire and pay you. Many consultants believe you are wasting your time if you cannot get in front of this person, because most likely you will be dealing with gatekeepers who can only say "no," never "yes." This may take a few iterations, but the customer is sending a signal they are not serious if they deny you access to the economic buyer, and you may want to invest your resources in more profitable opportunities—such as servicing existing customers.

It is important to have someone present at this conversation who is a member of the firm's value council. This is especially true if the relationship partner is not an effective listener and/or questioner, or if he is not a member of the value council. Team selling is usually more effective, and you want someone skilled at comprehending and communicating value to the customer. Too many partners have personal relationships with their customers that can obfuscate the goal of capturing value.

Avoid the ever-present temptation to provide solutions to the customer's needs and wants. That is not the purpose of the conversation at this stage. You are on a *value quest* with the customer, not in a venue to begin providing solutions. Your role at this point is to ask questions and have the customer formulate—or at least articulate—a vision of the future. Before doctors *prescribe*, they must *diagnose*, which is the role you must assume at this stage in the conversation. Anything less is malpractice.

Focus on Wants, Not Needs

Think of listening as having no preconceived notions of what the customer really wants. Karl Albrecht, in his book *The Northbound Train*, offers this axiom that is true of professionals: "The longer you've been in business, the greater the probability you do not really understand what's going on in the minds of your customers" (Albrecht 1994: 138). Professionals are so skilled at solving problems that they begin to believe they know what the customer needs better than the customer does. And this may be true with respect to needs. A lawyer certainly knows how to draft a contract to avoid future problems, and a CPA knows how to structure a tax-free exchange to defer paying tax. However, the focus is on *needs*. In contrast, when you are having the conversation, with the goal of creating value, the focus should be more on the customer's *wants*. If you want to command premium prices, solving the customer's needs is not enough; you have to improve the customer's condition. Moving up the value curve is easier when people get what they want rather than what they need.

How you sell is a free sample of how you *solve*, according to Mahan Khalsa in *Let's Get Real or Let's Not Play*. Active listening and effective questioning are two of the most important skills your firm can possess at this step in implementing value pricing.

Starting the Conversation

This is one of the most effective statements to utilize somewhere near the beginning of the conversation, regardless of whether you are meeting with a new or old customer:

Mr. Customer, we will only undertake this engagement if we can agree, to our mutual satisfaction, that the value we are creating is at least three (to ten) times the price we are charging you. Is that acceptable?

Do not get sidetracked by the multiple of three to ten, as it will obviously vary from customer to customer. In fact, sometimes you do not need to state a multiple, rather just state that the value needs to exceed the price.

This establishes the right tone near the beginning of the conversation that yours is a firm obsessed with value, along with the willingness to demonstrate the economic impact that your services can have for the customer—how it will improve the customer's life. It also subtly suggests that you will not enter into relationships that do not add value for both parties—the exact tone you want to set, as both sides to a transaction must profit if it is to be sustainable.

The distinction between *needs* and *wants* is important here, as the latter are almost always higher on the value curve than the former. My VeraSage colleague Daryl Golemb, CPA, begins all conversations by leading with customer wants because he says it is much easier to build a unique value proposition upon them.

Another important distinction should be made between *tangible* and *intangible* value. While *all* value is subjective, some value drivers can be quantified, which is what we mean by tangible value. This can include the size of the tax dispute, court case, risk exposure, size of the deal, economic impact on sales, profits, and so on. Certainly the customer and the firm need to quantify as many factors of tangible value that they can jointly uncover. This uncovering every rock of value is more likely to take place by using the opening statement above, as the focus will then be on value, not inputs, deliverables, costs, or hours, but actual results. Some examples of tangible value include:

- Increasing the customer's revenue, growth rate, profit, return on investment (ROI), market share, customer or team member loyalty, efficiency, effectiveness, cash flow
- Reducing the customer's expense, risk, turnover, bureaucracy
- Improving customer's process, systems, technology, information, technical quality

Yet many firms forget to include the *intangible* drivers of value—those characteristics that cannot be exactly quantified but are just as important nonetheless. The following is just a small sampling of the intangible factors a professional firm offers its customers:

- Specialist expertise or knowledge
- Unique social capital of the firm
- Brand and/or reputation of the firm
- Specialized proprietary technology not possessed by competitors

- Opportunity to achieve a unique result given time, circumstances, and specialized knowledge
- Reducing risk to the customer through business model innovations— offering fixed prices, payment terms, service and price guarantees, risk-sharing pricing strategies
- Minimizing risk to the customer on the engagement itself
- Providing education to the customer
- Assisting the customer in mitigating future risk
- Knowledge elicitation—transferring specialized knowledge to the customer so they can develop their own in the future
- Decrease conflict, complaints, time, or effort
- Increase morale, image, customer service, or reputation,
- Nature of the relationship with the firm, including comfort, convenience, and peace of mind
- Developing customer strategy, business model innovation, product or service design, Total Quality Service

These are in no way meant to be exhaustive lists. In fact, your firm's value council should develop its own list of ways it adds tangible and intangible value. You also need to factor in the future annuity of this value, as it will pay dividends over time. A discounted cash flow approach is appropriate for such calculations. In any event, both types of value need to be factored into your pricing; otherwise you are not capturing a fair share of the value you are creating for the customer.

Conversations Lower Asymmetrical Information and Adverse Selection

Customers will try to conceal from you how much they value your services and what they are willing to pay for them. This is especially true of professional buyers, such as procurement. Economists refer to *asymmetrical information as information concerning a transaction that is unequally shared between the parties to the transaction.*

Economists and actuaries also use the term *adverse selection*—the problem that arises when people know more about their own risk characteristics than others do (Landsburg 2002: 325). If you want to purchase maternity coverage, chances are an insurance company will not be willing to sell it to you. The person in the market for insurance is usually the worst type of risk, which is why insurance companies attempt to lower asymmetrical information and adverse selection risk by requiring medical checkups, fire inspections, higher deductibles, larger co-payments, and so forth.

The conversation provides a venue for a meeting of the minds to take place between the customer and professional when it comes to designing and valuing a firm's services. This is a tremendous opportunity to discover exactly what a customer values. Obviously, trust and transparency will lower asymmetrical information and adverse selection, which is the result of artful questioning.

Questions You Should Ask the Customer

If all patients were the same, medicine would be a science, not an art.

—Sir William Osler, one of the fathers of modern medicine

Something similar to Osler's statement can be said of questioning—it is an art and skill, not a science. Each customer is unique, and so must be your approach to questions. Just as with naïve listening, one should not be afraid to take the Lt. Columbo approach and ask simple questions. As English mathematician and philosopher Alfred North Whitehead wrote, "The 'silly question' is the first intimation of some totally new development."

Peter Drucker also taught an effective approach to assignments: approach the problem with your ignorance:

I never ask these questions or approach these assignments based on my knowledge and experience in these industries. It is exactly the opposite. I do not use my knowledge and experience at all. I bring my ignorance to the situation. Ignorance is the most important component for helping others to solve any problem in any industry (Cohen 2008: 58–59).

There are questions you should ask every customer to lower the level of asymmetrical information and assist you in determining just where on the value curve your customer is located. The more information you seek from customers, the better equipped you will be to assess their price sensitivity. Always ask open-ended questions to engage the customer in discussing goals, aspirations, fears, desires, and dreams of the future. This has a tremendous psychological impact, because most people's favorite topic is themselves. Start with the following questions:

- What do you expect from us?
- What is your business model? How do you make profit?
- What are your company's critical success factors and Key Predictive Indicators (KPIs)

- How will the services we provide add value to *your* customers?
- Which of our firm's offerings is of the highest value to you?
- Who is the next best alternative (competitor) to our firm?
- What characteristics do they have that we do not, and vice versa?
- What is your current pain?
- What keeps you awake at night?
- How do you see us helping you address these challenges and opportunities?
- What growth plans do you have?
- If price were not an issue, what role would you want us to play in your business?
- Do you expect capital needs? New financing?
- Do you anticipate any mergers, purchases, divestitures, recapitalizations, or reorganizations in the near future?
- We know you are investing in Total Quality Service, as are we. What are the service standards you would like for us to provide you?
- How important is our service and price guarantee to you?
- How important is rapid response on questions? What do you consider rapid response?
- Why are you changing firms? What did you not like about your former firm that you do not want us to repeat?*
- How did you enjoy working with your former firm?**
- Do you envision any other changes in your needs?
- Are you concerned about any of your asset, liability, or income statement accounts to which we should pay particularly close attention?
- If we were to attend certain of your internal management meetings as observers, would you be comfortable with that?
- How do you suggest we best learn about your business so we can relate your operations to the financial information and so we can be more proactive in helping you maximize your business success?
- May our associates tour your facilities?
- What trade journals do you read? What seminars and trade shows do you regularly attend? Would it be possible for us to attend these with you?
- What will the success of this engagement look like?
- What is your budget for this type of service?

*Do not denigrate the predecessor firm. First, this insults the customer and reminds the customer of a poor decision. Second, it diminishes respect and confidence in the profession as a whole.

**Even though the customer is changing firms, almost certainly the customer liked some characteristics of the predecessor. Find out what these were and exceed them. For instance, if they said the prior firm always returned phone calls within one day, return them within four hours.

For tangible value that can be measured and to move from mere evidence to economic impact, here are five questions suggested by Mahan Khalsa:

1. How do you measure it?
2. What is it now?
3. What would you like it to be?
4. What's the value of the difference?
5. What's the value of the difference over time? (Khalsa 1999: 81)

If the value is intangible, you can use the above questions and instead of financial measures, have the customer *qualify* the value on a scale of 1–10. This will help you prioritize what is really valuable to the customer.

Ordinal Value, Not Cardinal Value

The above questions also enable you to prioritize the customer's goals. This is done using an *ordinal* ranking, rather than a *cardinal* ranking. A cardinal ranking can be added, subtracted, multiplied, or divided. An ordinal ranking represents a position on a list of options, the difference, say, between being "fifth" and the number five. You can add five and five, but you cannot add "being fifth" to anything meaningfully. The British economist Lord Lionel Robbins explained it this way: "You can usually tell whether you love one person more than another, but you can't measure 'how much' in definable units."

This ordinal ranking is particularly important when dealing with intangible value, as it is simply a fact that customers will put different rankings of value on different characteristics.

Discussing Risk with the Customer

Recall from Chapter 7, any purchase entails risk. Services are relatively riskier than products, especially credence services discussed in Chapter 7 as well. If you buy a defective toaster, you take it back and get a new one. But if your veterinarian does more harm than good to your pet, there is not much you can do. This is one reason why there is greater loyalty to service providers than to product manufacturers. Some firms have begun to include the seven types of customer risk explained in Chapter 7 in their conversations, showcasing how their firm reduces these risks to the customer. This is always an excellent strategy, since risk to the customer and price premium to the firm is like a teeter-totter: The lower you can reduce risk to the customer, the more value you are creating, and hence the higher prices you can charge.

Summary and Conclusions

It is important to remember that customers are not necessarily trying to minimize their professional's price; what they are attempting to accomplish is maximizing the net value they receive from those costs. And net value is measured by taking the gross value of the services—both tangible and intangible—less its price. By engaging the customer in a conversation, and getting ego investment, you are offering a form of "participatory pricing" that in today's market customers expect. They can decide to fly first class or coach, shop at a department store or a discount store, and even place bids for travel at the price they desire through online services such as priceline.com. Customers make these and myriad other decisions in which they have total control over the price/value equation.

And they want to make that price/value comparison *before* they purchase, not during or after as with hourly billing. You cannot manage value retroactively, which is why the firm always wants to price when it possesses the leverage—that is, before the services have been delivered. A service *needed* is always worth more than a service *delivered*.

Now that you have learned the value drivers of the customer, it is time to take all of this reconnaissance back to the firm's value council and let it begin pricing the customer, the subject of the next step, and our next chapter.

CHAPTER 29

Step Two: Pricing the Customer: Questions for the Value Council

You can't sell your way out of unprofitable business. No business is better than bad business. More businesses fail chasing sales, rather than profit.

—Gary Sutton, *Corporate Canaries*, 2005

When was the last time you worried that your firm's prices were too low? When was the last time your competitors complained that your prices were too high? One of the vital roles of the value council is to experiment with different types of pricing while understanding that if it is going to err, it is almost always more advantageous to err with higher prices than lower ones. After all, if you are going to go bankrupt, it is much easier to get there from overpricing rather than underpricing.

It is far easier to establish a bad price than a good one. What constitutes a good price?

- Proper customer selection—there is no right way to value price the *wrong* customer.
- Understanding the customer's value drivers—both the tangible (measurable) and intangible (immeasurable)—learned in Step 1, Chapter 28.
- A good price is always established when the firm maintains the price leverage—before the work begins (Chapter 7).
- The firm must know the cost to serve *before* it begins the work, not after. Knowing costs is useless if your customer does not value the services (Chapter 19).
- Knowing what attributes of your value proposition your customer is willing to pay for—to assist you in developing options.

- Not confusing *mutual* gain (discussed in Chapter 3) with *equal* gain. Both parties must profit, but it does not always have to be in equal proportions.
- Realizing that the sooner a firm quotes a price, the lower it will be. The value council is a deliberate strategy to slow down the process of pricing to focus on value creation.
- Not allowing your dumbest competitors to set your price—your competition does not care about you or your customers.
- Appreciating that price competition is only good for weak competitors; it is all they have to differentiate themselves.
- Knowing that lowering prices requires no skill, unlike adding more value, offering Total Quality Service, a service guarantee, and so on.
- A relentless focus on the customer, not the firm's competition. Focusing on competition leads only to mediocrity and price wars.
- Comprehending that price is not the only negotiable aspect of a firm's offering—service, access, start date, turnaround time, risk, payment terms, talent, and a myriad of other factors are more strategic to negotiate.
- The firm is responsible for setting prices, not its customers. Customers are, no doubt, the ultimate arbiters of value, but firms are responsible for their pricing strategies.
- Only the firm cuts its prices—not its competition, or its customers. This is ballistic podiatry.
- Price is usually more important in the mind of the seller than the buyer.
- A good price is one that is established for the customer, not the service.

Questions to Ask before Establishing a Price

The following are questions the value council needs to answer before establishing the firm's price and options for any individual customer. The relationship partner and team responsible for serving the customer can be involved at this stage because they have much tacit knowledge about the customer that will be useful. These are internal questions only, though you may find some of them useful to ask the customer. However, this process is done *after* the conversation with the customer.

The objective of all of these questions is to determine the price sensitivity of the customer. A more price-sensitive customer requires a more competitive price as opposed to one who is higher on the value curve. Providing options is an optimal strategy to self-identify the more price sensitive customer, allowing the firm to remove value in exchange for offering a lower price. You will be able to see why having an in-depth conversation, from Step 1, is so critical to answering all of these questions.

Almost all of these questions look outside the firm to the customer, where value is created, rather than an internal focus on costs, efforts, hours, and so on.

Once again, this is not an exhaustive, or definitive, list. You will need to edit it for your own professional sector, experience, and customer strategies. Appendixes C through F do provide additional guidance for advertising, CPA, IT, and law firms, respectively, adding more targeted questions that are relevant to each sector. The list below, though, is a good starting point for all firms.

- What is the customer's cost of not solving this problem in dollars?
- What is the economic benefit to the customer if they solve this problem?
- How do we help the customer grow their business and be more profitable?
- How do we help make their business more valuable?
- How do we help the customer achieve their preferred vision of the future?
- How do we remove surprises for the customer?
- If the services entail risk, what is the worst that can happen if the customer does not take this risk? What is the worst that can happen if they do take this risk? Is this intolerable? What is the upside of taking this risk? Is there anything we can do to hedge the downside of this risk for the customer?
- Who on the organizational chart are we dealing with?
- Who referred this customer to us? Why were they referred?
- What is the nature of the relationship with the referral source?
- What is the timeline on the customer's decision to select a firm?
- Do they have any time-sensitive deadlines for the completion of this work? Why do they need it now and not in six months?
- Who's paying for the service? Are they spending other people's money? (Chapter 7, the four categories of spending.)
- Do we have any serious competitors competing for this work? How are we more valuable then them, justifying a higher price?
- What price information do we have about these competitors (bids, RFPs, etc.)? Have there been any recent changes in their firm that might cause them to price differently?
- Has the customer engaged another firm to do similar work?
- Who was the prior firm? Why are they changing?
- How profitable is the organization? How long has it been in business?
- How sophisticated is the customer with respect to our services?
- If the business is new, who is the banker, attorney, CPA, ad agency, and the like?

- If the customer did not select us, what is the price they are likely to pay to the next best alternative firm?
- Are the services we are providing wants or needs?
- What is the ratio of tangible (measurable) to intangible (immeasurable) value we are creating?
- What is the risk to the firm in dealing with this customer? (Actuary axiom: There's no such thing as bad risks, just bad premiums.)
- What is that risk over time? (Drafting a 15-year lease exposes the firm for 15 years.)
- Does this firm add to the firm's intellectual capital (IC)—human, structural, or social—or are we simply using existing skills?
- What is the profit to the firm's IC, not just its accounting profit?
- Does this customer open up a new niche or market segment for the firm?
- Is this a "boomerang customer"? (Usually an indicator that your prices are too low if customers return after trying the competition.)
- Do we like this customer? Is it a business we are interested in?
- What is the state of their restrooms?
- On what basis will we structure various pricing options for this customer—that is, which attributes do they value (service, access, priority access, quick start/turnaround times, specific talent assigned to their engagement, etc.)?
- Where is the customer on the value curve (Chapter 10)?
- Where are the customer's services on the Smile Curve (Chapter 10)?
- Which category is the customer in on the following price sensitivity diagram (Figure 29.1, page 249).

Price buyers are simply looking for the lowest price, with little concern for marginal value and low firm loyalty. They are a distinct minority in almost every category, usually comprising not more than 5 to 15 percent of professional firm customers. These customers should be allotted only so much capacity, and be offered a strip-down version of your offering. Curtailing services and/or features is another effective method of reducing value to these customers, thereby forcing them to make a price/value trade-off. Apple's cheapest iPod, the Shuffle, will only play songs randomly, not the first choice of the user. Look for ways to *remove* value from your core offering. Also, it may be possible to eliminate characteristics that reduce the firm's cost to serve these customers, such as self-service, pick-up rather than delivery, and other value-added offerings acknowledged and appreciated by other customer segments. Keep in mind that you deliberately want to make your lower-value offerings much less attractive, as they are only for the most price-sensitive—and least loyal—customers.

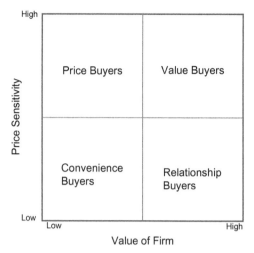

FIGURE 29.1 Customer Segmentation by Price Sensitivity
Source: Adapted from Nagle and Holden 2002: 106.

Value buyers are willing to pay more for marginal value and tend to be loyal to various brands or firms they perceive as offering more value for the same dollar, but only after doing extensive homework on competing offerings. This type of buyer may show a preference for, and be willing to pay more for, a particular firm, but remain ever vigilant that the marginal benefits must exceed the marginal cost. In planning a vacation, these buyers will study all of the alternatives and carefully weigh each trade-off. If they spot a special targeted offer, even if a nonpreferred brand, they are more likely to accept it. If a company offers a loyalty program, these buyers would usually be in the first or second tiers, because they will defect if more valuable offers are presented.

Convenience buyers are not very loyal but are more willing to pay a higher price for exactly what they want, when they want it. Time tends to be of the essence, since the offering is either urgently needed (your automatic garage door breaks over the weekend, or you need a locksmith) or too small an expenditure to justify high search costs. 7-11 thrives on these types of buyers. Since convenience buyers do not put much value in any one particular company, they are not usually candidates for loyalty programs, but are a profitable segment.

Relationship buyers place a high value on firm brand and are willing to pay for perceived value, as well as incremental value offerings. These buyers are usually in the top tier of any loyalty program and show strong loyalty, valuing the intangible services as well as the tangible offerings. Top-tier frequent flyers appreciate greatly how the airlines provide special check-in and security lines, let them board first, tag their luggage so it comes up first, guarantee a seat on flights even with short notice, provide airport lounges with business centers, and offer myriad other benefits for being loyal to one carrier.

Factors of Price Sensitivity

Analyzing price sensitivity is certainly an important task for any firm that wants to capture the value it receives from its offering. Taking into account the nine factors of price sensitivity, as detailed in Chapter 11, is a necessary exercise to accurately assess each customer's price sensitivity (the tenth factor, the Inventory Effect, is being excluded here, as services generally cannot be inventoried). Nagle and Holden offer a set of questions that need to be answered for each of the factors in preparing the analysis of price sensitivity.

1. Perceived Substitutes Effect
   - What alternatives is the customer typically aware of when making a purchase?
   - To what extent is the customer aware of the prices of those substitutes?
   - To what extent can the customer's price expectations be influenced by the positioning of one firm relative to particular alternatives, or by the alternatives offered them?
2. Unique Value Effect
   - Does the service have any unique (tangible or intangible) attributes that differentiate it from competing services?
   - What attributes does the customer believe are important when choosing a firm?
   - How much does the customer value unique, differentiating attributes?
   - How can we increase the perceived importance of differentiating attributes and/or reduce the importance of those offered by the competition?
3. Switching Cost Effect
   - To what extent has the customer already made investments (both monetary and psychological) in dealing with one firm that they would need to incur again if they switched?
   - For how long is the customer locked in by those expenditures?
4. Difficult Comparison Effect
   - How difficult is it for the customer to compare the offers of different firms? (Be sure to account for the Internet in your answer.)

- Can the attributes of a service be determined by observation, or must the product be purchased and consumed to learn what it offers— is it a search, experience, or credence service, as discussed in Chapter 7)?
- Is the service highly complex, requiring costly specialists to evaluate its differentiating attributes?
- Are the prices of different firms easily comparable, or are they stated for different value propositions that make comparisons difficult?

5. Price-Quality Effect
   - Is a prestige image an important attribute of the service?
   - Is the service enhanced in value when its price excludes some customers?
   - Is the service of unknown quality and are there few reliable cues for ascertaining quality before purchase?

6. Expenditure Effect
   - How significant are the customer's expenditures for the service in absolute dollar terms (for business buyers) and as a portion of income (for end consumers)?

7. End-Benefit Effect
   - What end-benefits is the customer seeking from the service?
   - How price sensitive is the customer to the cost of the end-benefit?
   - What portion of the end-benefit does the price of the service account for?
   - To what extent can the service be repositioned in the customer's mind as related to an end-benefit for which the customer is less price sensitive or which has a larger total budget?

8. Shared-Cost Effect
   - Is the customer paying the full price of the service?
   - If not, what portion of the price is the customer paying?

9. Fairness Effect
   - How does the service's current price compare with prices the customer has paid in the past for services in this category?
   - What does the customer expect to pay for similar services in similar purchase contexts?
   - Is the service seen as necessary to maintain a previously enjoyed standard of living, or is it purchased to gain something more out of life? (Nagel and Holden 2002: 111–14).

Pricing Questions

Once the above questions have been answered, the value council is now ready to begin assigning prices to the firm's value offerings. It is important to remember that the firm can price its services not only *above* the range the customer is willing to pay, but also *below* that range. We simply must get over the false idea that there is one optimal price for a customer. There is a *range* of optimal prices, commensurate with the value being created. Dutch psychologist Peter van Westendorp developed the van Westendorp Price Sensitivity Meter (PSM) by posing five questions, to which I have added two more:

1. At what price would this service be so expensive the customer would not consider buying it?
2. At what price would the service be expensive, but the customer would still buy it?
3. At what price would the service be perceived as inexpensive?
4. At what price does the service become so inexpensive the customer would question its value?
5. What price would be the most acceptable price to pay?
6. What costs can we afford to invest in at the target price and still earn an acceptable profit? (Price-led costing, as described in Chapter 19.)
7. At what price would the firm walk away from this customer (Reservation price)? What is the firm's Hope For price? Pump Fist price?

These questions are essential to go through for each customer. The last one is particularly important, as it establishes the Reservation price—the price at which the firm would rather decline the customer than reduce. Nothing raises your pricing self-respect like being willing to walk away from work. Here is the logic, and consequences, of establishing these three prices:

1. *Reservation price*—a price that will provide a *normal* profit to the firm relative to the risk it is assuming, and one you will not go one nickel below.
2. *Hope For price*—a price that will return a *supernormal* profit to the firm relative to the risk it is assuming, and a price you should receive more often than not.
3. *Pump Fist price*—a price that will return a *windfall* profit to the firm relative to the risk it is assuming. If a firm never quotes Pump Fist prices, it will never get them.

Think of the above three prices as a portfolio, much like a financial advisor would have you invest in a diversified array of investments. Some of your customers should be relatively risk-free, normal-profit engagements, while others should throw off supernormal and windfall profits. The objective is to monitor your pricing to ensure you are receiving a range of prices across these three categories. A firm will not be able to increase its profitability by working only with customers who pay Reservation prices. Establishing a Reservation price, and sticking to it, takes courage; but your firm's pricing integrity is on the line, which is far more important than any one customer because it affects what you can charge *all* of your customers.

Your portfolio of customers—like your investment portfolio—needs to have some higher-risk engagements to earn above-average profits. Remember: profits are derived from risk. Complacency and a world of *riskless risk* is not an option. In fact, a good KPI for the value council to track is what percentage of the firm's customers are in each of the above three price categories.

To illustrate how the above questions will assist the value council, allow me to tell a story from my days as a practicing CPA. One day I got a call from a bookkeeper who worked with one of my first-class customers and who had been a good referral source over the years. She had recently picked up a new customer, a limited liability corporation (LLC), that was in its first half-year of operations, had a fiscal year-end, and had a tax return due in approximately six weeks. The LLC was 25 percent owned by a company located in France and 75 percent owned by a local woman. The company needed a tax return, and the French company's CPA firm— one of the then Big Five—had quoted a price that the bookkeeper was asked to see if she could improve upon.

When the bookkeeper called, my mind raced to the above questions. First, this was a warm referral source, who knows me quite well, and therefore I am probably presold to the owner, as my abilities and service level had already been testified to by the trusted bookkeeper. Also, I would be dealing with the CEO of the company. The higher on the organizational chart the employee you are dealing with is, the less price sensitive that employee tends to be. A CEO does not have time to interview multiple CPAs, so if you are at that level, your chances are fairly good of landing the customer. A CEO also has other concerns, such as business growth, strategy, profitability, and adding value, of which a CFO, or controller, might not be aware.

Also, the company had an impending deadline. In six weeks the company had to file its first tax return. The owner would be traveling to France in two weeks to stay for another three weeks. Therefore, she was ready to make a decision immediately. The French company had infused some working capital into the company, which was a consideration because when spending someone else's money you are less price sensitive (see the four categories of spending from Chapter 7).

The bookkeeper told me that the then Big Five firm quoted $5,400 and the owner thought that "was a little steep." This was a new business and not very profitable, so I had to come in at less than $5,400. In this case, the prior CPA was not an issue (there was no prior CPA), but that is always a consideration in your prequalifying routine. Checking references is also important, but since this came from a person I knew and trusted I did not do the usual level of due diligence.

The owner was a first-time business owner, so she was not a sophisticated buyer of CPA services. Part of my job would consist of educating her about what a CPA can offer and communicating the value of these services. This particular customer would add to my firm's skills because LLCs were relatively new at the time, and this was a customer with some interesting issues that needed to be explored.

The bookkeeper sent me the financial statements, which consisted of a one-page balance sheet and a one-page income statement (this was a new business, only in operation for six months). Looking at the financials, I knew the tax return would take me or my team no longer than four hours (this is what is meant by relying on expertise, judgment, experience, and wisdom, not prior timesheets that most firms never look at anyway). At a theoretical "standard hourly rate" of $200, I would quote this job at $800.

I recalled a colleague had recently told me that, in a situation that was numerically similar to mine, he felt that the customer was being "ripped off" at $5,400, and he quoted the job at $1,000. He did not get it. He told me he learned a valuable lesson that day: Low prices command low respect. In the mind of the customer, his service could not be of equal quality at less than one-fifth the price. If all customers have is price to judge a service on, they will naturally assume that high price equals higher quality and better service.

Based on my answers to the above questions, I put together an FPA priced at $3,500 (my Hope For price), and the owner signed it and sent it back immediately. And I left money on the table! Realistically, I could have priced it at $4,000 and perhaps as high as $4,500 (my Pump Fist price). I simply did not have the confidence and courage at the time. Fortunately, this changes; over time, your courage increases dramatically. Nevertheless, with hourly billing I would have left $2,700 on the table. This is what is meant by pricing the customer and turning pricing into the art that it is, rather than an administrative task involving hours times rate.

How much would I have to increase "efficiency" to garner an additional $2,700 in bottom-line profit? What possible benefit will completing timesheets add to this engagement? Will they help me price better in the future?

In fact, this is how we know when a value council truly understands value pricing: when it stops fretting over the question "Did we make money on this engagement?" and instead worries incessantly over the question "How much money did we leave on the table?" This is a state of mind that is very difficult to understand until you have engaged in a few pricing decisions on your own. But the epiphany will happen, and when it does, you have crossed a meaningful threshold from billing hours to pricing on value.

You may (fairly) be asking: "What would happen if she goes to another CPA next year and gets the job for $1,000"? The answer is: "You do not let her defect to another CPA next year." You meet with her, educate her, and offer her more services, thereby increasing her switching costs. The value of any service is what someone is willing to pay for it. A CPA can command $3,500 for a tax return some competitors may be willing to perform for $1,000—if the CPA provides $2,500 more value through Total Quality Service, service and price guarantees, no surprise fixed prices, payment terms, and unlimited access, all of which were bundled into this customer's FPA.

What I did not do back then on this engagement was offer the customer various options. This is the next level in making pricing a core competency in your firm. We at VeraSage Institute have seen this strategy work so well—across all professional sectors—it is worthy of its own step in the pricing process and is the subject of our next chapter.

CHAPTER 30

Step Three: Developing and Pricing Options

> It cannot be too strongly emphasized that the deciding factor in price setting is the price which the consumer is willing, or can be induced, to pay.
>
> —R. Edwards, *Economica*, 1945

One of the most customer-centric strategies your firm can deploy is to offer an array of options to your customers. It is very "outer-directed," rather than just offering a one-size-fits-all, take-it or leave-it option. Customers prefer options, especially in today's world where they face a plethora of choices regarding who, when, what, and how to patronize a business. Contemplate these examples:

- Universal Studios Theme Park's standard admission price is $49, but for $99 you can get a "Front of the Line Pass" and for $129 a "VIP Experience," giving guests behind-the-scenes access.
- When the final book in the Harry Potter series was released, the publisher offered the regular version for $34.99 and the deluxe version for $65. They were ranked number one and two, respectively, on Amazon and Barnes and Noble Web sites.
- Tourists in New York can avoid the long lines to get to the observation deck of the Empire State Building for double the regular admission price, guaranteed to take no longer than 20 minutes.
- Guests can purchase a one-day pass to Walt Disney World, or add additional days for a progressively lesser price, down to the fifth day costing only a marginal $3—illustrating the economist's law of diminishing marginal utility.

The Psychology of Price

In addition to the benefits a firm offers its customers by utilizing options, there is strong empirical evidence—from both the rational and behavioral schools of economics—that offering customers different options can often result in them purchasing more, at a higher price, than merely offering one take-it-or-leave-it option. This simply recognizes that different customers have different value perceptions, and firms that engage in price searching are deploying a more optimal pricing model.

In his book *Predictably Irrational*, behavioral economist Dan Ariely illustrates the utility of offering options by illustrating *The Economist* magazine's offerings. First, he presented the following two options to 100 students at MIT's Sloan School of Management:

1. Economist.com subscription $59: One-year subscription to Economist. com, including access to all articles from *The Economist* since 1997— 68 students chose this option.
2. Print and web subscriptions $125: One-year subscription to the print edition of *The Economist* and online access to all articles from *The Economist* since 1997—32 students.

Now compare those results to the actual ad that *The Economist* offered, which contained *three* options, not two:

1. Economist.com subscription $59: One-year subscription to Economist. com, including access to all articles from *The Economist* since 1997—16 students chose this option.
2. Print subscription $125: One-year subscription to the print edition of *The Economist*—0 students.
3. Print and web subscriptions $125: One-year subscription to the print edition of *The Economist* and online access to all articles from *The Economist* since 1997—84 students (Ariely 2008: 5–6).

Ariely concludes that there is nothing *rational* about this change in choices. The mere presence of an option that was not desired affected behavior, leading to a potential 42.8 percent increase in incremental revenue for *The Economist*, or $3,432. You simply will not get that level of return by improving efficiency.

Offering pricing options creates the *anchoring effect*, whereby the customer is now comparing prices to your highest offering. This is why Victoria's Secret offers a diamond-ornamented bra for $6.5 million that no one probably ever bought; Prada stores always display one incredibly high-priced article that acts as an anchor for all the other products; and even

TABLE 30.1 Anchoring Effect

Microwave Oven Model	Group one	Group Two
Panasonic II, $199.99, sale price 10% off	-0-	13
Panasonic I, $179.99; sale price 35% off	43	60
Emerson, $109.99; sale price 35% off	57	27

Source: Itamar Simonson, and Amos Tversky, "Choice in Context: Tradeoff Contrast and Extremeness Aversion,"*Journal of Marketing Research* 29 (August 1992), 281–295.

some restaurants offer the "free" 72-ounce steak challenge. All of these high-priced items act as an anchor, even if the customer never buys them—throwing a halo effect over the other offerings, allowing for prices to be higher.

A similar experiment to the one Dan Ariely conducted was carried out for microwave ovens, with researchers asking half of research subjects to select between two models (Group One), while the other half were asked to select between three models (Group Two). The results are shown in Table 30.1.

The first lesson from the above is if you do not offer a high-end premium package, how could your customers ever select one? Second, list your most expensive option first. The third lesson is that by offering three options, you almost always sell more of the middle option, and less of the cheapest offering. Williams-Sonoma offered a fancy bread maker for $279, then added a higher-end model for $429. This model was a failure, but sales of the $279 model doubled. Had they offered a third choice, the economics probably would have been even better. We have seen some firms offer four and even five levels of service, nudging their customers subtly up the value curve into higher-priced options. Once again this confirms what most pricing experts know: People are not just price sensitive; they are value conscious.

Seven Generic Customer Segmentation Strategies

According to Tom Nagle and Reed Holden in their book *The Strategy and Tactics of Pricing*, there are seven effective segmentation strategies to specifically identify different types of customers in order to capture the consumer surplus:

1. *Buyer identification.* Senior discounts, children's prices, college students, nonprofits, and coupons are all examples of ways to identify different buyers with different price sensitivities.

2. *Purchase location.* Dentists, opticians, and other professionals sometimes maintain separate offices, in different parts of the same city, or
   in different cities, which charge different prices based upon the economic and demographic makeup of each. With the increasing use of
   the Internet to make purchases, being able to segment by location is
   becoming more difficult, but is still feasible.

3. *Time of purchase.* Theaters offering midday matinees, restaurants
   charging cheaper prices for lunch than dinner, and cellular and utility
   companies offering pricing based on peak and off-peak times are all
   examples of segmenting by time of purchase.

4. *Purchase quantity.* Quantity discounts are usually based on volume,
   order size, step discounts, or two-part prices. Customers who buy in
   large volumes tend to be more price sensitive but less costly to service,
   and they have more incentive to shop for a cheaper price. Two-part
   pricing involves two separate charges to consume a single product.
   Night clubs charge a cover at the door as well as for drinks and
   food.

5. *Product design.* Offering different versions of a product or service is
   a very effective way to segment customers, either by adding more
   features, or taking some away. Pricers call low-end products a *flanking
   product*, a signal to competitors not to start a price war in the higher-
   value segment.

6. *Product bundling.* Restaurants bundle food on the dinner menu as
   opposed to à la carte, usually at cheaper prices. IBM and Hewlett-
   Packard bundle hardware, software, and consulting services to increase
   the value of their respective offerings.

7. *Tie-ins and metering.* Razor blade manufacturers design unique razors
   requiring customers to purchase its blades for refill, and a certain toner
   must be used on various leased copy machines.

In addition to the above seven generic strategies, other characteristics
that can be used to offer different options to the customer include:

Guaranteed response time; start time; and turnaround time
Access to specific talent within the firm
Bundling education and training
Inclusion of the firm's newsletter, special events, seminars, and so
    forth
Automatic upgrades or updates (relevant if changes in the law or tech-
    nology are significant to your customer)
Offering older technology to achieve a lower price
Historical data conversion included or excluded

Prior tax or other government compliance requirements (e.g., bundling in five year's worth of prior tax return filings)

A systems review, risk audit, or other Needs & Diagnostics your firm offers

Attendance at the customer's board meetings

Intellectual Property ownership belongs to firm rather than to customer (mostly for advertising agencies)

Different risk-sharing methods based upon the outcome the customer achieves

Offering warranties, guarantees, and other forms of insurance

Varying payment terms

Various financing options—purchase, lease, rent, etc.

Once again, the above is not an exhaustive list of criteria that a firm could use to offer different levels of options to its customers. The process of creating these options is one of creativity and innovation; there are literally an infinite number of combinations, limited only by a firm's imagination. Here is how one chartered accounting firm in Australia created a menu offering for its business customers.

Silver Level

Preparation of:

- All tax returns for the group
- All necessary financial statements
- All statutory returns currently required by your business and previously prepared by us

Plus

- Unlimited phone discussions, advice, and meetings regarding day-to-day matters
- A free review of all your business and private loans
- Receipt of our quarterly newsletter

Additional fees for work outside the above description will be charged either as a VARIATION ORDER or on a newly agreed Value Pricing Agreement discussed with you before we commence work.

Gold Level

Based on our experience with your business we would like to tailor a package to suit you. This service, unlike Platinum Service, does not include unlimited consultation or input on day-to-day business, but it's more our expectation of your needs and wants. We will sit down with you and specify your needs and expectations.

It will typically include all services in Silver Service; plus additional components may be added such as:

- Annual reconciliation of BAS returns
- Preparation of quarterly BAS and IAS returns
- Tax planning assessment before the end of the year
- Providing trust account clearance of ATO refunds/checks for entities that don't have their own bank account
- Assistance with employee recruitment
- Assistance with wills
- Succession planning
- Business plans
- Team advisory board
- Client advisory board
- Marketing strategies
- Pension and superannuation plans
- Annual business performance review plus report
- Review of insurance both personal and business
- Liaise with you and your financial planner regarding wealth creation/protection
- Review and target growth in your business value
- Assess the profit improvement potential in your business
- Strategic review of your business

Platinum Level

All services included in Silver Service plus specified assignments from Gold Service PLUS:

- Unlimited meetings, advice, investigations, planning, and assistance as and when required regarding your current operations but excluding new ventures or extremely complicated matters which could not have been envisaged by either party prior to establishing this agreement.
- Priority enrollment in our soon to launch 2IC MBA
- 50 percent discount on all seminars conducted by 2IC
- 50 percent discount on any Principa systems implemented in your business
- Invites to our quarterly boardroom lunches

NOTE: Excluded from this package will be assistance in recruiting new employees for your organization. This will be dealt with as a Variation Order and a new Value Pricing Agreement drawn up before we commence work.

VARIATION ORDER
> Where you require services which are outside those envisaged by the above services we will before commencing work discuss with you the basis for our fee arrangement based on a Value Priced agreed fixed fee. We will document this arrangement so as to ensure no surprises.

NOTE RE POOR RECORDS SUPPLIED: If records or information supplied is in a format that is below the standard previously supplied or expected we will discuss options to get clients records to a suitable standard for the various service levels to be applicable. We reserve the right to return your books for more attention or arrange a Value Priced Agreement for us to review and correct the inaccuracies.

Pricing Options

Using the three prices developed in Chapter 29—Reservation, Hope For, and Pump Fist—the value council should construct a table similar to the following (see Table 30.2), utilizing the American Express Card offering levels for illustration purposes. This model is based upon the work of the obscure Austrian economist Barron Joseph von Neinbach.

Of course, the customer is not presented with all nine options, only the three options with one price next to each.

The logic behind this exercise is that it forces the value council to develop prices that reflect the value being created for each customer's level of price sensitivity. For example, if you know the customer is extremely price sensitive, you may present only the Reservation price for all three options. However, if there are some services that are adding marginal value, a Hope For price may be quoted for the Gold and Platinum levels. If extraordinary value is being created—the customer is at the top of the

TABLE 30.2 Barron Joseph von Neinbach Model

	Reservation Price	Hope For Price	Pump Fist Price
Platinum	$C	$B	$A
Gold	$N	$M	$L
Green	$Z	$Y	$X

TABLE 30.3 Van Westendorp Pricing Questions

	Too Expensive	Expensive	Cheap	Too Cheap
Platinum				
Gold				
Green				

value curve—quote the Pump Fist price on at least one or two of the offerings.

The value council is not finished yet. One more useful thought experiment to go through is the van Westendorp model (Table 30.3), based upon the last set of pricing questions in Chapter 29. Except now we will adjust the grid for the three—or four, or five, when you become more advanced—levels of offerings.

None of these grids should be completed in a vacuum. Customer input is essential, which is why Step 1—the conversation with the customer—is so critical to this process. The upper bound of these prices would be based upon the value being created, yet all will be lower than that value so as to ensure the customer also earns a profit. There is an art to these exercises, and the value council will get better with practice. What is known with certainty is this: One way never to get to this value is to continue to think and price based upon hours.

Firms that use this model report that it makes them "compete with itself." That may sound counterintuitive, but you will discover this to be true after pricing a few customers in this manner. After all, if your objective is to nudge the customer into the platinum offering at a Pump Fist price, what additional value are you adding? Why should the customer pay a premium for that option, forgoing a lower-priced alternative? This exercise forces you to answer these questions.

When you present the three options and prices to the customer, you are also subtly changing their psychology. Rather than thinking about whether they *will* do business with your firm, the options nudge them in the direction of thinking about *how* they are going to do business with your firm. For an excellent example of how this worked for one technology firm, see Case Study 30.1, "Do You Want Fries with That?"

Pricing Complex Projects

Attorney Christopher Marston, founder of Exemplar Law and fellow at VeraSage Institute, has refined a pricing process that works well in his law firm. At a seminar Chris and I taught together, Chris was asked how he

---

Case Study 30.1: Do You Want Fries with That?

By Karen Smart

There are many things that people do instinctively. One is to look for patterns. Our eyes are constantly searching for patterns. Think of those posters we use to see in the shopping malls in the late '80s. If you stared at it long enough, an image would emerge. Remember those? Well, I was staring at those "motivational" posters waiting to get excited about their message and beautiful images until Ed Kless womped me over the head. Another thing we do instinctively is *choose*. Options are in front of us everyday. We even give our children options. Do you want the red fire truck or the Sit-n-Spin™? You can't have both. Do you want fries with that? Himalayan Pink Salt or regular table salt? What size? I think the entire value model probably goes back to Adam and Eve. They had a choice too. But I don't have time to do all of that research because I'm so busy having fun at work these days trying to figure out what options I want to offer my customers on proposals. And yes, they "see" a pattern in my options and I can generally alter the text to have a specific pattern that is more pleasing to the eye. Read on.

I'd like to start off by presenting the first proposal I fashioned after coming back from an intense two-day training course that our company hired Ed Kless to do especially for our group (www.smarte-solutions.com). It was sort of like a mini consulting and leadership academy wedged in between two beautiful Florida sunrises and ocean sunsets.

I had previously submitted to our client an hourly based contract, which you will also see later. When I first submitted the hourly proposal, the client didn't purchase the upgrade due to some economic struggles and staff changes. A few months later (after Ed's training) the client wanted me to send over the proposal again because they lost the first one. Bless their little heart! What a great opportunity to try this new "value pricing" model. I was skeptical at first, and my business partner actually thought the idea was ludicrous and wanted no part of "ripping off our clients," as he deemed it. I looked him in the eye and said, "The customer now expects me to upgrade their system, install the new modules, train people, and work with their bank all within a two-week time frame." That meant I had to shift around my schedule and call other clients to move their scheduled updates, just to make this customer's deadline when we could have worked this in nicely

Continued

three months ago. So, I ventured into the "uncomfortable zone" by myself and with people scowling over my shoulder, mumbling something about hours and time tracking and losing customers.

I think it's important that you see an example of what options look like. Please keep in mind, this was my first time walking and it was hard to be creative. After looking at my first proposal, I am then going to show you how I previously went about doing this task. Seeing is believing.

Okay, as promised, below is my first value-priced proposal to upgrade a customer who was on a very old system. This customer also wanted to add the ability to do direct deposits.

Proposal for Client

What will be needed to configure EFT:

- Client to authorize their banking representative to talk directly with Karen Smart
- Karen Smart to obtain ACH file formatting specifications/sample from bank
- Configure EFT to generate ACH file in accounting/payroll software
- Generate sample ACH file
- Transmit sample file to bank for testing and make changes as necessary to form and or database structure

(This section imparts a skill level that will be required to do the EFT work. Most clients would not want to do this and that's the reason I put it in the beginning, before the pricing options.)

Option 1:
- Project to be completed by January 31, 2009
- Obtain product activations for new version of software from Sage
- Download software and all available service packs to client server
- EFT software installation and installation of accounting software
- Accounting software conversion, install all current service packs
- Configuring EFT (above steps) will be up to client
- $3,800

Option 2:
- Project to be completed by January 16, 2009
- All of Option 1 above plus
- Adjust check stock forms and invoice forms after upgrade
- ½ day of training on new product features
- Configuration of EFT as stated above by Karen Smart
- $4,900

Option 3:
- Completed by January 8, 2009
- Includes Options 1 and 2 above
- Create direct deposit form
- Full day of training (8 hours)
- Casual product use calls for one month
- $5,900

Option 4:
- Completed by December 31, 2009
- All of Options 1, 2, and 3 above
- Preconversion testing performed at Smart e-Solutions Inc, off business hours
- Transfer converted and service packed system to client server, reducing impact of system downtime.
- Database repair on data if needed
- $7,000

What you are about to see next is how we previously worked up our proposals.

Description	Done by	Consulting Hours	Programming Hours
Project Management and documentation	Karen Smart	1.50	
Analysis (Preconversion)	Karen Smart	4.00	
Check writing to be ported over to new version	Programming		1

Continued

Description	Done by	Consulting Hours	Programming Hours
Invoice form to be ported over to new version	Programming		0.5
Training on new features and direct deposit (EFT)	Karen Smart	4.00	
Performing MS SQL backup of all databases	Karen Smart	2.50	
Installation and conversion of accounting data to new version (for all company databases at client site)	Karen Smart & Programming	4.00	1.25
Workstation setups	Karen Smart	.75	
Configuration of EFT	Karen Smart	1	
Total		**17.75**	**2.75**

Note: This is not a fixed cost quotation. We work on a "Time and Material" basis. If the above quote goes under the amount actually worked, we only bill for the time worked. Same holds true for any time above the estimated hours.

Rates:

> Charges for programming hours: $150.00 **per hour**
> Charges for Karen Smart hours: $150.00 **per hour**

Notice that if you calculate the total estimated hours it only adds up to $3,075. My value pricing proposal started out at $3,800.

You want to know what option they chose? I'll get there, but let's talk about your business for a minute. If you're like me, you've been in business for a few years, you are experienced in your field of work, and you probably consider yourself to be among the best at whatever it is that you do. I had forgotten all of that. I was looking at things from an hourly standpoint and not from an experience level. Tasks that took me 30 minutes to complete ten years ago now only take 10 minutes. That is experience and knowledge and, folks, it shouldn't be defined by an hourly rate. If it is, I can guarantee your clients loathe getting bills from you. I also woke up to the fact that when people call me for help, it's because they seriously can't do the task themselves and my experience becomes invaluable to the customer, whether it takes 10 minutes or 10 hours.

As a result of my look back and more bonks on the head by our internal sales person, we are in the process of on-boarding all clients to service level agreements (SLA[1]), which is a whole story in and of itself. We have consultants and programmers in our group who have been applying their experience and knowledge to our customers for over 20 years. I started asking employees and contractors, What do you want out of life? What do you want to do in this position? What are your goals at work? Many came back with things like, "I want to earn over the yearly Social Security maximum taxable wage just once in my life," "Pay off my mortgage," "Go on a vacation without taking out a loan," and the list went on. I started off by looking at what bacon I was bringing home in a year. I took into consideration my college degree and the many years of being in this field and what knowledge I have as a result of those years of work. My yearly wage has never been where I want it to be. So, let's do the math. 40 hours × $150 = $6,000.00 × 52 weeks = $312,000.00. Now start calculating how many *actual* billable hours you have over a year, and it's nowhere near $312,000.00 per year. In fact, when you start putting a pencil to it, **maybe you're lucky you're still in business**. A good economy masks a poor business. If you're struggling in today's economy, maybe it's time for that change.

You know how much people despise looking at bills from lawyers, so you can imagine that your customers probably feel the same way about getting hourly bills from you. In fact, I know the customers abhor this because one of our clients, who is on plan (SLA), actually told me one day, during a technical support call, "I hated getting bills from you, even though the support was great. I didn't want to call you unless it was a real emergency." Reason: Hours = Pain, for the customer and for you. The conversation with my customer led me, of course, to review our SLA billings. I guess it's just easier to pay a yearly amount because I'm doing just fine on margin. As a result, communications with my client have actually increased. I'm building reports for them and talking to them about other products. They feel they can call me anytime, without the pain of an hourly billing rate. In fact, there's a lot less stress in the office as a result of having our clients on plan.

For recurring revenue streams that are consistent, and that will allow you to concentrate on your business, start looking at

---

[1]Ed Kless has been challenged on the use of this acronym, especially since we prefer Professional Knowledge Firm to Professional Service Firm. A superior name for these agreements is Access Level Agreement.

Continued

implementing and enforcing SLAs. You'll soon be working *on* your business instead of *in* it. We have four different levels on our SLAs and one of those levels is "NO PLAN." No plan means a higher incident fee when they call in for any help. Sage has been doing maintenance and support contracts for years, and it's amazing that for most of us, the lightbulbs didn't turn on to recurring revenues long ago. Sage depends upon those recurring revenues for over half their business, 52 percent to be exact. In 2009, it continued to increase!

I'm sure that there will be other methods developed in the future to woo us, but this plan is truly working for my company and we've never felt more secure in such a tough business environment. So when you're doing your next proposal, I encourage you to try the value pricing method. I've managed to work with two other companies on opposite ends of the nation and they were amazed at what options their customers chose on the proposals I created. They have now seen the light and how this really works! Implementing the SLAs (with options!) has also allowed me to relax and not worry about when the phone is going to ring, so that I can bill someone and make them feel horrible about using my services.

So, the client I did the quote for? They weren't as hot to get the job done before December 31 as they thought they were, and I really didn't want to call my other clients and reschedule them. They chose the option I wanted them to: Option 3. That was $2,825 above what I originally quoted using the hourly rate syndrome! You know how people frame one dollar bills and proudly display them as their first money earned? I have my first value pricing option proposal taped next to my desk for all to see we did it!

I have yet to prove my theory on pattern searching within my proposals, but I'm starting to keep track of the choices and outcomes.

scoped a project (especially complex litigation). He answered by drawing concentric circles, as shown in Figure 30.1.

This forces a firm to think about what they know for sure is going to happen—the "Yes" circle. Since the firm is the expert, they should know, at a minimum, the work that needs to be done in the first phase. If they do not know this, perhaps they do not know enough about the customer's objectives to be able to handle the project. Everything can be broken down into phases. Mechanics will sometimes charge a price just to diagnose a car's problem, or a doctor will charge for a biopsy. The same logic applies

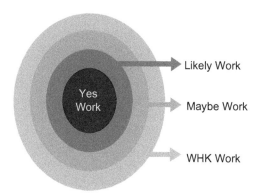

FIGURE 30.1 Chris's Concentric Circles

here—provide a scope for work you know will need to be done, no matter what.

Next, the firm should consider those elements that are "Likely" to be required. These are tasks with a high probability of being required to be performed, probably greater than 50 to 60 percent.

After that, the firm should consider those things that might be needed—the "Maybe" circle, showing work with less than a 40 to 50 percent chance of being required. This is where the process, from a pricing perspective, becomes creative, for it allows firms to begin offering various bundled options. Using the American Express Green, Gold, Platinum, and Black credit card analogy, a firm only scoping the "Yes" items could offer a Green card price—a stripped-down value proposition. This may be strategic if the customer is price sensitive, or if the economy is in a downturn.

Value pricing is not just about offering higher value and higher prices. It can also mean a lower price, but always for a lower value. There should always be a trade-off required from the customer. Moving beyond the "Yes" factors to the "Likely" factors could produce a Gold Card service option, at a higher price; including the "Maybe" factors would bring a Platinum card price. Not only are you offering various levels of comfort, you are also providing insurance to the customer against risk. You are also showcasing your firm's expertise, building confidence in the customer that you have done this type of work before and can project future scenarios, even though no one expects you to have a completely accurate crystal ball.

This is significant because people will pay "premiums" to avoid risk—it is what insurance companies are all about, and why electronic retailers such as Best Buy earn half of their profits from the sale of extended warranties. The firm is able to spread this risk over many customers, yet the customer usually only deals with one lawyer or other professional firm at a time, so the risk to them is much higher. Reduce that risk and you earn a price premium. It is similar to fixed-rate versus variable-rate mortgages. The higher interest rate is not because it cost the bank any more to process a fixed-rate loan; rather, it is for the value of reducing risk to the customer. Since profits come from risk, this is an opportunity for a firm to make supernormal or windfall profits.

If the firm can actuarially assess the risk of not only the "Maybe" factors, but then step beyond to cover what Chris calls "Who the Hell Knows (WHK)" factors, then it is offering an insurance premium with umbrella coverage for contingencies. Some customers will value this ultimate peace of mind and be willing to pay for it—the Black Card in American Express lingo. (The Black Card imposes a one-time $5,000 price to open, plus a $2,500 annual price; it is a charge card that comes with a 24/7/365 concierge, frequent flier miles, and other perks.)

Placing the project into phases, with creative scoping, leaves the opportunity for change orders when the scope changes. Once the professional is approximately 60 to 90 percent done with phase one, they can begin to scope phase two. The important point here is to discuss price, terms, scope, and get authorization from the customer for phase two *before* you are done with phase one. This maintains the firm's pricing leverage, as well as monetizes the customer's switching costs.

This method of analyzing scope applies to all firms, from advertising agencies, CPA, and law firms to software resellers. Give your customers options. Too many professionals get hung up that they are unable to foresee all the contingencies of a job. So what? If you feel anxious about that risk, imagine how your customers feel about it. Firms need to do what the insurance companies do: Use that risk actuarially and turn it into an opportunity to create and capture more value. Give your customers the option of choosing what level of risk they are comfortable with. Since risk is like price—it is completely subjective, different for each person—some customers will not value avoiding it, while others will. An actuary taught me another lesson: If there is risk involved, then your service is *certainly not a commodity.*

Chris's circles will help you analyze risk in a structured, logical manner, allowing you to absorb the level of risk you are comfortable with. As with pricing, this is a skill—the more you do it, the better you will get. Actuaries price risk for a living. If firms can develop a competency in this skill, they will be able to differentiate themselves in the market from their competition, as well as capture more of the value they create. That is the ultimate win-win. See Case Study 30.2 for an example of a risk-sharing agreement.

Case Study 30.2: Mission Impossible

Santa Monica Freeway

The January 1994 earthquake in Northridge, California, devastated the Santa Monica Freeway, leaving 350,000 daily commuters no access to Los Angeles. Early estimates predicted at least 12 months to rebuild, at a public cost of $1 million for each day the freeway was shut down.

Innovative constructor C. C. Myers saw it differently. He saw it as a 4.5-month project. Staking his wealth and reputation, C. C. Myers signed a $14.7 million contract with the city, which allowed a maximum completion time of 140 calendar days, with a penalty for late completion of $205,000 per calendar day and an incentive of $200,000 per day for early completion and opening the freeway to traffic.

Mission: Impossible
Approach: Change everything.
Results: Spectacular

Contract time commenced on February 5, with materials and equipment moving to the jobsite that same day and through the weekend, even though final construction plans were not available until February 26. C. C. Myers immediately went to work on a 24/7 schedule with up to 400 workers on the job. On-site inspectors were used to eliminate delay and rework. Workers were running on the job. Special quick-setting concrete was used. Subcontract bids and awards were made on a daily basis. Work flowed.

Sixty-six days after the contract was signed, the Santa Monica Freeway was opened to traffic, 74 days ahead of schedule.

Source: The Elegant Solution, Matthew E. May, 2006, p. 135.

Another model to assist you in breaking down projects into phases is FORD, as explained by my VeraSage Institute colleague Ed Kless.

FORD—A Model for Consulting

A dialogue once began in one of my consulting classes that I teach for Sage. The conversation focused around the levels (I am not convinced *levels* is the right word) of consulting. In the end, the group proposed the following four levels: Findings, Options, Recommendations, and Decision. Serendipitously, this yielded the acronym FORD. This model has served me quite well over the last few years, so I thought it worthy to briefly define each level and provide some overall thoughts about this model.

> **Findings.** These are the issues (problems, opportunities, and desired results) that the consultant uncovers through a question-and-answer process, referred to by most as discovery.
>
> **Options.** These are the different possibilities that the consultant proposes for solving the uncovered problems, seeking the opportunities, or achieving the desired results. A great consultant always includes "Do nothing" as an option.
>
> **Recommendations.** This is the option (or options) that the consultant believes would be the best course of action for the customer. Making recommendations would usually include a list of advantages and disadvantages (pros/cons, positives/negatives, strengths/weaknesses, whatever you want to call them) of each option and a rationale for why the option(s) was (were) selected.
>
> **Decision.** One of the various options or a variation of the options is selected for implementation.

A few observations about the model:

- Each incremental level increases the level of risk on the consultant and requires a higher degree of knowledge. Since risk and knowledge required are factors in setting price, an engagement to just collect findings will be less expensive than an engagement to present options, and an engagement to present options will be less expensive than an engagement to provide recommendation.
- If you are making the decisions you are not a consultant, but what Peter Block would call a surrogate manager. He defines this as "a person who acts on behalf of or in place of a manager." Surrogate manager-hood is not bad in and of itself, but it is way more risky and deserving of a premium price.
- Being a consultant or a surrogate manager is a strategic decision. Some people may choose never to enter the fray as a surrogate manager and only remain in the role of consultant.
- It is critical to have a conversation early on with every customer or prospective customer as to the level of consulting in which they would like to engage you. Failure to do so causes not only pricing problems, but myriad other problems that are beyond the scope of this explanation.

- I believe that all professionals are consultants of some kind. Doctors are consultants on the anatomy and physiology of the human body; lawyers, on the law and legal system; CPAs, on accounting practices, and so forth.

Using any of these models requires the ability to think, take risks, and be creative and imaginative. This is precisely why most firms do not do it; it is too hard. Yet, as Ed Kless likes to say, "If you suck at what you do, by all means price by the hour."

Dipping Your Toe in the Water

I can't understand why people are frightened of new ideas. I'm frightened of the old ones.

—John Cage

Are you still uncomfortable with the idea of implementing this model? You are not alone. Even when people are shown specific examples, similar to the Karen Smart case study above, they still have major trepidation. We recognize these ideas are revolutionary, especially for professional firms that have been mired in hourly billing for decades. Yet this model is not that revolutionary; it is actually *radical*—Latin for getting back to the root. The root in this case is value created for the customer—the source of all wealth.

Nevertheless, this model will be implemented over time, in an *evolutionary* manner. In workshops we have conducted around the world, when the participants get to that point of fear—and you can easily recognize this emotion from the looks on their faces and body language—it is time to do our "dipping your toe in the water" exercise.

Realistically, we are not going to eliminate hourly billing overnight, let alone timesheets. What we can do is emphasize how looking at hours needs to be done up front, *before* the work begins. In addition, it needs to be remembered that putting "expected hours" next to each deliverable is merely *costing* the work, not *valuing* it, nor *pricing* it.

But if we want to transition people, we must start with what they know. In that spirit, I am going to posit a formula for you to use to calculate your firm's Reservation price in the various models outlined above. Even though value is subjective, and there is no formula for it, we have found this exercise gives professionals comfort and the impetus to continue to experiment with value pricing. We know the more they experiment, the better they will get, until that point comes when they are no longer paranoid about hours and "Did we make money on this?" Eventually, they will have that epiphany, and then the concern becomes "How much money did we leave on the table?"

I am also illustrating this exercise to achieve another purpose. Recall how the billable hour places an artificial ceiling over professional's heads on how much they can earn. This is evidenced by the fact that most firms' realization rates are between 50 and 95 percent—in other words, we are writing down and writing off more than we are writing up profession-wide. We put this ceiling over our own heads; the customers did not place it there. Therefore, this formula I am about to share with you does something quite cunning with this ceiling—see if you can figure it out as we go through the exercise.

Formula for Calculating Reservation Price

We will start with hours x rate and then add various price premium percentages for lowering customer risk, as follows:

Hours × Rate
Fixed price premium %
Change Orders premium %
Service guarantee premium %
Price guarantee premium %
Payment terms premium %
Unlimited Access premium %
Price Sensitivity components premium %

I am going to explain each of the above factors, and then show you what an actual group of attorneys in a workshop in Australia said was the value price premium you could command—in percentage terms—for each one of the factors above. The idea is to think of that teeter-totter: If you can reduce the customer's risk of dealing with your firm, you will be able to command a value price premium, similar to how a fixed rate mortgage commands a higher rate of interest than a variable rate mortgage.

Hours × Rate

Even though this goes against everything I am arguing in this book, go ahead and look at hours. You know your hourly rate contains a profit margin, so this is not really cost accounting; it is *profit forecasting*. But for this exercise, fine—use your hourly rates and do your timesheets in advance. Multiply it out. You obviously are not going to get a premium for this calculation because we have not yet begun to reduce the customer's risk.

Fixed Price

What is a fixed price worth to your customer? The fact that they will not be surprised by an invoice, that they will authorize all work before it is undertaken, and that they will be able to budget with certainty their professional spend.

For example, a 2009 study conducted by the Utility Consumer's Action Network showed that cell phone users in San Diego paid an average of $3.02 per minute for calls (Poundstone 2010: 174). This premium is due to the fact that most cell customers select flat-rate plans, usually with more minutes than they use. Just another example of how people will pay a premium to avoid risk and uncertainty.

The group estimated that this one factor was worth somewhere between **10 and 20 percent.**

Change Orders

The fact that your firm uses Change Orders is a way to ensure the customer that work will never be performed without their authorization on price, payment terms, and scope. Customers are used to this level of service from their auto mechanics and contractors, and will appreciate being informed— as well as given the choice on how to proceed—when the anticipated scope of the work changes.

The group estimated that this factor was worth **5 to 10 percent.**

Service Guarantee

The service guarantee is one of the most effective ways of proving to your customer that you are serious about creating value. A service that is guaranteed is worth more than a service that is not. You already offer a guarantee—it is just *covert*, no one knows about it until they complain—so why not get some marketing and pricing power from it by making it *overt*.

The group estimated that this factor was worth **15 to 25 percent.**

Price Guarantee

This is the guarantee that says to the customer to ignore any invoice they receive in which they did not authorize price, payment terms, and scope of work. It is another way of ensuring the customer that your firm will never surprise them with an invoice because all work is priced in advance.

The group estimated that this factor was worth **5 percent.**

Payment Terms

The fact that you will structure payment terms based upon the cash flow cycle of your customer rather than the work-flow of your firm is greatly appreciated by business customers, and even individual customers. This is especially true if you offer different types of financing plans, such as with software firms offering financing or leasing plans.

The group estimated that this factor was worth **5 to 10 percent.**

Unlimited Access

This service tears down the "Berlin Wall" that exists between the customer and the firm, providing for unlimited telephone calls and meetings to discuss whatever the customer wants. This most often will lead to additional work. It is not free; you are bundling it in with the price of your other services. Like the flat-rate cell phone plans, this service is highly valued, even if the customer never uses it.

The group estimated that this factor was worth **10 to 20 percent.**

Factors of Price Sensitivity

Recall from Chapter 29 the nine factors of price sensitivity that were discussed. The value council would go through each one to determine what an appropriate addition, or subtraction, would be to the above formula. For purposes of this exercise, we will ignore these factors, even though they will provide substantial value to your customer.

Summary and Conclusions

Adding only the factors discussed above, a price premium of between 50 and 90 percent can be commanded, over and above your rate × hours. When this total was summed, the group was astounded, and still skeptical. All right, I said, what if *you* are wrong by 80 percent? (It was, after all, *their* estimates of the price premiums.) That still equates to a 10 to 18 percent price premium—and this is a premium that can be justified over your competition that is most likely not offering these benefits. Recall from Chapter 5 how much profit can be added to your firm's bottom line with just a 1 percent increase in price.

This is why it is so important to invest intellectual capital into the pricing function. I have yet to meet a firm that thinks too much about pricing; but I have encountered many who do not think at all about pricing.

Were you able to figure out what we did with the artificial ceiling of the billable hour?

We lowered it to a *floor*, since the above calculation is used to compute the Reservation price—the Hope For and Pump Fist prices would be even higher. This is important because there is no ceiling on value, except your imagination. Essentially, we have reduced the risk to the customer, and are able to charge a premium to cover this additional risk to the firm. This is a much more customer-centric approach than billing for hours. Once you have done this a few times, you are going to learn for yourself how tracking hours becomes superfluous, and a distraction from focusing on value creation.

Now that we have developed and priced options for the customer, it is time to proceed to the next step—presenting the options to the customer.

CHAPTER 31

Step Four: Presenting Options to the Customer

He knew the precise psychological moment to say nothing.

—Oscar Wilde

Stanley Marcus, of Neiman-Marcus, used to tell the story of selling high-priced items to customers, from fur coats to watches. He said you wanted the customer to be wearing the article when they asked the price. Once you stated the price, he advised: "Shut up." He never saw a good salesman *listen* himself out of sale, but saw many *talk* themselves out of one.

If your value council has done its job of understanding the customer's value drivers, along with offering options that cover those drivers and more, your firm's incidence of price objections should drop dramatically. After all, if the customer is price sensitive, they can always select the cheapest offering. If they are clamoring for the additional value of a higher priced option, they are self-identifying themselves as a customer who is not solely concerned with price.

Firms should never qualify their prices with statements such as, "Our usual price is ..." or "Our normal price is ..." and so forth, because these qualifiers are nothing more than an invitation for the customer to negotiate. Pricing is not negotiating. This is why it is important to have full confidence in your value council's ability to establish prices commensurate with value, and leave the pricing integrity of the firm in its capable hands.

Strategically, you want to become skilled at "testing" your price during the conversation (Step One). If you and the customers are far apart, it may be time to stop the sales process and move on to more advantageous opportunities. When you do encounter price objections, here are some strategies for effectively dealing with them.

Handling Price Objections

One of the questions professionals always ask about quoting a value price is what happens when the customer objects that it is simply too high? First, realize that price is always a consideration, and naturally every business-person is going to attempt to get the best price they can. Consequently, if you are to succeed in getting full value for your services you must learn how to handle price objections. It helps to keep in mind the following equation when dealing with price:

$$Value = \frac{Benefits\ Received}{Price}$$

If the customer is objecting to your price, perhaps you have not done an adequate job in educating the customer about the benefits of your services. The customer may not be objecting to the price as much as doubting the value. This is a critical distinction because the majority of a professional's customers are not price-sensitive. This is precisely why it is so important to discuss value first and set price last. The more you can build up the value, the higher the perceived value of your firm, and thus the higher the price you can command. One way to achieve this is to focus customers on the objectives they want to achieve rather than the price to be paid. In so doing, customers will focus on how to maximize the objectives rather than minimize the price.

In his book *Getting into Your Customer's Head*, Kevin Davis offers the following *value equation* that I believe also helps in determining a customer's price sensitivity (Davis 1996: 80):

$$Value\ Gained = \frac{Seriousness\ of\ Discontent}{Cost\ of\ Buying}$$

Think of the "Seriousness of Discontent" as the gap between where the customer is and where they want to be. If you can assist them in closing this gap, then the cost of buying is less of a factor.

With new customers, most price objections are due to inadequate prequalifying. When meeting with new customers, the following may occur:

- **The customer's only consideration is price.** This is, most likely, a customer you should not deal with at all. These customers are attracted to you solely because of price and they will be the first to defect when they can locate a cheaper service provider. Be wary of these customers, and do not waste your precious marketing resources on them. You are better off spending those resources on existing customers, who are more loyal and more valuable to your firm.

- **The customer never asks about your price.** Although this may sound like Nirvana, the reality is quite different. Price is always a consideration, especially with businesspeople. The person who never asks about your price is also the person who probably does not intend to pay your price. Always ask these customers for a large retainer up front to test their level of commitment.
- **The customer says price is no object.** Again, this is probably because the customer has no intention of paying you anyway. Price is *always* important.
- **The customer asks a lot of questions, seeking your advice.** If customers are unwilling to commit to an FPA, they are merely using you as an unpaid consultant. Avoid them.
- **The customer complains about the predecessor professional.** In another year, you will be the subject of this customer's wrath. Employ adverse selection. If this is such a great customer, why doesn't one of your competitors have this customer already?

Price objections with existing customers require a strategic approach. Most likely, these customers will require a good deal of education on the value of an FPA. Always remember that the FPA lowers the customer's risk and uncertainty, and that is one of its major value-added benefits that should be emphasized. If you are still encountering many price objections utilizing this approach, this is not a positive indicator. The popular view is that price objections are a good sign (who would object to your price if they were not serious about doing business with your firm?). Neil Rackham points out a different viewpoint in his classic sales book *SPIN Selling*:

> No, make no mistake about it, the more objections you get in a call, the less likely you are to be successful. It's a comforting myth for trainers to tell inexperienced salespeople that professionals welcome objections as a sign of customer interest, but in reality an objection is a barrier between you and your customer. However skillfully you dismantle this barrier through objection handling, it would be smarter not to have created it in the first place (Rackham 1988: 133).

Despite the best probing questions during the conversation, development of a future vision, a focus on the customers wants, and the offering of options, it is inevitable that you will receive at least some price objections. While getting many may be a sign of a deficient value communication approach, a few can usually be handled using some of the more common objection-handling techniques. One thing to keep in mind: The number of objections is finite. You have probably heard most of them already. How can we not have answers for *all* of them? Here are specific methods for overcoming objections to price (I am indebted to Troy Waugh, consultant to CPAs, for some of this content):

1. Postpone the price objection.
2. Use the lowest common denominations.
3. Use comparison.
4. To get volume up, sell down.

Postpone the Price Objection

You cannot intelligently discuss price until you know exactly what the customer needs and wants. Here are two responses that postpone the price objection until you have had a chance to build your firm's value:

- I can appreciate that you would be interested in the price, and I assure you we will discuss it completely, but before we even consider the price, I want to be sure that our firm can satisfy your needs. Will that be all right?
- Mr. Smith, your concern for price is quite understandable. The actual amount paid for the service, however, will depend upon the nature of the services you ultimately select. Let's consider the price for the services after we establish the specific services you will require. Is that fair?

If you discuss price at the beginning, the customer may think you have nothing else to talk about. Sometimes, a customer is insistent in knowing a ballpark amount, and in these cases you will not be able to postpone the objection. If you try, they may stay so focused on your reluctance to talk price that everything else you say regarding value will be mentally blocked out. If you have to mention price, err on the high side, for reasons that should be apparent by now.

However, there is not a customer alive who can force you to quote a price before you are ready. You control when price is discussed, not the customer! If they are that insistent, it is likely they are not serious about hiring your firm, but rather to use your price as "column fodder" against their existing firm.

Use the Lowest Denominations

One of the advantages of setting the payment terms in accordance with the customer's desires is that this breaks down the price into the lowest denominations, usually monthly. A monthly price is a much more manageable number to deal with than the total FPA price. Also, this is the time to reiterate your service guarantee and the fact that you will be available anytime to respond to the customer's needs, if you include an unlimited access clause in the FPA.

Use Comparison

An effective comparison to make is that of your customer's pricing policies, with a statement such as the following:

> Mr. Becker, your own company makes a high-grade product that commands an exceptionally high price, and deservedly so. Your tool-and-die products warrant their outstanding reputation because of the top-quality materials used to make them. Our high level of service and attention to helping you create more value in your business are naturally suited for you. Sure, you can buy less expensive financial help than ours, but you would not be satisfied with the performance.

This approach achieves a level of parity between your firm and your customer's business, which makes considerable sense, as most business owners are convinced of *their* product's superiority. Testimonials from your other customers can also help prove your case. One automotive supplier said to an automobile company executive, "How can you advertise your product as being the finest quality if you buy cheap parts?"

To Get Volume Up, Sell Down

All customers have a price they are *able* to pay and a price they are *willing* to pay. Do not project your own price sensitivity onto the behavior of your customer. Never assume that a customer is only willing to spend what you would spend in similar circumstances. A fascinating study conducted by Macy's of New York illustrates this lesson:

> Macy's gave ten professional shoppers $1,000 each with instructions to enter one of Macy's departments to buy merchandise without mentioning price. The shopper was to buy whatever was offered by the salesperson up to $1,000. Not one of the shoppers was able to get rid of more than $350. For example, when one shopper asked about ladies' hats, the sales person brought out a hat within her own price range—$75; the buyer could have bought a $200 hat.

This is another reason you should always present your most expensive price first. Men's clothing is sold in such a manner. The salesman will first show you a $3,000 suit, let you try it on, and when you choke, he'll then move down, gradually, to your price level. Once he has sold you the suit, he will then move down to sweaters, shoes, shirts, ties, and socks. It is easier to buy a $99 sweater after you have decided to purchase a $375 suit. Psychologically, this is a very effective method, as the anchor effect from behavioral economics has proven.

If price is still an objection, focus on the difference. Perhaps you are trying to price the FPA at $20,000, but the customer wants to pay $15,000. Do not focus on the $20,000; focus instead on the $5,000 difference. That is the real problem, and that puts the focus on the smaller, more manageable amount.

If price is still an objection, be slow to cut it, as you will lose creditability with the customer if you do not get a concession from them; you will also degrade your firm's pricing integrity. Instead, work on the other terms of the FPA first. Perhaps you can accelerate the payment terms; perhaps you can cut some services, or add additional services.

Getting the Best Deal

Most people think that the final decision in the buying process is one of risk—either the risk of not buying or of not making the right decision on a service provider. However, the very last buying decision is ensuring that you get the best deal. This is a separate issue from the value of the service; the customer is already convinced of the value or you would not be this far along in the buying process.

When customers are trying to ascertain whether they have gotten the best price, they will test you. As Michael Bosworth says in his excellent book, *Solution Selling*:

> At negotiation time, in the buyer's mind, the seller is a washcloth. ... And if that buyer has an IQ over 80, he's going to take at least one wrenching squeeze to see what happens. Am I right? And the squeezing will continue until the seller stops dripping. As long as the seller drips, the buyer squeezes.
>
> How does a seller stop the squeezing? By resolving to stop dripping, by resolving to walk out if the business is not right, and by resolving to walk away from the business. The seller must take his stand with conviction—enough conviction to convince the buyer he is getting the best possible deal (Bosworth 1995: 147).

If the buyer sees you panic, this reinforces their fear that they have not yet negotiated the best price. This is an emotional process, not a logical one; standing your ground is very important, which is why establishing your Reservation price is so critical.

Bosworth also suggests using the word "fair," such as "Is this a fair price to you?" People have an innate desire to be fair and it is a very powerful word. In fact, it is so powerful that you should use it sparingly.

Remember, after showing or stating your price, shut up. The ball is now in the customer's court. Do not panic because the customer is silent—they may be experiencing "sticker shock," for instance—as most people do go through a moment of silence before spending a relatively large amount of money. Think about the moment of hesitation you have experienced before agreeing to purchase a car, buy a piece of jewelry, and so forth. This is simple human nature, and Stanley Marcus understood it well. Do not interfere with it by saying anything.

Summation: Presenting Your Price to the Customer

Here is a summary checklist to consider before presenting your price to the customer:

- Always place a timeline on all proposals and request for proposal (RFP) responses. No price should last forever.
- Copyright all of your proposals to ensure you retain ownership of any intellectual property—this is especially relevant for advertising agencies performing "spec" work.
- Present your most expensive option first. Be proud of your highest price option.
- Do not use price qualifiers, such as "Our normal/standard/regular price is ..."
- Do not negotiate with yourself. State your price and be quiet. One lawyer presents the options to the customer, and then walks out of his office so they can decide in peace.
- Any bargaining worthy of the name has to take place between equals. Match professional buyers with professional pricers.
- You are an equal to your customer, not a supplicant.
- Be creative in using options. One IT firm selected the names of the Ferrari models since the CEO of the customer owned a Ferrari.
- Use the word *price*, not *fee*—the latter conjures up negative emotions.
- Use the word *agreement* rather than *contract*. "Authorize the agreement" is less threatening than "Sign the contract."

- Use one of the strategies above to deal with any price objections.
- Realize that the only way to command premium prices in the long run is to offer superior value.

We are now ready to proceed to the next step: memorializing the meeting of the minds into the Fixed Price Agreement.

CHAPTER **32**

Step Five: Customer Selection Codified into the Fixed Price Agreement

Once the customer has selected the option they desire, the Fixed Price Agreement (FPA) memorializes the meeting of the minds between the firm and the customer. It codifies in a plain-written agreement what services will be performed, the price, payment terms, scope of services, and the responsibilities of both parties, as well as other clauses that help the firm communicate value and reduce customer risk. A sample FPA is provided in Figure 32.1 for a CPA firm, to illustrate the various clauses in general.

Let us scrutinize each section of the FPA and explain why it is designed the way it is.

Date of the FPA

For most CPA firms, the date of the agreement is usually in the last quarter of the customer's calendar or fiscal year. It is advantageous to meet to agree on the terms of the FPA to clarify the customer's expectations before the new year begins, as well as to learn of opportunities that may be present to offer the customer additional services. Do not feel the need to rush this process. If it takes multiple meetings with the customer, as it sometimes does to get over price resistance and anxiety, do not panic and feel the need to draft something. The FPA is not a request for proposal (RFP). There are no surprises in an FPA because the customer is instrumental in the design and is involved every step of the way. The more customer involvement you obtain, the higher the level of commitment you will get, and the more likely the customer will act consistent with their commitment.

Some firms do stagger their FPAs to begin at different times, to lessen the burden of trying to meet with each customer in a given period of time. This will depend on the number of customers, the work flow, and other factors. The advantages of staggering the FPAs throughout the year is it smoothes out cash flow, as each FPA contains payment terms.

November 19, 2010

Dear Client:

In order to document the understanding between us as to the scope of the work that ABC CPAs will perform, we are entering into this **Fixed Price Agreement** with XYZ, Inc. To avoid any misunderstandings, this Agreement defines the services we will perform for you as well as your responsibilities under this Agreement.

PROFESSIONAL SERVICES
ABC will perform the following services for XYZ during 2011:
- 2010 XYZ S Corporation Tax Returns
- 2010 Financial Statement Review with PBC (Prepared by Client) schedules to be provided by XYZ by March 15, 2011
- 2011 Tax Planning
- Budgeting and cash flow projections for 2011
- Unlimited Access 2011*

TOTAL 2011 PROFESSIONAL SERVICES $XXX
*Included in the Unlimited Access are the following services to be provided by ABC to XYZ:
- Unlimited meetings, to discuss operations of XYZ, business matters, tax matters, and any other topic at the discretion of XYZ or its employees and/or agents.
- Unlimited phone support for XYZ personnel and/or independent contractors and agents regarding accounting assistance, general questions, and other matters that require no additional work.

Because our Fixed Price Agreement provides ongoing access to the accounting, tax, and business advice you need on a fixed-price basis, you are not inhibited from seeking timely advice by the fear of a meter running endlessly. Our service is built around fixed pricing, as opposed to hourly rates, and offers you access to the accumulated intellectual capital of the firm through CPAs with substantial experience, who can help enhance your company's future and achieve its business objectives.

Unanticipated Services
While the fixed price entitles your company to unlimited consultation with us, if your question or issue requires additional research and analysis beyond the consultation, that work will be subject to an additional price, payment terms, and scope to be agreed upon before the service is performed, and a Change Order will be issued to document this understanding.
Furthermore, the parties agree that if an unanticipated need arises (such as, but not limited to, an audit by a taxing agency, a financial statement audit required as part of a lender financing agreement, or any other exogenous service not anticipated in this agreement by the parties) that ABC CPAs hereby agrees to perform this additional work at a mutually agreed-upon price. This service will be priced separately to XYZ, using a Change Order.

Service Guarantee
Our work is guaranteed to the complete delight of the customer. If you are not completely satisfied with the services performed by ABC CPAs we will, at the option of XYZ, either refund the price or accept a portion of said price that reflects XYZ's level of value received. Upon payment of each of your scheduled payments, we will judge you have been satisfied.

Price Guarantee
Furthermore, if you ever receive an invoice without first authorizing the service, payment terms, and price, you are not obligated to pay for that service.

FIGURE 32.1 Sample Fixed Price Agreement

Payment Terms

The following payment terms are hereby agreed to between XYZ and ABC CPAs:

January 31, 2011	$X
February 28, 2011	XX
March 31, 2011	XX
April 30, 2011	XX
May 31, 2011	XX
June 30, 2011	XX
July 31, 2011	XX
August 31, 2011	XX
September 30, 2011	XX
October 31, 2011	XX
November 30, 2011	XX
December 31, 2011	XX
TOTAL 2011 PAYMENTS	*$X*

To assure that our arrangement remains responsive to your needs, as well as fair to both parties, we will meet throughout 2011 and, if necessary, revise or adjust the scope of the services to be provided and the prices to be charged in light of mutual experience.

Furthermore, it is understood that either party may terminate this Agreement at any time, for any reason, within 10 days written notice to the other party. It is understood that any unpaid services that are outstanding at the date of termination are to be paid in full within 10 days from the date of termination.

If you agree that the above adequately sets forth XYZ's understanding of our mutual responsibilities, please authorize this Agreement and return it to our office. A copy is provided for your records.

We would like to take this opportunity to express our appreciation for the opportunity to serve you.

Very Truly Yours,

BY: _____
     Allan Somnolent, partner, ABC CPAs

Agreed to and accepted:

BY: _____   DATE: _____
     Customer, president, XYZ, Inc.

FIGURE 32.1 *Continued*

Professional Services

The FPA is designed to take advantage of the economics of bundling. It will easily accommodate the *needs* of the customer—tax compliance, financial statements, and other required services. By adding at least one *want*—such as a consulting service or an estate plan—in the bundle you will be able to climb the value curve discussed in Chapter 10. This is especially important for veteran customers who you are transitioning from hourly billing to value pricing for the first time. It also makes comparisons with prior year's prices more difficult, since you have totally repackaged the price and terms of your services.

Be sure to explain all responsibilities of each party, as in the Example 32.1 FPA, the requirement in the Financial Statement Review that the customer is responsible for preparing any schedules and reconciliations by a certain date. The general rule is, the less sophisticated the customer, the more specific and detailed the mutual responsibilities should be outlined.

The "Unlimited Access 2011" is designed to break down the "Berlin Wall" between most firms and their customers. How many times have you looked at a customer and said something to the effect, "Why didn't you call me before you did this? If we would have structured it this way or that way, we could have saved [or prevented] $XXX." This is all too common in CPA and law firms, and when we have asked customers in customer advisory boards why they did not contact their professional before undertaking some significant transaction, they usually respond with some variant of, "Tick, Tock; I knew I'd be on the clock and don't like getting charged $100 for a phone call." Now that might not be the most rational response—the $100 probably would have been one of the best investments they could have made—but you cannot always rely on the customer to be intellectually rational. Emotions rule, and very few people like to be charged for phone calls.

When customers do not call, it is a lose-lose all the way around because the point at which the firm can add the most value to a transaction is *before* it takes place, not after. If the customer does not contact you until after, you can only mitigate any damages. This is not the highest point on the value curve.

We are always asked whether customers will abuse this clause, and the answer is a resounding no. However, if a customer was to place excessive demands with phone calls and meetings, then you have a basis for increasing your firm's price in the FPA. After all, if they are calling on you that often, you must be adding more value than originally anticipated.

But the reality is that most phone calls or meetings that are initiated by the customer will result in your firm getting more work. And this is where the Change Order comes into use. How do you draw the line of demarcation between what is included in the Unlimited Access and a Change Order? The general rule is, if you hang up the phone or walk out of a meeting and do not have to do any further work—no research, no further analysis, and so on—that is included in the Unlimited Access service. If you have to do something further as a result of the phone call or meeting, then you have a Change Order, and that needs to be discussed and priced *before* you do the work, as well as signed and authorized by the customer.

Notice that the Unlimited Access service is not *free*; it is bundled in with the other services, becoming part of the total price. Because the customer is paying for it, she is more likely to use it, which will translate to a narrower value gap since the firm will cross-sell more services. Furthermore, there is only one price for the entire bundle of services, rather than line-item pricing that makes it easier for the customer to shop each service. This changes the focus from pricing each service, to pricing the value of the total offering to the customer, allowing you to command higher prices than individual item pricing.

Many professionals object that they cannot quote a price up front because they do not know how long a specific project will take. But this is Marx's labor theory of value, which is completely irrelevant. The fact of the matter is, your customer does not care how long it takes you to complete a project. If you quote prices—and do not mention hours—the customer can focus on the value proposition, rather than an inflated hourly rate they cannot relate to.

Let me be blunt: If you cannot quote a price up front to the customer *before* the work begins, you have no business doing that work. I stand by this statement, even though many professionals whom I've confronted with it recoil. In the real world, prices are quoted up front, before any purchase decision is made. Once again, attorney Jay Shepherd makes this point powerfully in his Blog post "A One-question Test for Your Law Firm," reproduced in Case Study 32.1.

Case Study 32.1: A One-Question Test for Your Law Firm

By Jay Shepherd

To figure out how good your lawyer is, give him or her the following test. It only has a single question, so it will only take about three seconds to administer. On the other hand, it will take considerably longer to answer. And it should.

Here it is:

Question One How much will this cost?

That's it. Five words only, but it's the whole ballgame. If your lawyer can't correctly answer it, then you've got the wrong lawyer.

Now for the Teacher's Guide:

1. Every case, every matter, every job will have a different answer.
2. The answer your lawyer gives you won't necessarily be the same as the answer he or she gives another client.
3. "It depends" is not an acceptable answer. Neither is "Well, there are variables. ..."

One of the commonest complaints I hear from CFOs and general counsels is that law firms pitching their wares always talk about how

Continued

good they are and how experienced they are. Unlike other vendors, they never talk about how they're going to save the company money. That's because the law-firm business model doesn't provide a means for doing that. In the billable-hour system, costs are passed on to the client, meaning that there is no incentive to reduce them. Meaning that they won't.

A fixed price avoids that problem, and requires the law firm to be efficient. But a fixed price also requires the law firm to know and understand the value of its services, something it can only do well if it really knows its business.

Many lawyers have insisted to me that you can't put a fixed price on litigation. There are variables, they whinge. We can't control the costs. What if the other side hits us with a bunch of discovery? What then?

What then indeed.

If your law firm knows its business well, then it should know the value of the service it provides. Hiding behind a fear of variable costs is an admission that you don't really know your business. An airline doesn't say "There are variables" when charging you for your ticket. And yet headwinds, storms, airport congestion, and overtime can dramatically increase the airline's cost of a particular flight. But your ticket price won't change after they sell it to you.

The Red Sox won't say "There are variables" when selling you a ticket for tonight's game against the Yankees. Yet Sox-Yankees games tend to be much longer than other games; plus it's raining lightly with more weather expected. A longer game, especially one with rain delays, means increased costs for the Red Sox in wages, overtime, electricity costs, and so on. But your ticket price won't change after they sell it to you.

The Red Sox know their business. The airline knows its business. Does your law firm? Give it the one-question test.

Source: www.clientrevolution.com/2009/06/a-onequestion-test-for-your-law-firm.html. Accessed January 31, 2009.

Many professionals will also object that on many engagements where they do not know the full scope the customer trusts them to simply do what it takes and charge by the hour. This confusion between trust and pricing comes up all the time. But just because the customer trusts you does not negate the necessity of pricing up front. I trust United Airlines with my *life*, yet they provide me a price up front, *before* I fly. Pricing and trust are not necessarily related, and in fact, I would argue you generate a higher level of trust by pricing up front because it avoids surprising the customer with an invoice they are not prepared for. If you insist on pricing by the hour, after the work is completed, you will never command a value price for your services because value cannot be managed retroactively.

Of course there will be projects where the scope is not well defined, but that does not obviate the need to quote a price up front. It does, however, require the scope be carefully crafted, which will be discussed in Chapter 33.

Unanticipated Services

This is the Change Order clause, which is a way of communicating to your customers that yours is a firm that utilizes Change Orders for additional services that arise during the course of the year, or for scope changes on services already included in the FPA. This clause is also essential to manage your customer's expectations and make your pricing policies transparent. The axiom to live by in a value pricing culture is "no surprises." The customer should never be shocked by an invoice or a price, because they have authorized it up front, *before* the work began.

The Change Order is also advantageous because most of them will deal with customer *wants*, not merely *needs*. The majority of customer needs will be dealt with in the FPA; hence when additional services are needed, they are more likely to deal with wants—such as a merger or acquisition, consulting service, estate planning, and so forth. An example Change Order is illustrated in Chapter 34.

Service and Price Guarantee

The advantages of the service guarantee are many. Similar to Nordstrom and FedEx, a service guarantee will enable your firm to command premium prices. To put a finishing point on it, upon payment of each of the scheduled payments, it is assumed the customer is satisfied. Normally, if any customer is not satisfied, you will discover this far ahead of the final payment being due. When I first began offering the service guarantee, I left it open until the final payment was made per the terms of the FPA. Theoretically, any customer could have asked for a total refund on December 31, and I would have had to comply. This never happened. Since then, many firms have worded the guarantee to apply only to the last payment. You will have to use your judgment on this matter. The important point is not to bog down the language in legalese. Keep it simple.

The next paragraph of the FPA is the price guarantee, which forces the firm to price everything up front when it possesses the leverage. This is essential to creating a no-surprises culture in your firm. Literally no work is performed until authorized by a customer. Period. No exceptions. Otherwise, you are risking firm resources on customers who may be unable—or more likely—unwilling to pay your price. This clause also sends the message to team members and customers alike that your firm is one that takes its pricing policies seriously, and prices on purpose.

Professionals are uncomfortable confronting the pricing issue up front with customers, but customers feel better knowing the price in advance— even if it's just for the first phase of a project. Make no mistake about it, you will have a price discussion with your customer. The question is *when* will it take place, before or after the service is performed? Having it before assures you maintain the leverage, which is essential in commanding premium prices.

Payment Terms

Payment terms are price, and they should be agreed upon before any work is performed, just as much as the overall price of the FPA (or Change Order) is. The sample FPA shows monthly payments, but payments could be on any basis—biweekly, quarterly, semi-annually, and so on. In fact, get the customer involved in the timing of the terms, so as to coincide the terms with the cyclical cash flow of the business, as long as the FPA is cleared to zero by the end of its term (usually one year, but it can be longer). You should also require a retainer, or deposit, for all new customers to gain their ego investment in the relationship. If the customer is not willing to pay a portion of your price up front, why should you believe they will pay you in full when you are done? A retainer solidifies the relationship and demonstrates the customer is serious about doing business with you.

Revisions to the FPA

This is an effective clause for veteran customers you are putting onto an FPA for the first time and for new customers about whose work you may not have a complete understanding of the nature and scope. Agreeing to meet weekly, monthly, or on some other periodic basis ensures that you will have an understanding of your customer's expectations and that problems that arise will be dealt with expediently. This clause not only lowers the customer's risk; it lowers the firm's as well, since you will always have an opportunity to modify the price, terms, or scope of the FPA. Lowering the customer's risk is an essential element in overcoming the three pricing emotions we explored in Chapter 7.

Termination Clause

The FPA is an at-will agreement, meaning either party can terminate it, at any time, for any reason (subject to professional responsibilities and state laws, of course). This is another way to lower the customer's—and the firm's—risk of doing business with you.

Because you are offering a packaged price, if either party terminates before the completion date of the FPA, one party will owe the other a sum of money, and you will have to work that out with the customer. That said, do not let the tail wag the dog; do not line-item-price your services out of fear of termination. The FPA makes it less likely that any customer will defect. Besides, if they "pull the trigger" on the service guarantee, they can get their money back anyway. You will reach a settlement perceived fair to both parties.

Another advantage of the termination clause was explained to me by a CPA, who said, "I actually got notified I was being terminated! Usually, like a husband, I'm the last to find out."

Other Issues Regarding the FPA

Note how the FPA is a rather simple document, yet it contains some relatively radical ideas (recall *radical* is Latin for "getting back to the root"). You are offering a fixed price for a *bundle* of services customized to each customer's needs and wants, not line-item-pricing each service. Bundling is an excellent way to get customers not only to focus on the totality of your service offering, but it also forces them to acknowledge the value of your services.

For instance, one CPA firm has a minimum price of $1,000 for personal tax return work. For this price, the customer receives their tax return preparation and Unlimited Access. For perhaps $1,500, the customer would receive tax planning, and for $1,800 the firm provides audit representation in the event of an Internal Revenue Service audit. It is not necessary—nor is it desirable—to set standard prices for the levels beyond the minimum, since that would depend on the individual circumstances of each customer. The point, rather, is to offer the customer a range of services and let them select the investment they are most comfortable with. As most marketers have learned, the majority of customers select the middle options, since very few customers consider it desirable to buy the cheapest offering, proving most customers are *value-conscious*, not *price-conscious*.

The FPA is *not* designed to replace your firm's standard engagement letter. You still need this letter as required by your insurance carrier or professional ethics. However, where the engagement letter discusses price, simply refer to the FPA, dated such and such.

As stated earlier, most FPAs in CPA firms are for a one-year term, though we have seen multiple-year FPAs utilized in some accounting firms. This is an effective method of increasing the customer's switching costs, thereby increasing their loyalty.

Also, we have begun to see what are being called *perpetual* FPAs, whereby the CPA firm covers the basic compliance and other needs of the customer on a fixed-price basis, which runs in perpetuity. This is an effective way to handle most of the customer's needs; then in the annual FPA meeting, you focus on the customer's *wants*, which are usually less price-sensitive. It also has the added advantage of removing the core services from the annual pricing so the customer only has to focus on the incremental value you are offering. This can be advantageous in difficult economic times, since the entire price is not put up for evaluation each year.

A lot of firms utilizing FPAs do not even send invoices to customers. What would be the point? They know, and you know, exactly what is to be done, what the payment terms are, and what the price is, so why send a periodic invoice? Think of all the time you would save from not preparing and reviewing invoices, time you could spend strengthening your customer relationships.

We also know firms who have *negative work* in process; in other words, they have received full payment in advance of performing any work. This is particularly the case in tax practices. I always point out in my seminars that United Airlines currently holds several thousand dollars of my money for future flights. There is really only two ways your firm will ever get paid before it does any work: It has to set the price up front, and it has to ask for the payment. Many firms do this when they send out the annual tax organizer, engagement letter, and a cover letter stating the price, and a credit card authorization. When the organizers are returned, they contain the payment, in full. Think of the invoicing, collection, interest on financing accounts receivable, write-down, and write-off costs you will avoid by employing this method. It is another salutary effect of up-front pricing.

The firm is now ready to do the work. No matter how you price—even if you use the antiquated billable hour—proper project management is an essential skill to get work through the firm in the most efficacious manner, the subject of the next step and chapter.

CHAPTER **33**

Step Six: Proper Project Management

Think of the end before the beginning.

—Leonardo da Vinci

Try this experiment: The following Roman-numeral equation is comprised of ten sticks, but it is also incorrect. Try to correct the equation by moving as few of the sticks as possible:

$$\textbf{XI} + \textbf{I} = \textbf{X}$$

Did you begin immediately moving sticks around? Perhaps you moved only one and came up with X + I = XI. But as Matthew E. May points out in is book *The Elegant Solution,* you *satisficed.* He argues for the elegant solution: "Zero. You don't need to move a single stick. Turn the book upside down" (May 2006: 152).

When professional firms are engaged, they have a tendency to jump right to the *scope of work,* without spending enough time on diagnosing and planning the engagement. Nor do they spend enough time in conversation with the customer on the *scope of benefits.* My VeraSage colleague Ed Kless offers this admonition: "Prescription before diagnoses is malpractice."

Many professional firms are finally beginning to recognize one of the gaps in their competencies, in addition to pricing—project management. Even law firms are beginning to invest in this skill, especially with the increasing use of alternative pricing engagements. Yet an important point needs to be made:

Pricing is not project management.

The factory foreman at Toyota may be an expert in project management, planning the just-in-time inventory, production runs in the correct colors, options, and so on, but he *does not do the pricing of the cars*. We have learned that pricing skills and project management skills are usually not found in the same person (there are exceptions), even though both functions must communicate with each other.

Another important point must be made:

Project management is necessary, regardless of how a firm prices.

Even if your firm only "bills by the hour" project management is vital, as you must plan how work that comes in is allocated, what resources are devoted to it, what are the deadlines, and the myriad other issues that proper project management deals with. This is simply a table stake of operating an effective organization; it is not at all tied to pricing.

Fortunately, we have the wisdom of Ed Kless. Ed is a Senior Fellow at VeraSage Institute, and is certified by the Project Management Institute. He has written, and teaches, extensively on this topic as it relates to professional firms (his specialty being IT firms), and has helped countless firms increase their effectiveness, along with their value, by making project management a core competency. I am grateful to Ed for contributing the following sections, based upon his teachings and wisdom.

Case Study 33.1: Defining the Word "Project"

By Ed Kless

Sometimes, we need to go back to the very basics. While facilitating a class on project management, I always take the opportunity to spend a few minutes defining some basic concepts, since as Plato said, "All knowledge begins with the definition of terms." Of course, for a project management course, the first term would be project.

What Is a Project?

According to the Project Management Institute (PMI), a project is "a temporary endeavor undertaken to create a unique product, service, or result."

In my experience, further refining two words in this definition provides tremendous insight into the topic of project management. They are: *temporary* and *unique*.

To understand a project as *temporary* is to understand that it must have a clearly defined end. Too many projects are allowed to continue on seemingly *ad infinitum*. More often, professionals struggle to obtain sign off from a customer to clearly end the project. These two situations are caused by a lack of, or poorly defined, project objectives. One metaphor that has helped me over the years is to think of a project as a temporary company—one that comes into existence for the sole purpose of obtaining the objectives of the project and then goes out of business.

To comprehend a project as *unique* is to know that while you have participated in many similar projects, each one is truly different. There is no such thing as the "plain vanilla" or standard project, especially in professional knowledge firms. Each project has a different set of goals, objectives, constraints, and of course, personalities. Customers who ask you for the "plain vanilla" project are ignorant of these facts. (Note that the same customer who asks for the "plain vanilla" project will likely state, often only five minutes later, that their company does this "very differently" from others you may have encountered.)

Projects Have Characteristics

In addition to these important clarifications about the definition of a project, there are other characteristics of projects that are not stated outright in the definition. These include:

- Are often focused around a team drawing from multiple departments or disciplines
- Are in most cases business critical
- Can vary widely in budget, team size, duration, and expected outcomes
- Have conflict

Regarding this last item, I always pause to give some tough-love advice. People who are truly conflict averse should not be project managers. Projects by their very nature are agents of change. Change in people and in organizations creates conflict. A conflict-adverse person will often not address people problems in a timely fashion, ultimately resulting in the failure of the project.

Projects Are Not Process

Firms often fail to recognize that they do in fact have a project that requires better project management. One way to assist firms in

Continued

302 Eight Steps to Implementing Value Pricing

recognizing projects is to see if the tasks they are working on fit into any of their normal business processes. Whereas *projects* themselves are linear and have a clear beginning, middle, and end, *processes* recur at regular intervals. A process could happen once an hour, day, week, month, or even year. A project clearly happens only once.

Projects Have Processes

While projects are not processes, projects have processes. It is the consistent application of these individual simple processes that makes even the most complex project attainable. Project management processes call for the identification of inputs, tools, techniques, and outputs. Inputs are the source of the information, which can be new, meaning they never existed before this beginning of the process, or they can be from reuse, meaning their creation happened during a previous process. This input data is gathered and then acted upon by the project team using the tools and techniques. The results are the outputs.

Projects Have a Life Cycle

To improve project management control, project managers divide projects into three or more phases. Together, these phases are known as the project management life cycle. The initial phase is devoted to initiating and possibly some planning. The intermediate phase or phases are for detailed planning and execution, while the final phase is centered almost exclusively on closing the project.

Projects Are Progressively Elaborative

Progressive elaboration is the constant comparing of the progress made during a project against the original plan and then making changes and updates to the plan through the use of change requests. (Change Orders and requests will be discussed in Chapter 34.) When you really think about it, it is through progressive elaboration that project managers really do their work. An important point is that progressive elaboration is an *art,* not a science. This is why estimates of project costs are less accurate at the beginning of a project than at the end. It is also why the vast majority of projects should have at least several change requests. Project managers are not psychics, and even if they were we should recall that, as comedian Denis Leary put it, "Psychic friends network went out of business. Ya think they shoulda seen that comin'."

The Difference between Goals and Objectives

There is clearly a difference, in good project management, between goals and objectives. *Goals* are what we hope to attain by undertaking the project; however, they are not always attained by project end because there may be other external influences that factor into their achievement or lack thereof. *Objectives* are, well, objective, in that they can clearly be checked off as having been attained by project end.

For example, "increase sales by 10 percent" would be a goal of the project, not an objective. An objective would be the "installation of the new accounting system." The acid test question to distinguish one versus the other is, "Can this (goal or objective) be clearly accomplished when we consider the project to be completed?"

I am not saying that we should not continue to track project goals post completion; I am just noting that they need not be accomplished in order for us (and the customer) to consider the project done.

Finally, if a customer wants you to guarantee the attainment of goals, then I would have you consider contingency pricing. For example, if they do increase sales by 10 percent, you should be paid at least 30 percent of that number. In a sense, a customer asking you to guarantee goals is like that customer asking a lawyer to guarantee winning a case and therefore subject to a contingency arrangement. I would, however, guarantee meeting all objectives.

Now that we have defined some basics of project management, let us put it all together into the Triangle of Truth.

The Triangle of Truth

One of the basic principles of project management is what is known as the triple constraint. Some call this the scope, resource, time triangle. However, when I was the practice manager of a software implementation consulting firm, one of the guys on the team, Dave Franz, dubbed it the Triangle of Truth. (Franzy, if you are out there, you should know I give you credit whenever I talk about it.)

The concept is simple. A project consists of three interrelated variables: scope, resource (some say cost), and time. These variables are like the angles of a triangle. If you recall from geometry class in high school, in order for a polygon (shape) to be considered a triangle, the three angles must add to 180 degrees—in other words, Angle A (Scope) + Angle B (Resource/Cost) + Angle C (Time) = 180. If these do not add to 180, you do not have a triangle. So, if you make a change

Continued

to the value of one of the angles, one of the other two or both must also change to compensate or else the figure is broken.

The big problem with most professionals is that they are lousy and lazy about scope development. They prefer to concentrate on the second two elements, cost and time. In some cases, the professional feels pressure from the customer or prospect to give answers to the cost and time questions first. To me, this would be the equivalent of purchasing the lumber for a new house before going to an architect for plans; or a doctor writing a prescription before performing a diagnosis. Remember: prescription before diagnosis equals malpractice!

To refute this poor practice further, I need to reference one of the giants of the consulting profession, Peter Block. In his landmark book *The Answer to How Is Yes!*, Block posits that consultants (read: professionals) are usually presented first with what he calls "How" questions. "How much will it cost?" and "How long will it take?" are two of these questions—angles B and C in our triangle of truth as shown in Figure 33.1. Block argues that while these are relevant questions, when asked too early, they "express our bias for what is practical, concrete, and immediately useful. It assumes we do not know and this in itself becomes a defense against action."

Scope (angle A), however, is a "What matters?" or "Yes!" question according to Block, specifically the question is "What do we want to create?" In order to properly begin a project with a balanced (or equilateral) triangle we must ask and fully answer this question first. Why do we need a balanced triangle? If we go back to the analogy and take it one step further, let us draw a circle inside this triangle; the size of the circle represents the quality of the work performed. The largest

FIGURE 33.1 The Triangle of Truth

perfect circle can be drawn inside a triangle that is equilateral—that is, all sides the same—and therefore all angles equal to 60 degrees.

This is an important point because for a professional knowledge firm (PKF), quality is defined exclusively by the customer, not the professional. The professional cannot say that they do quality work. Rather, their customers say that about them. What happens in most firms is that scope is often poorly or not at all defined. I am sent an e-mail a week from someone asking me to assist them with scope creep on a project. My first response is to ask them to send me a copy of their scope document. In almost all cases, I am sent back a *proposal* with a range of hours. In replying to this I tell the poor sap that I have some good news and some bad news. "The good news is you do not have scope creep; the bad news is you are over budget." What I mean is that since they never defined scope to begin with they are not outside of scope. This leads us to the scope document.

Elements of a Scope Document

I submit the following as the required elements (consultants call them inclusions) of a scope document:

- Scope statement
- Objectives
- Constraints
- Project structure
- Roles definition
- Project team definition
- Assumptions
- Deliverables
- Scope details or functional requirements
- Project change control
- Future projects list
- Approval

I will now briefly examine each of these elements.

Scope statement. The scope statement defines in one sentence what the project will accomplish. It should support either the mission statement of the customer or be tied to at least one strategic objective of the firm. An example scope statement would read: To (*infinitive*) (*something*) on or before (*date*) and

Continued

at a price of (*dollar amount*). Notice how this statement addresses each of the three angles of the Triangle of Truth. While this statement appears first in the document, it will usually be written last.

Objectives. Objectives answer the specific question "What does success look like?" They are high-level statements that explain exactly what the desired results of this project are. Since they are general actions, they should begin with verbs. For example: train, create, develop, followed by specific, measurable, attainable, relevant, and time-sensitive (SMART) items to be accomplished. A general rule is that a project should not have more than eight objectives. If you have more than eight, you probably have more than one project.

Constraints. Constraints are limitations to the successful completion of the project due to affecting the scheduling of activities. They are things that could prevent work from getting accomplished. Common constraints are found in the following areas: technical, financial, operational, geographic, time, resource, legal, political, and ethical. Note that while similar categories exist for risk, constraints are *not* risks. Constraints are known facts; risks are uncertain events. A constraint may evolve into or cause a risk, but at least early on in the project they are different. An example constraint might be the lack of availability of data from current systems.

Project structure. Each project must have an overall organization. In short, your project structure is the organization chart for the project. Usually, this organization is in some conflict with the normal regular structure of the firm and, therefore, creates a temporary matrix-type organization. While there are some advantages to matrix organizations, the main weakness is lack of authority of the project manager since the functional manager has more say in the work performed by the individual.

Roles definition. Once you have outlined the project structure, it is important to define each role within the project. For each role you must define the specific responsibilities. These can and will change from project to project. Some roles requiring definition are:

- Steering committee member or executive sponsor
- Project manager
- Project owner
- Team leader
- Team member
- Project advisor

Team definition. This is simply the list of people who are functioning in what role on the project. Once you have the structure and role defined you need to assign people to the roles. In large projects this is part of resource planning.

Assumptions. Assumptions are beliefs about the relationship that serve as the starting point for project definition. Be sure to evaluate each assumption in terms of it being true, real, and certain. Another way of looking at them is that they answer the question "what should we not leave unsaid?" Do not have too many assumptions. If you do, you probably need to refine your scope—having more than ten assumptions looks careless. One example of an assumption relates back to the Triangle—in order for success to be attained the relationship between scope, costs, and time must be maintained. A change to any one of these three interrelated variables will affect the other two. For example, adding to the scope of the project will require an adjustment to either the cost of the project or the commencement date.

Deliverables. Deliverables are the tangible results—the products or services of the project. If objectives are verbs, as we stated earlier, deliverables are the nouns. They are usually things you can physically touch. There are two types of deliverables: intermediary, meaning they are to be used in subsequent tasks on the project, and final deliverables, meaning they are turned over to the customer at the end of the project. Examples of deliverables include the project plan, a training schedule, and training manuals.

Scope details or functional requirements. These will change depending on the project, but this is a critical section, which expounds on the scope statement's *infinitive*. Think of this section as the detailed definition of that *infinitive*.

Project change control. This section is like Article V of the United States Constitution, which describes how amendments are to be made. This section simply says that the scope document can be changed (amended) and defines the process for doing so.

Future project list. In addition to the obvious of being a list of possible future projects and major tasks that will be deferred until after this one is complete, the future projects list is important in that it defines what is not included in this project. It is important to list these additional projects as they are identified

Continued

during the planning process, since they are the future business of a professional knowledge firm.

Approval. The scope should be signed and dated by the project manager and the project sponsor.

If you do not have each of these elements, it is my belief that you do not have scope. If you do not have scope, you cannot have scope creep. Even when firms do a decent job of developing scope, some professionals get caught in true scope creep. This happens when, after having defined a good scope, the project manager allows more scope to be added to the project without rebalancing the triangle. In other words, they take on more "What" and they squeeze the "How." This is exactly what a change request is for.

Elements of a Change Request

In almost all of the small and medium business information technology projects that I have been associated with there have been usually dozens of change requests. In fact, I cannot think of a single project, however small, that there were none. I believe it would be *Twilight Zone* weird that any project would have no change requests. Any project worth scoping will be, by definition, one that lends itself to changes. If a customer expects that a project will not have any change requests, he is probably not a good customer to have. No one can predict the future.

Please note that the language that I use for these is *change request*, not Change Order. They are, by definition, requests and may be accepted or rejected by the project sponsor (steering committee, on a larger project). A change request is simply an acknowledgment that something that affects the Triangle of Truth needs to be adjusted. In some cases there may not be any budgetary or price change. For example, during an implementation of software the controller may leave the company. The resolution for this may be to push the "go-live" date of the project out, rather than adjust the financial resources. Even if there is no change to the budget, this is still a change request and needs to be approved by the project sponsor. Let us look at the elements of a change request with some commentary.

- Project name.
- Change number.
- Project manager name.
- Requestor name. In my view on small projects anyone on the project (customer or consultant) can request a change. In many

cases the project manager would assist in the creation of the change request document and would most certainly review it before presenting it to the executive sponsor.

- Requested date.
- Resolution requested by date. "ASAP" is not an allowed date. ASAP means different things to the sender and receiver. To the sender it means *now*, emphasis on the word *soon*. To the receiver it means *whenever*, emphasis on the word *possible*.
- Description of change.
- Business reason for change. This section must describe the economic benefit that the change will create. In short, if the economic benefit does not exceed the cost section below, it is unlikely the change will be accepted.
- Impact on scope—In a sense a change request is a mini scope document. Please remember that when scope changes there must be a change to cost and/or time in the Triangle of Truth.
- Impact on price—This would detail the pricing change needed to perform the change.
- Impact on time.
- Impact on quality—Remember if quality is affected, all three of the other elements (scope, cost, and time) must also be affected.
- Change accepted or rejected.
- Reason for rejection, if rejected.
- Signatures and dates.

Finally, change requests should be listed in a separate change request log if the changes are great in number.

Most professionals continue to bill by the hour because they are afraid of scope creep. Between Ed Kless's project management and Chris Marston's circles, they have provided you a way to avoid that fear while adding tremendous value to your customers. Like pricing, proper project management needs to become a core competency in the firm of the future.

Customers do not care about the amount of time spent on their work—or *effort*. They do, however, care about the *duration* of that work. *Duration* is the number of days or weeks that a project will take to complete. It is the window of time in which the result must be achieved. *Effort* is the actual amount of work, usually expressed in resource hours. A task can have a duration of 8 hours; however, the effort could be only 15 minutes. Alternatively, a task with duration of 8 hours could also have 24 hours of effort. Project management is more concerned about *duration* than effort.

Turnaround time would emphasize when a project or case will be done, not how many hours will go into its completion. It is similar to FedEx guaranteeing the package will arrive on your doorstep by 8:30 a.m. It is the result that counts. Hence, turnaround time is an example of a Key Predictive Indicator that measures what customers care about.

Let us now proceed to the next step and discuss scope creep, a sample Change Order (or Change Request, if you prefer Ed's term), and how this concept fits strategically with value pricing.

CHAPTER **34**

Step Seven: Scope Creep and Change Orders

Imagine you hire a contractor to build a game room in your home. After he walks around the house taking measurements and drafting preliminary plans for the job, chances are at some point you are going to ask what every customer wants to know: "How much?" If the contractor could not quote you a price up front, but said instead, "Well, I'm not sure, but I will keep fastidious track of the time and the cost of materials, and will bill you when I'm done" my conjecture is you would find another contractor. More likely he would quote you a fixed price for the job and you would enter into an agreement.

Assume then, that on the first day his crew begins the job, while tearing out one of your walls, they discover dry rot and termites. They will immediately stop work, inform you of the problem, tell you what the price would be to fix it, and let you decide how you want to handle the issue. This is what separates a contractor (or auto mechanic) from a professional. In contrast, professionals would simply plow ahead and fix the problem, with no input or authorization from you, track the time spent, and simply send the invoice when the work is complete. At that point, the firm would lose the pricing leverage and would be at risk for a write-down, or sometimes, a write-off. This is not an effective way to sell your services or keep customers happy.

Notice you expect the contractor to quote you a price *before* he begins work, even while knowing that myriad problems could arise that would cause the job to go beyond the original estimate—what we term *scope creep*. Simply because you do not know everything that might arise on a particular customer engagement does not mean you are released from the obligation to set a price for the parameters you are aware of. It simply means you must define the scope of the job and be diligent about issuing Change Orders when scope creep occurs.

Change Orders originated in the contracting industry and are one of the most sophisticated pricing strategies ever devised (this should dispel, once and for all, the notion that professionals have a monopoly on knowledge and cannot learn from other industries). When the contractor makes you aware of the dry rot and termites, he is putting you in charge of making the decision of how to handle the problem. Drafting a Change Order produces the best of both worlds, from a seller's perspective. It keeps the customer in charge of the buying process (which is always imperative since no one likes to be *sold*, but they do decide to *buy*), while the contractor *retains* the pricing leverage.

Change Orders should be used anytime scope creep appears in a project included in the FPA, which is why it is essential the team members know exactly what the responsibilities of each party are and the scope of the project. It is team members on the front lines who are usually the first to spot scope creep, and once they do, they need to inform the manager or partner on the engagement of the problem, the remedy, and the resources required to solve the problem. This way, the partner can contact the customer to determine how she wants to move forward. Do not allow team members to commit firm resources by providing work the customer has not yet authorized. A sure prescription for write-downs and ill will among customers, and for not maximizing your profit potential, is to perform work they have not agreed to in advance. Figure 34.1 is a sample Change Order for a service that is included in the FPA where the firm has encountered scope creep.

My VeraSage colleague Daryl Golemb, CPA, uses an effective question for simple to moderate projects and/or scope creep, such as tax research, lease versus buy analysis, and the like: "Mr. Customer, what's *my* budget for this?" Chances are high, according to Daryl, your customer will not insult you with a ridiculously low price, but rather quote a price that will be above your Reservation price. He discovered the effectiveness of this question after testing the first iteration: "What's *your* budget for this?" This was less effective, as the customer rarely has a budget for unexpected contingencies. For more complex Change Orders, obviously, this method will not be as effective, but those Change Orders should be priced by the value council.

Also, utilize Change Orders for projects that arise that are not included in the FPA, such as an audit, consulting service, and so on. The advantage of combining FPAs with a Change Order strategy is that, as noted previously, because the FPA deals with most of the customer's needs, Change Orders will mostly be used for wants, which are less price sensitive to the customer. This allows you to utilize some innovative pricing strategies, such as the TIP clause. Figure 34.2 is a sample Change Order for a service that has not been included in the FPA.

Customer:

Date:

Project description and scope [and estimated completion date, if appropriate]:

During fieldwork of the audit for the year ended [insert date], ABC CPAs discovered that the Prepared By Customer (PBC) Schedules were not accurately completed, in a timely manner, as specified in the FPA dated [insert date of FPA].

To complete the audit in a timely manner, both parties agree that ABC CPAs will hereby complete the PBC Schedules.

Since this service was not originally anticipated by ABC CPAs in its FPA for the audit, both parties agree to the mutually acceptable price for this service as stated below.

Price: $_____

Terms: Payable upon authorization of this Change Order (or upon completion of the work, or any other acceptable terms agreed upon).

We believe it is our responsibility to exceed your expectations. This Change Order is being prepared because the above project was not anticipated in our original Fixed Price Agreement, dated [insert date of FPA].The price for the above project has been mutually agreed upon by XYZ, Inc. and ABC CPAs. It is our goal to ensure that XYZ is never surprised by the price for any ABC CPAs service, and therefore we have adopted the Change Order Policy.

If you agree with the above project description and the price, please authorize and date the Change Order below. Thank you for letting us serve you.

Sincerely,

Allan Somnolent, partner, ABC CPAs

Agreed to and accepted:

BY: _____
        Customer, president, XYZ, Inc.

Date: _____

FIGURE 34.1 Sample Change Order: Service Specified in the FPA; Scope Change Due to Customer Not Fulfilling an Obligation

I have used the term Change Order throughout this book since that term is widely understood, but some firms have modified this term. Some have labeled it a work order or work request.

My VeraSage colleague Ed Kless recommends the term *change request.* This is because someone is always recommending the change—either the customer or the firm. The chain looks like this:

Customer:

Date:

Project description and scope [and estimated completion date, if appropriate]:
ABC CPAs will hereby represent XYZ, Inc. before the Internal Revenue Service for the
audit of its [year] Corporate Tax Return, for the issues as described in the IRS letter dated
[insert date].

XYZ, Inc. hereby agrees that its accounting department will provide all records,
documentation, and schedules as deemed necessary by ABC CPAs.

Based upon ABC CPA's knowledge of the IRS's concerns and issues to be examined, we
hereby agree to represent XYZ, inc. for the fixed price stated below.

If, in the course of the audit, other issues are raised that are outside the scope of the IRS
letter mentioned above, ABC CPAs and XYZ, Inc. hereby agree to enter into another
Change Order at that time, at a mutually agreed upon price.
Price: $_____
Terms: 50% payable upon commencement of the IRS audit.
       50% payable upon completion of the audit.

We believe it is our responsibility to exceed your expectations. This Change Order is
being prepared because the above project was not anticipated in our original Fixed Price
Agreement, dated [insert date]. The price for the above project has been mutually agreed
upon by XYZ, Inc. and ABC CPAs. It is our goal to ensure that XYZ is never surprised
by the price for any ABC CPAs service, and therefore we have adopted the Change
Order Policy.

If you agree with the above project description and the price, please authorize and date
the Change Order below. Thank you for letting us serve you.

Sincerely,

Allan Somnolent, partner, ABC CPAs

Agreed to and accepted:

BY: _____
          Customer, president, XYZ, Inc.

Date: _____

FIGURE 34.2 Sample Change Order: Service Not Specified in the FPA

- Scope creep is encountered, either by the customer or the firm; or
- A change is initiated, either by the customer or the firm;
- Communication takes place between the parties, which leads to
- A change request, which leads ultimately to a
- Change Order

Whichever name you choose, the important point is the process this puts the firm through before performing any additional work not authorized by the customer.

We are always asked, "Do customers get upset by the firm triggering too many Change Orders?" The answer is no. Customers appreciate the communication and being given the authority of determining how to handle the issue. This is not to say you can be lazy regarding determining the scope of projects because you know you can rely on Change Orders. You still have to do proper project management and learn as much as you can about the customer's situation. By managing the customer's expectations from the beginning, and informing them that your firm utilizes Change Orders to implement the no-surprises policy, you will not experience resistance from them when you use this strategy.

We are now ready to proceed to the last step in the process—the value council performs an After Action Review on value created and price captured.

CHAPTER 35

Step Eight: Pricing After Action Reviews

You always learn by doing, but you also learn by learning, if you know what I mean.

—Yogi Berra, *When You Come to a Fork in the Road, Take It!*, 2001

Recall the discussion of After Action Reviews (AAR) from Chapter 25, which focused on the technical knowledge that firms can convert from human to structural capital by utilizing the AAR.

The value council also needs to conduct AARs on the pricing of each major engagement. Again, follow the Pareto Principle: Only perform AARs on that 20 percent of customers who generate 80 percent of the revenue. One of the major problems with pricing is we can only see *what we priced*, yet what we really want to know is *what we could have priced*. My VeraSage colleague Michelle Golden summed it up nicely when she said, "This is how we refine the art of pricing—one word: Regret." AARs will add enormously to your firm's pricing competency and intellectual capital.

The following are questions the value council—along with the team members who worked on the customer engagement—should answer after the job is done. As always with the checklists contained in this book, it is not meant to be exhaustive but rather a beginning for you to modify to fit your firm's needs and that of your customers.

Sample Value Council After Action Review
- Did we add value for this customer?
- How could we have added more value?
- Did we capture a fair portion of that value?
- Could we have captured more value through a higher price?
- How much money did we leave on the table?

- If we were doing this engagement again, how would we do it?
- What are the implications for product/service design? Did we learn any new intellectual capital that we could leverage across other customers?
- Should we communicate the lessons on this engagement to our colleagues and how?
- How could we have enhanced our customer's perception of value?
- What did we teach this customer?
- What other needs does this customer have and are we addressing them?
- Did this engagement enhance our relationship with this customer?
- What impact has this engagement had on developing our customer's trust in us?
- How would you rate our customer's price sensitivity before and after this job?
- How has this engagement advanced us?
- Did we have the right team on this engagement?
- How high were the costs to serve?
- What could we do better next time?
- Do we need to update our customer complaint register?
- How could we thank this customer for their business?

The AAR process forces firms to devote a portion of their time to *improving* the work rather than just *doing* the work. Experience is what we get when we did not get what we expected, which is what the AAR is suited to capture with a formal method. It forces firms to *reflect* on what they have learned, *capture* it, and then be able to *reuse* it when needed in the future.

Recall from our discussion of price-led costing and cost accounting that we advocate that cost accounting needs to be done *before* the work is started. It does no good to know your costs to the penny if your customer does not agree with your price. How do you know if your upfront cost estimates were accurate? The question included in the AAR above—How high were the costs to serve?—is the firm's opportunity to ask the team how long they spent on the engagement as a check to see if the upfront estimate was accurate. This does not have to be exact. Cost accounting is not an exact science. Anyway, if you price on value, you are going to soon come to the conclusion that hours are insignificant. What matters is customer yield and profit, which are driven by price, not cost accounting accuracy.

PART VI

Inflection Point

Inflection point: A time in the life of a business in which its fundamentals are about to change.

—Andy Grove, founder, Intel

CHAPTER 36

No One Can Forbid Us the Future

If we want things to stay as they are, things will have to change.

—Giuseppe Tomasi di Lampedusa, *The Leopard*, 1958

Evolutionary biologists have proven that the more adapted (i.e., comfortable) you are in your existing environment, the less able you are to adapt to environmental changes. Struggle is good for us. Rigidity is what organizations manifest when they are faced with either superior competition or outdated business models. They blindly cling to "that is the way we have always done it" in defiance of the evidence that this way is no longer relevant to success. Charles F. Kettering, the automotive inventor and pioneer said it best: "If you have always done it that way it is probably wrong."

This is the history of business. New ideas, inventions, and business models from the tinkerer in the garage change the world, while rendering obsolete the existing modes of production, infrastructure, and business models. The automobile replaced the horse and buggy, the calculator replaced the slide rule, the personal computer replaced the typewriter, iTunes replaced CDs, and so on in a never-ending "perennial gale of creative destruction," as described by economist Joseph Schumpeter. Clayton Christensen writes, "Generally, the leading practitioners of the old order become the victims of disruption, not the initiators of it."

Change and creativity always take us by surprise. If it didn't, we wouldn't need it, because we could simply plan on it and incorporate it into our existing strategies and processes. Nassim Nicholas Taleb makes this very point in his book *The Black Swan*:

Chapter title is the inscription on the base of the monument to Léon Gambetta (1838–1882) in Paris, c. 1883.

We do not know what we will know. Invention and creativity is always a surprise. If we could prophesy the invention of the wheel, we'd already know what a wheel looks like, and thus we could invent it (Taleb 2007: 173).

The professions, however, have been slow to adapt to the realities of an intellectual capital economy. Never before has this mentality been such a hindrance to success in today's rapidly changing, globalized marketplace. *How many CPAs does it take to change a light bulb? Ten. One to change it and nine to talk about how great the old one was.*

Experts rarely innovate. G. K. Chesterton wrote, "The argument of the expert, that the man who is trained should be the man who is trusted, would be absolutely unanswerable if it were really true that the man who studied a thing and practiced it every day went on seeing more and more of its significance. But he does not. He goes on seeing less and less of its significance." Here are some all-time best blunders on the part of the "experts":

- In 1886, the Gottlieb Daimler Company predicted the ultimate size of the world's automobile market to be an eventual total of one million, rationalizing that there could be no more than one million trained chauffeurs in the world.
- "Flight by machines heavier than air is impractical and insignificant, if not utterly impossible." (Simon Newcomb, an astronomer of some note, 1902)
- "There is no likelihood man can ever tap the power of the atom." (Robert Millikan, Nobel Prize winner in physics, 1920)
- "We don't like their sound. Groups of guitars are on the way out." (Decca Recording Company executive, turning down the Beatles a second time, 1962)
- "Get your feet off my desk, get out of here, you stink, and we're not going to buy your product." (Joe Keenan, president of Atari, responding to Steve Job's offer to sell him rights to the new personal computer he and Steve Wozniak had developed, 1976)

Business Model Innovation

History is not a teacher, but an overseer, a *magister vitae*: it teaches nothing, but only punishes for not learning its lessons.

—Russian historian Vasily O. Kliuchevsky

In a meeting with Harvard Business School professor Clayton Christensen, former Intel CEO Andy Grove made the point that "disruptive threats came inherently not from new technology but from new business models" (Johnson 2010: 191). Perhaps this is why Grove titled his own book *Only the Paranoid Survive.*

Clayton Christensen's partner in his consulting firm Innosight is Mark W. Johnson, author of the compelling book *Seizing the White Space.* He points out that most successful innovative business models are forged by start-ups. Johnson studied approximately 350 business model innovations in the past ten years, with more than 30 percent being enabled by Internet technology (Johnson 2010: 95). Fourteen companies founded since 1984 have entered the *Fortune* 500 between 1997 and 2007 through business model innovation, including:

Amazon.com
AutoNation
eBay
Google
Qualcomm
Starbucks
Yahoo! (Johnson 2010: 19)

Thinking about the history of innovation, creative destruction, and business models in the context of professional knowledge firms, in combination with the radical business model proposed in this book—from "We sell time" to "We sell intellectual capital"—Figure 36.1 provides an interesting look at where any firm can be at a given point in time. Since competitive advantages are built based on effectiveness, not efficiencies, I have chosen to highlight each as the axes of the exhibit.

Luddites: Firms that resist technological advances and other innovations that are merely table stakes risk being Luddites. They have both low efficiency in doing things right and low effectiveness at doing the right things—not a bright future. Fortunately, not many firms are in this category. If you are here, you are dead already and the funeral is a mere detail.

Buggy whips: Usually when an industry is at the apogee of its efficiency, it is at risk of being made obsolete by new technologies or business models. As Peter Drucker said, no amount of efficiency gains would have saved the buggy whip manufacturers from the automobile.

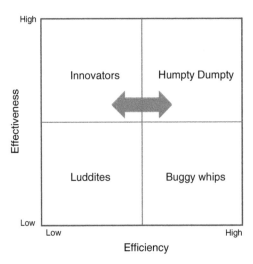

FIGURE 36.1 The History of Innovation

Innovators: As George Gilder wrote in *Forbes,* "Knowledge is about the past; entrepreneurship is about the future. If creativity was not unexpected, governments could plan it and socialism would work. But creativity is intrinsically surprising and the source of all real profit and growth" ("The Coming Creativity Boom," November 10, 2008, www.forbes.com/forbes/2008/1110/036.html). Innovators are firms that are willing to invest some of today's profits into tomorrow, while at the same time sacrificing efficiency for effectiveness. Innovation, creativity, and Total Quality Service are the antithesis of efficiency—ideas such as Google Time (team members can spend 20 percent of their time innovating), research and development, investing in education, all reduce efficiency metrics. But if firms do not make these essential investments they are simply coasting on their existing intellectual capital, and in today's economy, knowledge becomes obsolete more rapidly.

Humpty Dumpty: This is a precarious future. This represents firms that are highly efficient *and* effective. I am arguing that if you are here, you better be sliding back to the Innovators position and start sacrificing some of that efficiency for innovation and making the firm more valuable to its customers. Humpty Dumpty eventually falls and ends up like the industries mentioned under Buggy Whips. Efficiency is not the answer. Effectiveness is.

The Diffusion of Theories

Each of us should realize that one possesses within oneself the formidable capacity to construct an explanatory system of the world and along with it a machine for rejecting all facts contrary to this system.

— Jean-François Revel (1924–2006), French philosopher, author, journalist, politician, *The Flight from Truth*, 1991.

Despite the economic pressure that is presently being applied to the old business model of professionals firms, the reasons for the resistance to change have deeper roots. The billable hour—a direct descendent of the labor theory of value—was falsified in 1871, so why has it had an uninterrupted era since at least 1919? Even though there are more firms today operating under an alternative business model, the "We sell time" theory predominates.

I believe it is because we are not simply talking about a technology change, or a business model change. Instead, we are talking about a new theory that has yet to diffuse into the professions. And theories do not diffuse at the same pace as new technologies, or even business models. As professionals, the history we should study is that of medicine, because the parallels are eerily similar.

David Wootton is a historian at the University of York and author of *Bad Medicine: Doctors Doing Harm Since Hippocrates*, one of the most important books I have read in a long time. He is no medical profession basher, thanking modern medicine for saving his life and also proudly announcing that his daughter is a doctor.

Not only is the book incredibly well written—even if, like me, you have no particular interest in the history of medicine—it is a mesmerizing look at how a supposedly scientific and evidence-based profession rejected new innovations, knowledge, and theories while stubbornly clinging to their old—and completely ineffectual, if not downright lethal—therapies.

Bad Medicine Drives Out Good Medicine

The history of medicine begins with Hippocrates in the fifth century B.C. Yet until the invention of antibiotics in the 1940s doctors, in general, did their patients more harm than good. In other words, for 2,400 years patients believed doctors were doing good; for 2,300 years they were wrong.

From the first century B.C. to the mid-nineteenth century, the major therapy was bloodletting, performed with a special knife called a lancet. Interestingly enough, that is the title of today's prestigious English medical journal *The Lancet*. Bad ideas die hard.

Bloodletting had its opponents, of course, but the debate was over *where* in the body to draw the blood from, not over its effectiveness.

The Case against Medicine

The author makes three devastating arguments. First, if medicine is defined as the ability to cure diseases, then there was very little medicine before 1865. Prior to that—a period the author calls Hippocratic medicine— doctors relied on bloodletting, purges, cautery, and emetics, all totally ineffectual, if not positively deleterious (no matter how *efficiently* they were administered).

Second, effective medicine could only begin when doctors began to count and compare, such as using clinical trials.

Third, the key development that made modern medicine possible is the germ theory of disease.

We all assume that good ideas and theories will drive out bad ones, but that is not necessarily true. Historically, bad medicine drove out good medicine, as Wootton explains:

> We know how to write histories of discovery and progress, but not how to write histories of stasis, of delay, of digression. We know how to write about the delight of discovery, but not about attachment to the old and resistance to the new (Wootton 2006: 14–15).

This is not to say that advances in *knowledge* were not made prior to 1865. Unfortunately, those advances had no pay-off in terms of advances in *therapy*, or what Wootton calls *technology*—that is, therapies, treatments, and techniques to cure. So until the 1860s, doctors had knowledge of what was wrong but could only use it to predict who would live and who would die. Wootton describes how the advances in knowledge did not change therapies, in perhaps the most devastating conclusion in the book:

> The discovery of the circulation of the blood (1628), of oxygen (1775), of the role of haemoglobin (1862) made no difference; the discoveries were adapted to the therapy [bloodletting] rather than vice versa.

> … [I]f you look at therapy, not theory, then ancient medicine survives more or less intact into the middle of the nineteenth century and beyond.

> Strangely, traditional medical practices—bloodletting, purging, induc- ing vomiting—had continued even while people's understanding of how the body worked underwent radical alteration. *The new theories were set to work to justify old practices.* [Emphasis added] (Wootton 2006: 17)

In a reversal of the scientific method, the therapies guided the theory, not the other way around. Diffusing a new theory into a population is no easy task, nor is it quick. Wootton describes in captivating detail how various innovations in medicine were rejected by the medical establishment (this list is much longer):

- Joseph Lister is credited with positing germ theory in 1865, yet there was considerable evidence for this theory dating back to 1546, and certainly by 1700. Prior to this, infections were thought to be caused by stale air and water (even Florence Nightingale believed this).
- Even though by 1628 it was understood that the heart pumped blood through the arteries, the use of tourniquets in amputations didn't happen until roughly a century later.
- The microscope was invented by 1677—simultaneously with the telescope, which lead to new discoveries in astronomy—yet as late as 1820 it had no place in medical research, believed to be nothing more than a toy.
- Penicillin was first discovered in 1872, not 1941, as popularly believed. Its effectiveness was doubted for nearly 70 years.

Why the Delay?

Wootton believes the primary obstacle to progress was not practical, nor theoretical, but psychological and cultural—"it lay in doctors' sense of themselves." Consider the psychological obstacles:

Medicine has often involved doing things to other people that you normally should not do. Think for a moment what surgery was like before the invention of anesthesia in 1842.

Imagine amputating the limb of a patient who is screaming and struggling. Imagine training yourself to be indifferent to the patient's suffering, to be deaf to their screams. Imagine developing the strength to pin down the patient's thrashing body (Wootton 2006: 21).

To think about progress, you must first understand what stands in the way of progress—in this case, the surgeon's pride in his work, his professional training, his expertise, his sense of who he is (Wootton 2006: 23).

The cultural obstacles, Wootton believes, are based on a somewhat counterintuitive observation: institutions have a life of their own. All actions cannot be said to be performed by individuals; some are performed by institutions. For instance, a committee may reach a decision that was nobody's first choice.

This is especially true for institutions that are shielded from competition and hermetically sealed in orthodoxy. In a competitive market, germ theory would have been tested in a competing company, diffusing into the population much faster than it did within the institutions of the medical community. Wootton also cites Thomas Kuhn's book *The Structure of Scientific Revolutions*, wherein he distinguished between periods of "normal science" and science that takes place during periods of crisis. Germ theory was adopted because the medical profession knew it was in crisis.

Why Is This Relevant to the Professions?

The similarities between bad medicine, the billable hour, timesheets, Frederick Taylor's efficiency religion, and value pricing are illustrative. Even today the U.S. Centers of Disease Control reports that 2 million people get infections in hospitals, and of those 90,000 die. The largest cause? Failure to properly wash hands.

In physics the key barriers to progress are most likely theoretical. In oceanography they might be practical. What are the key barriers to progress in the professional knowledge firm? My VeraSage colleague Tim Williams remarked about Wootton's book, "It makes me think about Stephen Covey's premise [in his book *The Seven Habits of Highly Effective People*] that if you want to make incremental changes, work on practices. If you want to make significant changes, work on paradigms." The problem is, minds are slower to change than markets, especially in the professions.

If a supposed scientific and evidence-based profession is this slow to change, what chance do lawyers, CPAs, and other professionals have to move away from the discredited labor theory of value—the modern-day equivalent of bloodletting?

Will the professions resist change for as long as doctors did? Are the cultural and institutional legacies that entrenched? Do professionals really want to define themselves by how many hours they log on a timesheet?

I do not know, but the evidence seems to indicate in the positive. Obviously, burying the billable hour and the timesheet is going to be a very long process indeed. Nonetheless, I remain a paranoid optimist. It may not be within reach, but it is certainly within sight.

Firm of the Future or Firm of the Past?

He who wants to improve conditions must propagate a new mentality, not just merely a new institution.

—Ludwig von Mises

Voltaire wrote, "The great consolation in life is to say what one thinks." This book has certainly provided me that opportunity. You have read my beliefs, values, and convictions (from the Latin word *convictum*, "that which is proven or demonstrated"). I have attempted to demonstrate with empirical evidence the superiority of the new business model over the old one for professional knowledge firms of the future, all the while wishing that this *will not* be the only business model the professions innovate. But this radical business model challenges the conventional wisdom of the ages because truth is not defined simply by seniority, or popularity. You can be alone and be right.

I have offered you a testable hypothesis, one that is subject to the falsification principle described by Karl Popper, which is how all knowledge progresses. As a writer I would desire nothing more than having these theories and ideas accepted as part of the conventional wisdom—not to mention practices—of the professions. I have stated what I believe is the truth, and I am now ready to accept the consequences, hoping that what is false will be exposed and that what is true will be admitted.

Clare Boothe Luce used to say, "The only difference between an optimist and a pessimist is that a pessimist is usually better informed." When it comes to the professions, I certainly hope she was wrong. But the road not yet traveled is long, and it seems the professions, to paraphrase Winston Churchill's exhortation of America, will do the right thing—once they have exhausted the alternatives.

Embracing a new business model requires leadership and vision. It requires knowing you are doing the right things, not just doing things right. It requires focusing the firm on the external value it creates for the customer and simultaneously building the type of firm people are proud to be a part of and contribute to—the sort of organization you would want your son or daughter to work for. It requires a sense of dignity and self-respect that you are worth every penny you charge, and you will only work with customers who have integrity, whom you enjoy and respect. It requires an attitude of experimentation, not simply doing things because that is the way it has always been done. It requires less measurement, less fear, and more trust. It requires boldness and risk-taking—there has yet to be a book written titled *Great Moderates in History*.

As science fiction writer William Gibson quipped, "The future is here. It's just not widely distributed yet." The firms mentioned herein are proof that the ground beneath the feet of the professions is beginning to shift. New and more effective business models are being developed and refined every day that recognize the realities of our intellectual capital economy, while treating professionals like the knowledge workers they are. It is an idea whose time has come.

Resembling lightning rods, the first wave of firms that truly understand the difference between knowledge workers and service/manual workers will have an enormous window of opportunity to attract, develop, inspire, and profit from their human capital investors. The firms that do not will continue to struggle in the competition for talent.

Skeptics will call for an incremental approach, which is how they maintain the status quo. But how will these optically challenged skeptics make incremental changes to an existing business model that is already dying? The late economist John Kenneth Galbraith wrote, "All successful revolutions are the kicking in of a rotten door," not—I would add—merely oiling the hinges to make it swing more efficiently.

There is no limit to what we can achieve, as long as we do not lose faith in ourselves. It is the difference between remaining a firm of the past, or, like a chrysalis, emerging as a firm of the future. The choice is yours.

CHAPTER 37

Declaration of Independence

Action January 1, 2001.
The UNANIMOUS DECLARATION of the FOUNDERS of VeraSage Institute of the PROFESSIONS ASSEMBLED,

WHEN in the Course of Economic Evidence, it becomes necessary for one group of Professionals to dissolve the Traditional Bands which have connected them with another, and to assume among the Powers of the Free Market, the separate and equal Station to which the Laws of Economics entitle them, a decent Respect to the Opinions of the Profession requires that they should declare the causes which impel them to the Separation.

We hold these Truths to be self-evident, that all Value is Subjective, the Customer is sole arbiter of the Value which we in the Professions create, and Price determines Costs, not the opposite—That to secure these Truths, Policies and Procedures are instituted among members of the Profession, and that whenever any Policy becomes destructive of these Principles, it is the Right of the Profession to alter or to abolish it, and to institute new Policies, laying its foundation on such Principles as to them shall seem most likely to effect their Professionalism, Dignity, Self-respect, and Happiness. Prudence, indeed, will dictate that Traditions long established should not be changed for light and transient Causes; and accordingly all Experience hath shewn, that the Professions are more disposed to suffer than to right themselves by abolishing the Policies and Procedures to which they are accustomed. But when a long Train of Pernicious Effects evinces a Design to reduce them under absolute Despotism, it is their Right, it is their Duty, to throw off such Traditions, and to provide new Procedures for their future Security. Such has been the patient Sufferance of these Founders; and such is now the Necessity which constrains them to alter the former anachronistic Systems of Firm Management. The History of the present Time Accounting is a History of repeated Injuries and Deleterious Effects, all having in direct Object the Establishment of an absolute Tyranny over the Professions. To prove this, let Facts be submitted to a Candid World.

Time Accounting is a descendant of the thoroughly discredited Marxian Labor Theory of Value, which has never adequately explained Value in a Free Market and has no jurisdiction to control the Pricing of Intellectual Capital of which the Professions are engaged in Creating.

Time Accounting has foisted onto the professions the implicit assertion that Time × Rate = Value. This Equation is emphatically false, and is in need of being rejected as without Reason. The Notion that Time is Money is hereby directly rejected.

Time Accounting misaligns the interests of the Professional and the Customer whom it is pledged to Serve.

Time Accounting has focused the Professions solely on hours, not Value, thereby keeping the Professional Mired in Mediocrity at the expense of Entrepreneurial Excellence in the pursuit of opportunities.

Time Accounting places the voluntary transaction risk entirely on the Customer, in direct defiance of the Customer's interests the Professions have pledged to Serve.

Time Accounting fosters a production mentality, not an Entrepreneurial Spirit, thereby hindering the Professions in their attempt to innovate and contribute to the dynamism of the Free Market.

Time Accounting has called together Management and Partners at Places unusual, uncomfortable, and distant from the Professionals and Customers they are bound to Serve, for the sole Purpose of fatiguing them into Compliance with these arbitrary Measures.

Time Accounting creates a subsidy system whereby some Customers will pay for the learning curve of others, and the allocation of Value to any one Customer is completely arbitrary and capricious.

Time Accounting transmits no useful information, as it is definitely not a Critical Success Factor or a Key Predictive Indicator for any member of the Profession, as defined by the Customer whom it is Pledged to Serve.

Time Accounting produces information that is Suspect and subject to inaccuracies and nonfeasance.

Time Accounting has made Owners dependent on Its will alone for the Tenure, Promotion, and the Amount of Payment of Professional Salaries rendered, irrespective of the Value they Create.

Time Accounting has erected a Multitude of new Ominous forms, and internal Bureaucracies, and sent hither Swarms of Officers, Nefarious Cost Accountants, Superfluous Lean and Six-Sigma Belts of various Colors, and Activity Based Costing Neophytes to harass our People, and eat out their Substance, in fifteen minute increments, and sometimes less.

Time Accounting encourages the Hoarding of Hours with no attention paid to the internal efficacious utilization of a Firm's Resources.

Time Accounting has conspired with others to subject us to a Measurement foreign to the Laws of Economics, and unacknowledged by our Self Evident Truths; giving Its Assent to the importance of pretended consequences.

Time Accounting focuses on Efforts, not Results. Customers don't buy efforts, and they don't buy hours, making Time Accounting a measurement of precisely the wrong things.

Time Accounting has become a tool, enhanced by modern technology, already rife with circumstances of Cruelty and Perfidy, scarcely paralleled in any other industry, and totally unworthy of a Proud, and Intellectual Capital based, Profession.

Time Accounting penalizes Technological Advances, as the Professions continue to invest in more and efficient technology, in order to produce more work in less Time, thus lowering Revenue in a Time Accounting Pricing Paradigm.

Time Accounting's Hourly Rates are set by paying attention to competitors, who have no quantifiable interest in the success of any competing enterprise, thereby depriving a Firm's Owners from being compensated for the Value They create.

Time Accounting is a Cost-plus Pricing method that has been thoroughly discredited throughout its inglorious history, and is no longer relevant in a world where wealth is created by Free Minds in Free Markets. It is not the Customer's duty to provide the Professions with a Desirable Net Income; it is the duty of the Professions to Provide a Service that is so good, the Customer Dutifully Pays a Profit in Recognition of what was done for them. Profit is a Lagging Indicator, at best, and is a Result of a Job well done, an Applause. In a Free Market, costs do not determine price, rather, price determines costs and value determines price.

Time Accounting defies the imperative rule of private, Free Market Transactions; that is, the Price is known to the Customer before they purchase a product or service. The Professions Defy this well-known Law at their Own Peril.

Time Accounting does not Differentiate one firm in the Profession from another. Rather, it transforms the Crown Jewels of any one Firm—the human and social capital, experience, wisdom, professional judgment, and intellect—into one completely arbitrary Hourly Rate, viewed as a Commodity by the Public.

Time Accounting imposes an arbitrary ceiling on the Income Potential of the Professions, as there is only a fixed quantity of hours in any given day, week, month, year, or life. This ceiling has been imposed by Time Accounting, not the Public the Professions are Pledged to Serve.

Time Accounting diminishes the Quality of Life of the Professional, by viciously segregating His or Her Time into Billable and Non Billable segments. Rather than being a device for tracking the Inventory of Time, Time Accounting has become the Inventory.

In every stage of these Oppressions we have Petitioned, Pleaded, and Exhorted the Profession's Leaders and Consultants for Redress in the most humble Terms: Our repeated Petitions have been answered only by repeated Injury and Ridicule. A Master, whose Character is thus marked by every act which may define a Tyrant, is unfit to be the arbitrary Ruler of a free Profession in a Free Market.

Nor have we been wanting in Attentions to Leaders and Consultants of the Profession around the world. We have warned them from Time to Time of Attempts by their anachronistic Practices to extend an unwarrantable Jurisdiction over us. We have reminded them of the Circumstances of our Emigration and Conception of a radical business model for Professional Firms. We have appealed to their native Justice and Magnanimity, and we have conjured them by the Ties of our common Knowledge and Interests to disavow these Usurpations, which, would inevitably interrupt our Connections and Correspondence and hinder the Future of the Professions. They too have been deaf to the Voice of Justice, Economics, and of Consanguinity. We must, therefore, acquiesce in the Necessity, which denounces our Separation, and hold them, as we hold the rest of the Professions, wrong in the Marketplace of Ideas.

We, therefore, the Representatives of VeraSage Institute, in GENERAL CONGRESS, Assembled, appealing to the Supreme Judge of the World for the Rectitude of our Intentions, do, in the Name, and by Authority of the good People of this Institute, solemnly Publish and Declare, That this Institute is, and of Right ought to be, FREE AND INDEPENDENT FROM THE TYRANNY OF TIME; that it is absolved from all Allegiance to the Past Traditions as they relate to Time Accounting, and that all Measurements and Procedures between them are and ought to be totally dissolved; and that as FREE AND INDEPENDENT PROFESSIONALS, they have full Power to Price on Purpose and for Value, levy Ideas in the Free Market, contract Alliances, establish Commerce, engage in Capitalist Acts between Consenting Adults, and to do all other Acts and Thoughts which INDEPENDENT PROFESSIONALS may of right do. And for the support of this Declaration, with a firm Reliance on the Protection of divine Providence, we mutually pledge to each other our Lives, our Fortunes, our Energies, and our sacred Honor.

Signed by Order *and in* BEHALF *of* VeraSage Institute,

RONALD J. BAKER, California
JUSTIN H. BARNETT, California
DANIEL D. MORRIS, California
SCOTT ABBOTT, Utah
PETER BYERS, New Zealand
MICHELLE GOLDEN, Missouri

DARYL GOLEMB, California
BRENDON HARREX, New Zealand
PAUL KENNEDY, England
ED KLESS, Texas
CHRISTOPHER MARSTON, Esq., Massachusetts
TIM McKEY, Louisiana
PAUL O'BYRNE, England
TIM WILLIAMS, Utah
YAN ZHU, New Zealand

Bibliography

Albrecht, Karl. *The Only Thing That Matters: Bringing the Power of the Customer into the Center of Your Business.* New York: HarperBusiness, 1992.

Albrecht, Karl. *The Northbound Train: Finding the Purpose, Setting the Direction, Shaping the Destiny of Your Organization.* New York: American Management Association, 1994.

Albrecht, Karl, and Ron Zemke. *Service America in the New Economy.* New York: McGraw-Hill, 2002.

Albrecht, Karl. *Practical Intelligence: The Art and Science of Common Sense.* San Francisco: Jossey-Bass, 2007.

American Bar Association, Economics of Tort and Insurance Law Practice Committee of the Tort & Insurance Practice Section, *Alternative Billing: The Sequel.* San Francisco: Fairmont Hotel, March 13, 1997 Seminar and Material.

Aquila, August J., and Allan D. Koltin. "How to Lose Clients without Really Trying." *Journal of Accountancy,* May 1992: 67–70.

Ariely, Dan. *Predictably Irrational: The Hidden Forces That Shape Our Decisions.* New York: Harper, 2008.

Baker Ronald J., and Paul Dunn. *The Firm of the Future: A Guide for Accountants, Lawyers, and Other Professional Services.* Hoboken, NJ: John Wiley & Sons, Inc., 2003.

Baker, Ronald J. *Professional's Guide to Value Pricing,* 6th ed. Chicago: CCH Incorporated, 2005. [Out of print].

Baker, Ronald J. *Pricing on Purpose: Creating and Capturing Value.* Hoboken, NJ: John Wiley & Sons, Inc., 2006.

Baker, Ronald J. *Measure What Matters to Customers: Using Key Predictive Indicators.* Hoboken, NJ: John Wiley & Sons, Inc., 2006.

Baker, Ronald J. *Mind Over Matter: Why Intellectual Capital is the Chief Source of Wealth.* Hoboken, NJ: John Wiley & Sons, Inc., 2008.

Bateson, Charles. *The Convict Ships: 1787–1868.* Glasgow: Brown, Son and Ferguson, 1969.

Beauchemin, Timothy J. "No More Begging for Work: Self Esteem Is the Key to a Better Practice." *CPA Profitability Monthly*, Volume 1996, Issue 8, August 1996.

Becker, Gary S. *Human Capital: A Theoretical and Empirical Analysis, with Special Reference to Education*, 2nd ed. Chicago: University of Chicago Press, 1980.

Bergstrand, Jack. *Reinvent Your Enterprise: Through Better Knowledge Work*. Atlanta: Brand Velocity, no date.

Bernstein, Peter L. *Against the Gods: The Remarkable Story of Risk*. Hoboken, NJ: John Wiley & Sons, Inc., 1998.

Berra, Yogi, with Dave Kaplan. *When You Come to a Fork in the Road, Take It!: Inspiration and Wisdom from One of Baseball's Greatest Heroes*. New York: Hyperion, 2001.

Berry, Leonard L., and Kent D. Seltman. *Management Lessons from the Mayo Clinic: Inside One of the World's Most Admired Service Organizations*. New York: McGraw-Hill, 2008.

Bethune, Gordon. *From Worst to First: Behind the Scenes of Continental's Remarkable Comeback*. Hoboken, NJ: John Wiley & Sons, Inc., 1998.

Blaug, Mark. *Not Only an Economist: Recent Essays by Mark Blaug*. Cheltenham, United Kingdom: Edward Elgar Publishing Limited, 1997.

Block, Peter. *The Answer to How Is Yes: Acting on What Matters*. San Francisco: Berrett-Koehler Publishers, Inc., 2003.

Boress, Allan S. *The "I Hate Selling" Book*. New York: AMACOM, 1995.

Bosworth, Michael T. *Solution Selling: Creating Buyers in Difficult Selling Markets*. Chicago: Irwin Professional Publishing, 1995.

Bosworth, Michael T., and John R. Holland. *Customer Centric Selling*. New York: McGraw-Hill, 2004.

Bowie, Norman E. *Business Ethics: A Kantian Perspective*. Oxford, UK: Blackwell Publishers Ltd, 1999.

Boyd, E. Andrew. *The Future of Pricing: How Airline Ticket Pricing Has Inspired a Revolution*. New York: Palgrave Macmillan, 2007.

Boyle, David. *The Sum of Our Discontent: Why Numbers Make Us Irrational*. New York: Texere, 2001.

Brafman, Ori, and Rom Brafman. *Sway: The Irresistible Pull of Irrational Behavior*. New York: Doubleday, 2008.

Branden, Nathaniel. *The Six Pillars of Self-Esteem*. New York: Bantam, 1994.

Branden, Nathaniel. *Self-Esteem at Work: How Confident People Make Powerful Companies*. San Francisco: Jossey-Bass Publishers, 1998.

Brandenburger, Adam M., and Barry J. Nalebuff. *Co-opetition: The Game Theory That's Changing the Game of Business*. New York: Currency Doubleday, 1996.

Brandt, Richard L. *Inside Larry and Sergey's Brain*. New York: Portfolio, 2009.

Callahan, Gene. *Economics for Real People: An Introduction to the Austrian School.* Auburn, AL: Ludwig von Mises Institute, 2002.

Cerf, Christopher, and Victor Navasky. *The Experts Speak: The Definitive Compendium of Authoritative Misinformation.* New York: Villard, 1998.

Chinn, Mark A. *Dumping the Billable Hour: One Lawyer's Experience.* E-Book, available at www.chinnandassociates.com/store.html.

Christensen, Clayton M., Scott D. Anthony, and Erik A. Roth. *Seeing What's Next: Using the Theories of Innovation to Predict Industry Change.* Boston: Harvard Business School Press, 2004.

Cialdini, Robert B. *Influence: The New Psychology of Modern Persuasion.* New York: Quill, 1993.

Cialdini, Robert B. *Influence: Science and Practice*, 4th ed. Needham Heights, MA: Allyn and Bacon, 2001.

Coens, Tom, and Mary Jenkins. *Abolishing Performance Appraisals: Why They Backfire and What to Do Instead.* San Francisco: Berrett-Koehler Publishers, 2000.

Cohen, PhD, William A. *A Class with Drucker: The Lost Lessons of the World's Greatest Management Teacher.* New York: AMACOM, 2008.

Collins, James C. *Good to Great: Why Some Companies Make the Leap ... and Others Don't.* New York: HarperBusiness, 2001.

Covey, Stephen R. *The 7 Habits of Highly Effective People: Powerful Lessons in Personal Change.* New York: Fireside, 1989.

Covey, Stephen R. *The 8th Habit: From Effectiveness to Greatness.* New York: Free Press, 2004.

Cram, Tony. *Smarter Pricing: How to Capture More Value in Your Market.* London: Prentice Hall, 2006.

Cross, Robert G. *Revenue Management: Hard-Core Tactics for Market Domination.* New York: Broadway Books, 1997.

Darling, Marilyn, Charles Parry, and Joseph Moore. "Learning in the Thick of It." *Harvard Business Review.* July–August 2005: 84–92.

Davenport Thomas H. and Laurence Prusak. *Working Knowledge: How Organizations Manage What They Know.* Boston: Harvard Business School Press, 1998.

Davenport, Thomas H. *Thinking for a Living: How to Get Better Performance and Results from Knowledge Workers.* Boston: Harvard Business School Press, 2005.

Davenport, Thomas H. *Competing on Analytics: The New Science of Winning.* Boston: Harvard Business School Press, 2007.

Davis, Kevin. *Getting Into Your Customer's Head.* New York: Times Books, 1996.

Dawson, Ross. *Developing Knowledge-Based Client Relationships: The Future of Professional Services.* Boston: Butterworth Heinemann, 2000.

deKieffer, Donald E., Esq. *How Lawyers Screw Their Clients and What You Can Do About It.* New York: Barricade Books, Inc., 1995.

DeLong, David W. *Lost Knowledge: Confronting the Threat of an Aging Workforce.* New York: Oxford University Press, 2004.

Deming, W. Edwards. *The New Economics: For Industry, Government, Education,* 2nd ed. Cambridge, MA: MIT Press, 1994.

Disney Institute. *Be Our Guest: Perfecting the Art of Customer Service.* New York: Disney Editions, 2001.

Docters, Robert G., Michael R. Reopel, Jeanne-Mey Sun, and Stephen M. Tanny. *Winning the Profit Game: Smarter Pricing, Smarter Branding.* New York: McGraw-Hill, 2004.

Drucker, Peter F. *The Effective Executive.* New York: HarperBusiness, 1993.

Drucker, Peter F. *Adventurers of a Bystander.* New Brunswick, NJ: Transaction Publishers, 1994.

Drucker, Peter F. *Managing in a Time of Great Change.* New York: Truman Talley Books/Dutton, 1995.

Drucker, Peter F. *Management Challenges for the 21st Century.* New York: HarperCollins, 1999.

Drucker, Peter F. *Managing in the Next Society.* New York: Truman Talley Books, 2002.

Drucker, Peter F. *Peter Drucker On the Profession of Management.* Boston: Harvard Business Review, 2003.

Drucker, Peter F., with Joseph A. Maciariello. *The Daily Drucker: 366 Days of Insight and Motivation for Getting the Right Things Done.* New York: HarperBusiness, 2004.

Drucker, Peter F., and Joseph A. Maciariello. *The Effective Executive in Action.* New York: HarperCollins Publishers, 2006.

Drucker, Peter F. *People and Performance: The Best of Peter Drucker on Management.* Boston: Harvard Business School Press, 2007.

Drucker, Peter F., et al. *The Five Most Important Questions You Will Ever Ask About Your Organization.* San Francisco: Jossey-Bass, 2008.

Dyson, James. *Against the Odds: An Autobiography.* New York: Texere, 2003.

Ebenstein, Alan. *Hayek's Journey: The Mind of Friedrich Hayek.* New York: Palgrave Macmillan, 2003.

Edersheim, Elizabeth Haas. *The Definitive Drucker.* New York: McGraw-Hill, 2007.

Empson, Laura, ed. *Managing the Modern Law Firm: New Challenges, New Perspectives.* Oxford, UK: Oxford University Press, 2007.

Ferguson, Marilyn. *The Aquarian Conspiracy.* New York: St. Martins Press, 1987.

Flaherty, John E. *Peter Drucker: Shaping the Managerial Mind.* San Francisco: Jossey-Bass Publishers, 1999.

Florida, Richard. *The Rise of the Creative Class: And How It's Transforming Work, Leisure, Community and Everyday Life.* New York: Basic Books, 2002.

Florida, Richard. *The Flight of the Creative Class: The New Global Competition for Talent.* New York: HarperBusiness, 2005.

Ford, Henry, and Samuel Crowther. *My Life and Work.* Kessinger Publishing, www.kessigner.net, 1922.

Freiberg, Kevin, and Jackie Freiberg. *Nuts! Southwest Airline's Crazy Recipe for Business and Personal Success.* Austin, TX: Bard Press, 1996.

Friedman, David D. *Hidden Order: The Economics of Everyday Life.* New York: HarperBusiness, 1996.

Friedman, Milton, and Rose Friedman. *Free to Choose: A Personal Statement.* New York: Harcourt Brace, 1980.

Gandossy, Robert P., Elissa Tucker, and Nidhi Verma. *Workforce Wake-Up Call: Your Workforce Is Changing, Are You?* Hoboken, NJ: John Wiley & Sons, Inc., 2006.

Garvin, David A. *Learning in Action: A Guide to Putting the Learning Organization to Work.* Boston: Harvard Business School Press, 2000.

Gawande, Artul. *The Checklist Manifesto: How to Get Things Right.* New York: Metropolitan Books, 2009.

Gilder, George. *Wealth and Poverty.* New York: Basic Books, Inc., 1981.

Gilder, George. *The Spirit of Enterprise.* New York: Simon and Schuster, 1984.

Gilder, George. *Recapturing the Spirit of Enterprise: Updated for the 1990s.* San Francisco: ICS Press, 1992.

Gilder, George. *Wealth and Poverty: A New Edition of the Classic.* San Francisco: ICS Press, 1993.

Gladwell, Malcolm. *Outliers: The Story of Success.* New York: Little, Brown, 2008.

Godin, Seth. *Purple Cow: Transform Your Business by Being Remarkable.* New York: Portfolio, 2002.

Golden, Michelle. *Social Media Strategies for Professionals and their Firms: The Guide to Establishing Credibility and Accelerating Relationships.* Hoboken, NJ: John Wiley Sons, Inc., 2010.

Goldstein, Noah J., Steve J. Martin, and Robert B. Cialdini. *Yes!: 50 Scientifically Proven Ways to Be Persuasive.* New York: Free Press, 2008.

Gray, Scott. *The Mind of Bill James: How a Complete Outsider Changed Baseball.* New York: Doubleday, 2006.

Gregorsky, Frank, ed. *Speaking of George Gilder.* Seattle, WA: Discovery Institute Press, 1998.

Gregory, John Milton. *The Seven Laws of Teaching.* Grand Rapids, MI: Baker Books, 1995.

Hamel, Gary. *Leading the Revolution*. Boston: Harvard Business School Press, 2000.

Hamel, Gary, with Bill Breen. *The Future of Management*. Boston: Harvard Business School Press, 2007.

Hart, Christopher W. *Extraordinary Guarantees: Achieving Breakthrough Gains in Quality and Customer Satisfaction*. Brookline, MA: Spire Group, Ltd., 1998.

Hoffer, Eric. *Reflections on the Human Condition*. Titusville, NJ: Hopewell Publications, 2006a.

Hoffer, Eric. *The Ordeal of Change*. Titusville, NJ: Hopewell Publications, 2006b.

Holcombe, Randall G. *15 Great Austrian Economists*. Auburn, Alabama: Ludwig von Mises Institute, 1999.

Holden, Reed K., and Mark R. Burton. *Pricing with Confidence: 10 Ways to Stop Leaving Money on the Table*. Hoboken, NJ: John Wiley & Sons, Inc., 2008.

Hopkins, Tom. *How to Master the Art of Selling*. New York: Warner Books, 1982.

Howey, Richard S. *The Rise of the Marginal Utility School, 1870–1889*. New York: Columbia University Press [Morningside Edition], 1989.

The Imagineers. *The Imagineering Way: Ideas to Ignite Your Creativity*. New York: Disney Editions, 2003.

Johnson, H. Thomas, and Robert S. Kaplan. *Relevance Lost: The Rise and Fall of Management Accounting*. Boston: Harvard Business School Press, 1991.

Johnson, H. Thomas, and Anders Bröms. *Profit Beyond Measure: Extraordinary Results through Attention to Work and People*. New York: Free Press, 2000.

Johnson, Mark W. *Seizing the White Space: Business Model Innovation for Growth and Renewal*. Boston: Harvard Business Press, 2010.

Johnson, Robert Early. *Kick Your Own Ass: The Will, Skill, and Drill of Selling More Than You Ever Thought Possible*. Hoboken, NJ: John Wiley & Sons, Inc., 2010.

Kames, Jeffrey A. *Inside Drucker's Brain*. New York: Portfolio, 2008.

Kay, John. *Foundations of Corporate Success: How Business Strategies Add Value*. New York: Oxford University Press, 1995.

Kay, John. *Culture and Prosperity: The Truth About Markets—Why Some Nations Are Rich but Most Remain Poor*. New York: HarperBusiness, 2004.

Kay, John. *Everlasting Light Bulbs: How Economics Illuminates the World*. London: Erasmus Press, 2004.

Kay, John. *The Hare and the Tortoise: An Informal Guide to Business Strategy*. London: The Erasmus Press Ltd., 2006.

Kehrer, Daniel. *Doing Business Boldly.* New York: Time Books, 1989.

Khalsa, Mahan. *Let's Get Real or Let's Not Play: The Demise of Dysfunctional Selling and the Advent of Helping Clients Succeed.* Salt Lake City, UT: White Water Press, 1999.

Koch, Charles G. *The Science of Success: How Market-Based Management Built the World's Largest Private Company.* Hoboken, NJ: John Wiley & Sons, Inc., 2007.

Koch, Richard. *The 80/20 Principle: The Secret of Achieving More With Less.* New York: Currency Doubleday, 1998.

Koch, Richard. *The Natural Laws of Business: How to Harness the Power of Evolution, Physics, and Economics to Achieve Business Success.* New York: Doubleday, 2001.

Kolassa, E.M. (Mick). *The Strategic Pricing of Pharmaceuticals.* The PondHouse Press, 2009.

Krass, Peter, ed. *The Book of Entrepreneurs' Wisdom: Classic Writings by Legendary Entrepreneurs.* Hoboken, NJ: John Wiley & Sons, Inc., 1999.

Kurtz, David L., and Kenneth E. Clow. *Services Marketing.* Hoboken, NJ: John Wiley & Sons, Inc., 1998.

Lafley, A.G., and Ram Charan. *The Game-Changer: How You Can Drive Revenue and Profit Growth with Innovation.* New York: Crown Business, 2008.

Landsburg, Steven E. *The Armchair Economist: Economics and Everyday Life.* New York: Free Press, 1993.

Landsburg, Steven E. *Price Theory and Applications,* 3rd ed., St. Paul, MN: West Publishing, 1996.

Landsburg, Steven E. *Fair Play: What Your Child Can Teach You About Economics, Values, and the Meaning of Life.* New York: Free Press, 1997.

Landsburg, Steven E. *Price Theory and Applications,* 5th ed. Cincinnati, OH: South-Western, 2002.

Lanning, Michael J. *Delivering Profitable Value: A Revolutionary Framework to Accelerate Growth, Generate Wealth, and Rediscover the Heart of Business.* Cambridge, MA: Perseus Books, 1998.

Lapin, Rabbi Daniel. *Thou Shall Prosper: Ten Commandments for Making Money.* Hoboken, NJ: John Wiley & Sons, Inc., 2002.

LeBoeuf, Michael. *How to Win Customers and Keep Them for Life: Revised and Updated for the Digital Age.* New York: Berkley Books, 2000.

Lev, Baruch. *Intangibles: Management, Measurement, and Reporting.* Washington, DC: Brookings Institution Press, 2001.

Levitt, Theodore. "Marketing Myopia." *Harvard Business Review* 53 (September–October 1975).

Lewis, Michael. *Moneyball: The Art of Winning an Unfair Game.* New York: W.W. Norton & Company, 2003.

Maister, David H. *True Professionalism: The Courage to Care about Your People, Your Clients, and Your Career.* New York: Free Press, 1997.

Maister, David, Charles H. Green, and Robert M. Galford. *The Trusted Advisor.* New York: Free Press, 2000.

Marcus, Stanley. *Quest for the Best.* New York: Viking Press, 1979.

Marcus, Stanley. *The Viewpoints of Stanley Marcus: A Ten-Year Perspective.* Denton, TX: University of North Texas Press, 1995.

Marcus, Stanley. *Minding the Store: A Memoir.* Denton, TX: University of North Texas Press, 1997 (facsimile edition, originally published 1974).

Marcus, Stanley. *Stanley Marcus from A to Z: Viewpoints Volume II.* Denton, TX: University of North Texas Press, 2000.

Marn, Michael V., Eric V. Roegner, and Craig C. Zawada. *The Price Advantage.* Hoboken, NJ: John Wiley & Sons, Inc., 2004.

Marriott, Jr., J. W., and Kathi Ann Brown. *The Spirit of Service: Marriott's Way.* New York: HarperBusiness, 1997.

Marshall, Alfred. *Principles of Economics.* Amherst, NY: Prometheus Books, 1997.

Marx, Karl. *Value, Price and Profit.* New York: International Publishers, 1995 (paperback edition; originally published 1865).

Maxwell, Sarah, PhD. *The Price Is Wrong: Understanding What Makes a Price Seem Fair and the True Cost of Unfair Pricing.* Hoboken, NJ: John Wiley & Sons, Inc., 2008.

May, Matthew E. *The Elegant Solution: Toyota's Formula for Mastering Innovation.* New York: Free Press, 2006.

McCloskey, Donald N. *The Applied Theory of Price,* 2nd ed. New York: Macmillan Publishing Company, 1985.

McCloskey, Deirdre. *How to Be Human—Though an Economist.* Ann Arbor, MI: University of Michigan Press, 2000.

McKenna, Patrick J., and David H. Maister. *First among Equals: How to Manage a Group of Professionals.* New York: Free Press, 2002.

McKenzie, Richard B. *Why Popcorn Costs So Much at the Movies: And Other Pricing Puzzles.* New York: Copernicus Books, 2008.

Menger, Carl. *Principles of Economics,* trans. James Dingwall and Bert F. Hoselitz. New York: New York University Press, 1976 [1871].

Micklethwait, John, and Adrian Wooldridge. *The Witch Doctors: Making Sense of the Management Gurus.* New York: Times Books, 1996.

Miniter, Richard. *The Myth of Market Share: Why Market Share Is the Fool's Gold of Business.* New York: Crown Business, 2002.

Mintzberg, Henry. *Mintzberg on Management: Inside Our Strange World of Organizations.* New York: Free Press, 1989.

Mintzberg, Henry. *Managers Not MBAs: A Hard Look at the Soft Practice of Managing and Management Development.* San Francisco: Berrett-Koehler Publishers, Inc., 2004.

Mintzberg, Henry. *Managing.* San Francisco: Berrett-Koehler Publishers, 2009.

Mohammed, Rafi. *The Art of Pricing: How to Find the Hidden Profits to Grow Your Business.* New York: Crown Business, 2005.

Mohammed, Rafi. *The 1% Windfall: How Successful Companies Use Price to Profit and Grow.* New York: HarperBusiness, 2010.

Monroe, Kent B. *Pricing: Making Profitable Decisions,* 3rd ed. New York: McGraw-Hill, 2003.

Morgan, J. Harris. *How to Draft Bills Clients Rush to Pay.* Chicago: American Bar Association, 1995.

Mourkogiannis, Nikos. *Purpose: The Starting Point of Great Companies.* New York: Palgrave Macmillan, 2006.

Murray, Charles. *Human Accomplishment: The Pursuit of Excellence in the Arts and Sciences, 800 B.C. to 1950.* New York: HarperCollins Publishers, Inc., 2003.

Nagle, Thomas T., and Reed K. Holden. *The Strategy and Tactics of Pricing: A Guide to Profitable Decision Making,* 2nd ed. Upper Saddle River, NJ: Prentice-Hall, 1995.

Nagle, Thomas T., and Reed K. Holden. *The Strategy and Tactics of Pricing: A Guide to Profitable Decision Making,* 3rd ed. Upper Saddle River, NJ: Prentice-Hall, 2002.

Nagle, Thomas T., and John E. Hogan. *The Strategy and Tactics of Pricing: A Guide to Growing More Profitably,* 4th ed. Upper Saddle River, NJ: Prentice-Hall, 2006.

Neuhaus, Richard John. *Doing Well and Doing Good: The Challenge to the Christian Capitalist.* New York: Doubleday, 1992.

Nonaka, Ikujiro, and Hirotaka Takeuchi. *The Knowledge-Creating Company: How Japanese Companies Create the Dynamics of Innovation.* New York: Oxford University Press, 1995.

Novak, Michael. *The Catholic Ethic and the Spirit of Capitalism.* New York: Free Press, 1993.

Novak, Michael. *Business as a Calling: Work and the Examined Life.* New York: Free Press, 1996.

O'Brien, Robert. *Marriott: The J. Willard Marriott Story.* Salt Lake City, UT: Desert Book Company, 1989.

Ogilvy, David. *Ogilvy on Advertising.* New York: Vintage Books, 1985.

O'Rourke, P.J. *On The Wealth of Nations.* New York: Atlantic Monthly Press, 2007.

Pallotta, Dan. *Uncharitable: How Restraints on Nonprofits Undermine Their Potential.* Medford, MA: Tufts University Press, 2008.

Pascal, Blaise. *Pensées and Other Writings.* Oxford, UK: Oxford University Press, 1995 (paperback edition; originally published 1670).

Peters, Tom. *The Tom Peters Seminar: Crazy Times Call for Crazy Organizations.* New York: Vintage Books, 1994.

Pine, B. Joseph, II, and James H. Gilmore. *The Experience Economy: Work Is Theatre and Every Business a Stage.* Boston: Harvard Business School Press, 1999.

Pigou, Arthur Cecil, and Nahid Aslanbeigui. *The Economics of Welfare.* New Brunswick, NJ: Transaction Publishers, 2001 (originally published 1920).

Poundstone, William. *Priceless: The Myth of Fair Value (and How to Take Advantage of It).* New York: Hill and Wang, 2010.

Previts, Gary John, and Barbara Dubis Merino. *A History of Accountancy in the United States: The Cultural Significance of Accounting.* Columbus: Ohio State University Press, 1998.

Rackham, Neil. *SPIN Selling.* New York: McGraw-Hill, 1988.

Rackham, Neil, and John DeVincentis. *Rethinking the Sales Force: Redefining Selling to Create and Capture Customer Value.* New York: McGraw-Hill, 1999.

Raju, Jagmohan, and Z. John Zhang. *Smart Pricing: How Google, Priceline, and Leading Businesses Use Pricing Innovation for Profitability.* Upper Saddle River, NJ: Wharton School Publishing, 2010.

Reed, Richard C., Ed. *Beyond The Billable Hour: An Anthology of Alternative Billing Methods.* Chicago: American Bar Association, 1989.

Reed, Richard C., Ed. *Win-Win Billing Strategies: Alternatives That Satisfy Your Clients and You.* Chicago: American Bar Association, 1992.

Reed, Richard C. *Billing Innovations: New Win-Win Ways to End Hourly Billing.* Chicago: American Bar Association, 1996.

Reichheld, Frederick F., and Thomas Teal. *The Loyalty Effect: The Hidden Force Behind Growth, Profits, and Lasting Value.* Boston: Harvard Business School Press, 1996.

Reichheld, Frederick F. *Loyalty Rules! How Today's Leaders Build Lasting Relationships.* Boston: Harvard Business School Press, 2001.

Reichheld, Fred. *The Ultimate Question: Driving Good Profits and True Growth.* Boston: Harvard Business School Press, 2006.

Ressler, Cali, and Jody Thompson. *Why Work Sucks and How to Fix It.* New York: Portfolio, 2008.

Revel, Jean-François. *The Flight from Truth: The Reign of Deceit in the Age of Information.* New York: Random House, 1991.

Richards, Jay W. *Money, Greed, and God: Why Capitalism Is the Solution and Not the Problem.* New York: HarperOne, 2009.

Roberts, Kevin. *Lovemarks: The Future Beyond Brands.* New York: PowerHouse Books, 2005.

Robertson, Mark A., and James A. Calloway. *Winning Alternatives to the Billable Hour: Strategies That Work,* 3rd ed. Chicago: American Bar Association, 2008.

Rosenzweig, Phil. *The Halo Effect...and the Eight Other Business Delusions That Deceive Managers.* New York: Free Press, 2007.

Ross, William G. *The Honest Hour: The Ethics of Time-Based Billing by Attorneys.* Durham, NC: Carolina Academic Press, 1996.

Semler, Ricardo. *Maverick: The Success Story Behind the World's Most Unusual Workplace.* New York: Warner Books, 1993.

Semler, Ricardo. *The Seven-Day Weekend: A Better Way to Work in the 21st Century.* London: Arrow Books, 2003.

Sewell, Carl. *Customers for Life: How to Turn That One-Time Buyer into a Lifetime Customer.* New York: Pocket Books, 1990.

Simon, Herbert A., *Models of My Life.* New York: BasicBooks, 1991.

Simon, Hermann, Frank Bilstein, and Frank Luby. *Manage for Profit, Not for Market Share: A Guide to Higher Profitability in Highly Contested Markets.* Boston: Harvard Business School Press, 2006.

Simon, Julian. *A Life Against the Grain: The Autobiography of an Unconventional Economist.* Piscataway, NJ: Transaction Publishers, 2002.

Sinek, Simon. *Start with Why: How Great Leaders Inspire Everyone to Take Action.* New York: Portfolio, 2009.

Sirico, Robert A. *The Call of the Entrepreneur: Study Guide.* Grand Rapids, MI: Acton Institute, 2007.

Skousen, Mark, and Kenna C. Taylor. *Puzzles and Paradoxes in Economics.* Cheltenham, UK: Edward Elgar Publishing, 1997.

Skousen, Mark. *The Making of Modern Economics: The Lives and Ideas of the Great Thinkers.* Armonk, NY: M.E. Sharpe, 2001.

Skousen, Mark. *The Power of Economic Thinking.* New York: Foundation for Economic Education, 2002.

Smith, Adam. *An Inquiry into the Nature and Causes of the Wealth of Nations.* Introduction by Ludwig von Mises. Washington, DC: Regnery Publishing, Inc., 1998 (originally published 1776).

Smith, Adam. *The Theory of Moral Sentiments.* Amherst, NY: Prometheus Books, 2000 (originally published 1759).

Smith Reginald Herber. *Law Office Organization,* 11th ed. Chicago: American Bar Association, Section of Economics of Law Practice, 1983 (originally published 1943).

Snyder, Tom, and Kevin Kearns. *Escaping the Price-Driven Sale: How World-Class Sellers Create Extraordinary Profit.* New York: McGraw-Hill, 2008.

Sowell, Thomas. *Knowledge and Decisions.* New York: Basic Books, 1996.

Sowell, Thomas. *Basic Economics: A Citizen's Guide to the Economy.* New York: Basic Books, 2000.

Sowell, Thomas. *Basic Economics: A Citizen's Guide to the Economy,* revised and expanded edition. New York: Basic Books, 2004.

Steinmetz, PhD, Lawrence L., and William T. Brooks. *How to Sell at Margins Higher Than Your Competitors: Winning Every Sale at Full Price, Rate, or Fee.* Hoboken, NJ: John Wiley & Sons, Inc., 2006.

Stewart, Matthew. *The Management Myth: Why the Experts Keep Getting It Wrong.* New York: Norton, 2009.

Stewart, Thomas A. *Intellectual Capital: The New Wealth of Organizations.* New York: Currency, 1997.

Stewart, Thomas A. *The Wealth of Knowledge: Intellectual Capital and the Twenty-First Century Organization.* New York: Currency, 2001.

Sullivan, Gordon R., and Michael V. Harper. *Hope Is Not a Method: What Business Leaders Can Learn from America's Army.* New York: Broadway Books, 1996.

Susskind, Richard E. *The End of Lawyers?: Rethinking the Nature of Legal Services.* New York: Oxford University Press, 2008.

Sutton, Gary. *Corporate Canaries: Avoid Business Disasters with a Coal Miner's Secrets.* Nashville, TN: Nelson Business, 2005.

Sveiby, Karl Erik. *The New Organizational Wealth: Managing and Measuring Knowledge-Based Assets.* San Francisco, CA: Berrett-Koehler Publishers, Inc., 1997.

Swartz, James B., and Joseph E. Swartz. *Seeing David in the Stone: Find and Seize Great Opportunities Using 12 Actions Mastered by 70 Highly Successful Leaders.* Carmel, IN: Leading Books Press, 2006.

Taleb, Nassim Nicholas. *The Black Swan: The Impact of the Highly Improbable.* New York: Random House, 2007.

Tedlow, Richard S. *Giants of Enterprise: Seven Business Innovators and the Empires They Built.* New York: Harper Business, 2001.

Thaler, Richard H. *The Winner's Curse: Paradoxes and Anomalies of Economic Life.* Princeton, NJ: Princeton University Press, 1992.

Thaler, Richard H., and Cass R. Sunstein. *Nudge: Improving Decisions About Health, Wealth, and Happiness.* New Haven, CT: Yale University Press, 2008.

Toffler, Alvin, and Heidi Toffler. *Revolutionary Wealth.* New York: Alfred A. Knopf, 2006.

Weiss, Alan. *Value-Based Fees: How to Charge—and Get—What You're Worth.* San Francisco: Jossey-Bass/Pfeiffer, 2002.

Williams, Tim. *Positioning for Professionals: How Professional Knowledge Firms Can Differentiate Their Way to Success.* Hoboken, NJ: John Wiley & Sons, Inc., 2010.

Winston, William J., ed. *Marketing for CPAs, Accountants, and Tax Professionals.* New York: Haworth Press, 1995.

Wootton, David. *Bad Medicine: Doctors Doing Harm Since Hippocrates.* New York: Oxford University Press, 2006.

World Bank. *Where Is the Wealth of Nations? Measuring Capital for the XXI Century.* Washington DC: The International Bank for Reconstruction and Development/The World Bank, 2006.

Yutang, Lin. *The Importance of Living.* New York: Quill, 1998 ed. (originally published 1937).

Index